Assessing Music Performance

A valid system for measuring student performance and growth

Assessing Music Performance

A valid system for measuring student performance and growth

By

Kevin McNulty, Sr.

Copyright © 2018 KMC PUBLISHING COMPANY, INC. (5th Edition)
All rights reserved. No part of this publication may be reproduced, distributed, or transmitted in any form or by any means, without the prior written permission of the publisher, except in the case of brief quotations embodied in critical reviews and certain other noncommercial uses permitted by copyright law. For permission requests, write to the publisher.

ISBN 13 978-0-9897965-8-3

DEDICATION

To my good friends and mentors

Paul Litteau
And
Bob Wenderski

TABLE OF CONTENTS

Section One

Standards & Testing in American Schools

PART I   The Landscape

Education in America	13
Testing in Schools	16
The Nature of Music Performance and Testing	21

PART II   Music Performance Teaching

Music Performance in the Academic World	30
Our grading legacy	39
Do we assess?	43
State of music performance assessment today	50

PART III   Measuring the Aesthetic

Musical Meaning – Langer	62
Musical Context – McNulty	69
Musical Judgement – Green	74

Section Two

Toward Credible & Methodological Judging

PART IV   Foundations of Performance Adjudication

Genesis of Judging Technique	80
School Music Contest Judging	87
The Evaluator's Background, Experience & Bias	90

PART V   Methodology

Take Away and Build up	96
Criteria Reference versus Rubrics	99
"The Linear Scale" & Impression, Analysis, Comparison	102

PART VI Scoring

Using the Scale	116
How Judges Judge	117
Scoring Assessments and Analyzing Results	128
Performance Profiles	130
Assessment Disciplines	134

Section Three

Applying Linear Scales to Auditions, Testing, and Grading

PART VII   Assessment Design Considerations

System Review	148
Designing Linear Scales & Score Sheets	149
Applying "Take-Away" & "Build-Up" Properly to Desired Outcomes	152
Aligning the Linear Scale with Grading Systems	154

PART VIII   Programing & Curriculum Considerations

Literature	162
Compulsories	166
Establishing Your Book	170

PART IX Student, Ensemble, Program & Professional Growth

Individual, Ensemble & Program Assessment	174
Resetting year-to-year Standards	176
Personal Assessment	177

PART X Single District, Unit District & Custom Applications

Prelude to Part X	180
Establishing Standards and Linear Scales in School Programs	181
Ranking and grading using the Grade Level Method	198
Ranking and grading using the Ensemble Level Method	215

Appendix

References-

FORWARD

I began teaching in 1974. Over these past 44 years, I have seen an incredible number of changes. As a new teacher, I could have never imagined the landscape upon which we teach and perform today.

Of course, there are many things that have remained the same throughout my teaching career. Kids are still kids. Their energy, excitement, and capacity to learn and be inspired are still immense. Music is still as powerful as ever. It still has the power to teach, inspire, excite, energize, and frustrate. Music still, as Bernstein said, "can name the unnameable and communicate the unknowable," and in so doing to lead students to a deeper understanding of self, beauty, and a better world.

Not all of the unchanged things are good, however. The world of education often still suffers from a lack of understanding of the uniqueness of the arts and especially of music. Administrators and legislators who try to find a way to measure success often feel the need to create a "one size fits all" common ground where all things can be measured and judged by the same ruler. As music educators, we have often been forced to justify our class's value by adjusting how and what we teach to fit into a definition of achievement that is created for other subject areas. While these curricular plans and assessments are fine for many areas, for music they are at best generic, often completely off target, and can even be detrimental.

During my teaching career, I have had many conversations (debates) with administrators who cared deeply and were sincerely trying to do what is right, but because of their lack of understanding of the subject were unable to make insightful judgments and corrections. They cannot envision a situation where assessment can be an instant and ongoing continuum as it is with performance-based music.

In his new book, *"Assessing Music Performance…A Valid System for Measuring Student Performance and Growth,"* Kevin McNulty, Sr. uses research and his forty-plus years in education, judging, performing, business and management to provide background, insight, information, and a plan for assessing music performance in today's educational landscape. Using the ideas and methods proposed here can provide the key to finding common ground between administrators' "one size fits all" landscape and our quest to teach students to make, understand and love great music.

Greg Bimm
Director of Bands
Marian Catholic High School
Chicago Heights, Illinois

PREFACE

All across the education landscape today, music performance teachers are being asked how students in band, orchestra, and choir students are being graded. For some time now, teachers in other disciplines have been addressing the same question. An entire industry has grown up around this topic, but the solutions are designed to serve academic subject matter in the traditional classroom.

Teachers teach methods, skills, and understanding to the entire class with the hope that each individual will gain an understanding of the subject matter. They then issue an assessment to determine if each student *has* "retained what they've learned." When a student takes accounting in high school, he or she is tested. Upon graduation, they study further, hopefully, graduate from accounting school, and land a job where they can apply "all they have learned."

Music performance teachers teach performance. Our students do not have to wait to apply their methods, skills, and understanding of music. They do it immediately, just as every professional musician does, every day. We assess their performance as soon as the music occurs. We give a downbeat, we hear something, we cut off the ensemble, and we assess. We do this all day long. Assessing is the only thing we do. In fact, our mode of teaching *is* assessment. We assess more than any teacher in the school building.

The fact that we instantly apply what we teach is the primary reason why we are different from all other subjects and why the assessment methodology deployed in non-performing classrooms does not work for us.

But what, then, *is* our system of assessment? I'm afraid our answer to that question has many answers, and many of them are not sound. Some of us do not formally assess individual students at all. Many grade on attitude, behavior, and something called, "esprit de corps." Pressed to provide something to administrators or comply with school policy, we create assessment tactics that appear recognizable to non-music performance curriculum directors and assessment committees. We offer defenses such as "no time," "it's busy work," "too many kids," and many other reasons.

Having a system that really measures what we are teaching in schools is not only important, it is a tool that will make our performing groups better, and it is critical to our continued presence in the school setting. But the system must be ours and one that actually measures what we teach.

"*Assessing Music Performance…A Valid System for Measuring Student Performance and Growth*" brings together the science of professional adjudication, acquired over more than forty years of application, with the science and art of assessing students in their pursuit of musical agility, expression, and artistry.

ACKNOWLEDGMENTS

In 1975, I attended my first meeting of the Central States Judges Association, in Chicago. There, I witnessed a group of professional judges who were creating and recreating the judging system used by drum and bugle corps and band contests. I've dedicated this book to two great CSJA judges, Paul Litteau and Bob Wenderski who had a profound influence on my judging career and my perspective on life.

Paul is a sage. He was one of the "new generation of judges" that documented and enhanced so many of the practices invented by people like Earl Joyce, Lenny Piekarski, and others twenty years earlier. He is the "judge's judge" and a genius in business. Bob was a man of process. He could read your mind simply by reading your scores. He was a pragmatist and spoke in precise terms. Bob taught me more about "numbers management" and "spread" than anyone since. He is a superior manager. He also taught me the importance of assessing "how things are," more than "how I'd like them to be."

I want to thank the hundreds of judges I've worked with for over forty years. I'd also like to thank my old friend Joe Miller who always kept one foot in reality and one firmly planted in whimsy. Thank you to James Elvord for teaching me beauty and Hugh Mahon for just being Hugh. To Rick Maass, my buddy Walt Kubiak, and Scottie Wild who were all bigger than life. To my first judge-trainers, Lance Lovejoy and Karson Klund for teaching me the fundamentals.

I'd like to thank my colleagues at Bradley-Bourbonnais Community High School, in Bradley, Illinois, especially, Bill Dyche, Cheryl King, Cindy Altenberger, Chris Lord, Katie Bretzlaff, Christine Hosek and Tori Cohagan. I'd also like to thank their principal Dr. Brian Wright for his tireless efforts to change the way student-learning is assessed in high school. My experience at BBCHS helped me become familiar with the latest in school reform.

I remember my wonderful education professor William Zeller at Illinois State University who had as much passion for testing authenticity as I did for music. I remember Mary Hoffman, Charles Leonhard, and Richard Cowell at the University of Illinois for their inspired and intuitive teaching.

I'd like to thank my good friend Greg Bimm of Marian Catholic High School for his forward to this book, teaching my kids about life and music, and letting me help when I ever could.

Finally, I want to thank my son Kevin McNulty, Jr. for his great help and the students of Keller Central High School in Fort Worth, Texas and Bradley-Bourbonnais Community High School. I'd like to thank all my students over the years that bore the burden of my testing experiments.

INTRODUCTION

The fact that you are reading this book indicates that the word "assessment" has entered your world – or is about to. Perhaps your school has just launched what I call "the conversion process" or maybe you've been at it for a few years. Re-writing curriculum, incorporating standards-based principles, writing assessments, and unifying teaching practices within departments and across a district is a lengthy and challenging process. Some schools have been at it for a while. Some have not yet started.

If you've had your first meeting on "the conversion," you have begun the process, and you may find yourself in strange territory. You see, nearly all the work done in this area has been done outside the area of music. Certainly, there are some initiatives within music education, which have begun to address assessment practices. But a large percentage of those engaged are general music people – not music performance people. Even music performance people who *are* engaged do not address the core differences between music performance and non-performance classes. When it comes to assessment, they try to adopt general music models, and it doesn't work.

The books, papers, panel discussions, symposia, and other formal reports about assessment in music education tend to be little more than 1) reports on the status quo, 2) documents that describe course content, 3) a dissection of performance skills by grade level, 4) what to put in handbooks 5) descriptions of what students do when performing 6) existential discussions linking assessment models to "what we do," and 7) warnings that music teachers need to "get on board." Despite all the work done in assessment, there has been no foundational system put forward that explains how to go about measuring what we teach in our classrooms – namely performance.

It is not my intent to report on the details of numerous symposia, university-sponsored workshops, state music association reports, arts education societies, the current state of curriculum development, standards setting, or assessment within music education. I shall only reference such things as a means to contrast this work. Nor is it my intent to present to you schools with models already in place that your school could adopt. To begin with, they are few and far between. Secondly, those schools that have put their ideas on paper skim over an important question yet to be addressed by most music assessment efforts to date:

> *Is it possible that performing arts content, which is the act of producing the very content itself, is so unique from all other subjects taught in our schools, that the assessment strategies and tools used by other disciplines are fundamentally unrelated to music performance and, therefore, useless as an assessment tool?*

"Assessing Music Performance...A Valid System for Measuring Student Performance and Growth" is intended to demonstrate the following:

1) Music performance is an active art form that is not simply the presentation of musical elements but the human demonstration of abilities and an expression of ideas, beliefs, moods, emotions, and visions, using musical elements.

2) Musical qualities within a composition or performance are proportional, not equivalent. A top-rated performance is not merely the presence of all qualities at maximum levels. It is an expressive performance with musical qualities at appropriate levels as set by the composer, displayed by the performer and is transparent to the listener.

3) The only way to accurately measure the desired outcomes of music performance is through the prism of a music performance teacher's background and experience as a musician, and not simply against a list of criteria or an extraneous written exam.

4) All music directors must possess and be cognizant of their musical standard for all forms, idioms, and genres of music. They must also possess standards for each instrument or voice. Standards do not simply apply to ultimate performances; they also identify the lowest-level performance ever heard by a director. It follows, then, that standards also imply an average, below average and above average performance - and all gradients of performance in between. Possessing standards and being able to assess against those standards, requires the use of a linear scale designed not only to rate but, more importantly, to rank performances.

5) While other disciplines in schools use rating almost exclusively, rating and ranking are required in music performance evaluation. Ranking not only establishes program standards but also provides distinction, fine-tunes teacher tolerance, provides data for seating and ensemble placement, allows for program measurement, and facilitates the escalation of performance standards year-to-year.

6) Though rubrics can be implemented, they are merely a musical prospectus and are not the primary means to assess the quality of a performance. They are incapable of fully defining achievement in musical performance. They can clarify teacher impressions but are not a substitute for the standards of the evaluator or music director doing assessments.

7) Grading is different from assessing. Assessment measures performance against a musical standard. Grading measures a student's achievement against benchmarks established for grade levels or ensembles. Benchmarks are natural divisions within the range of achievement by all students in the program or ensemble. They are set for an entire school year based on ensemble or seating auditions at the end of the previous school year.

8) To rate, rank, and eventually grade music performance students, directors must use a system that allows them to move from a subjective synergistic impression to an objective numerical assessment. It must allow the director to experience the expressive aesthetic, realize its significance, perceive technically artistry, and calculate the ranking and rating of each performance. It must be capable of assessing students at all levels.

9) When evaluating student-musicians, directors should react to the overall performance of the student first, to determine a broad impression range of achievement. They then analyze the basis for their reaction, referencing the elements present in the musical performance. They then check for any personal bias, reflect on previous impressions collected over time, and assign an initial raw number to the performance.

10) In the final stage of evaluation, directors narrow their impression range, determine a tentative final number and then place that number on a ranking scale that allows for comparison to other performers. If, through their own cognition, the rating, ranking or number spread to other performers is incorrect, directors must repeat the impression and analysis phase to determine how their impression or analysis was flawed. Once rectified, evaluators return to the comparison step again and set the final number and ranking.

11) Formative skills should also be measured using this system. Written tests are not a substitute for music performance achievement assessment. Formative and summative assessments should only be determined through live performance.

12) To accommodate students with lower or advanced musical abilities (the talent debate), directors can tailor individualized growth targets to measure achievement from a student's starting point at the beginning of the year. This individualized assessment strategy aligns with the notion of individualized instruction and is accommodated by ensemble placement and/or part-assignment within an ensemble. The percentages of students who need these accommodations are minimal. They should be designed to facilitate the lower ability student with the goal of achieving their grade level over time. Accelerated students who might exceed the demands of their ensemble can be assigned higher targets through advanced studies.

13) Regardless of the grading system used in a school district (percentage, letter grade, numerical rating), music performance directors can align the proposed numerical scale-based system presented here with any grade reporting system used in their district. The system utilizes a linear scale, divisible by five ranges of achievement. Five levels can overlap any number of grading levels be it a four-year high school or four years of elementary-middle school training.

14) Selection of literature each year should exceed the capabilities of all students based on the assessment of the ensemble at the end of the previous year. This assures student growth and raises program standards over time.

15) Competent music-performance teachers must regularly seek out performances of other school music programs and professional performances outside education in order to expand and better understand the wide range of achievement potential in music performance as it relates to their school district's current level of achievement.

The purpose of this work is to explain the unique nature of music performance as it relates to assessment. It presents a process best suited to quantify the subjective nature of music performance into objective data that best measures achievement of desired outcomes in music performance classes.

Student assessment in our schools has ignored the realities of performing music. At the same time, music performance teachers have looked away from a formal method to report on individual music performance achievement - despite the fact that they make informal assessments every minute of their teaching day and, in fact, know the abilities of their students.

Music performance classes have a long tradition of issuing grades based on behavioral outcomes rather than musical outcomes. While behaviors such as attendance, attitude, practice and adherence to procedures are vital to successful and professional music performance, they should not be the primary basis for how we assess student achievement in the performing arts.

Work done in the area of music assessment has borrowed heavily from the machinations of the non-performing academics. Education has invested significant time and research to a process that works for them but not for us. General music has borrowed from non-music subjects, but their outcomes align with those of non-music disciplines, not music performance classes.

Music performance disciplines need to put forth assessment methods that actually measure what we teach and are based on the applied principles that have created the finest school performing arts organizations in the world.

"Assessing Music Performance...A Valid System for Measuring Student Performance and Growth" is presented as a principled and workable method for music directors to execute accurate assessments of their student-performers. At the same time, it is intended to provide school districts with a well-founded method for grading students in music performance on a par with all other subjects.

Section One

Standards & Testing in American Schools

Part 1 - Landscape
The formation of schools, involvement of our communities and government, and the common practice of testing students over the years provides a backdrop for which to discuss the music-performance exception. It does us well to remember that the essential question all parent-tax payers have asked since our founding is – "How is my child doing? Our discussion of how music performance is measured is designed to best answer this question.

Part 2 - Music Performance Teaching
Understanding how music ensembles came to be part of our school curricula also puts the proposed system into context. Assessing how musicians play did not begin with the arrival of music-performance in schools. An understanding of what conductors and directors have done for years, in every rehearsal, reveals that our teaching method *is* to assess.

Part 3 - Measuring the Aesthetic
Our system is based on "philosophical logic," established by the key aesthetic and educational thinkers and on a "common sense logic" understood by all who engage in the production of music at all levels.

Part 1

Landscape

Education in America

In 1635, the first Latin Grammar School opened in Boston, Massachusetts, designed for sons of certain social classes who were destined for leadership positions in the church, state, or the courts. One year later, Harvard College, the first higher education institution, opened in Newtowne (now Cambridge), Massachusetts. That same year, the first "free school" opened in Virginia. But most schooling in the Colonies was provided at home by parents or tutors.

Massachusetts passed the "Old Deluder Satan Act" in 1647 which decreed that every town of at least 50 families hire a schoolmaster who would teach the town's children to read and write and that all towns of at least 100 families should have a Latin grammar schoolmaster who would prepare students to attend Harvard College. Thus, the first governmental action on education passed 140 years before the American Constitution.

When the Bill of Rights was approved in 1791, the tenth amendment stated that "powers, not delegated to the federal government are reserved to the States, respectively, or to the people." Thus, education became a function of the state rather than the federal government. That would change. The 1800's was a century of higher education, as significant universities cropped up all across the country, due mainly to the "Land Grant Acts of 1861 and 1890. The first public high school opened in 1821 in Boston and the first community college in Joliet, Illinois in 1901. The work of Horace Mann, who promoted free, universal public education for all, made a significant impact on the minds of all Americans.

Shortly after the end of the Civil War, the federal government increased its role in shaping education by creating the Department of Education. But it would not be raised to a cabinet-level department until 1979. Its goal was to help states establish effective school systems. Its creation increased the involvement of the federal government in local education. It also paved the way for national standards dictated to the states from Washington, D.C.

In the 20th Century, teaching methods began to receive scrutiny. The Carnegie Foundation for the Advancement of Teaching was founded in 1905. It had a significant impact on education, including class time recommendations, and the founding of the Educational Testing Service. The organization would merge with the American Council on Education and the College Entrance Examination Board, birthing the notion that testing was best performed by independent, nonprofit organizations outside the school system. Today, we have tests like ACT, SAT, and PARCC.

Between 1900 and 1932, 1,300 achievement tests were on the market, as compared to about four hundred tests of "mental capacities," ninety-two high school tests covering vocational aptitude, and assessments of athletic ability. State-sponsored testing programs were becoming more common during this time, as well.

Teacher groups, most notably the NEA, got involved in recommending curricula. Their Commission on the Reorganization of Secondary Education in 1918 produced seven cardinal principles of secondary education. Music, along with social studies, literature and art were mentioned as best suited to teach "those qualities that make the individual a worthy member of a family." Though teaching music has been part of an education curriculum since Greek times, it's been, more often than not, relegated to a "nice thing to learn," or "a way to make life more pleasant." Music was not, however, seen as being an educational discipline on par with mathematics or the literary arts.

Since the end of World War II, the federal government has taken on the issue of education, often setting achievement targets but with little instruction on how to carry things out at the state and local level. National initiatives such as "National Defense Education Act" (1958), "National Education Improvement Act" (1963), "No Child Left Behind Act" (2001), and "Every Student Succeeds Act" (2015), have all legislated "sweeping reforms" that were intended to upgrade and standardize education in America. Few commented on form or execution. That would be left up to the states and local school districts.

Yet, in 1989, President George H. W. Bush called together 49 Governors in Charlottesville, Virginia with the primary aim of addressing the 1983 report that came out of President Ronald Reagan's National Commission on Excellence in Education. The report was called "A Nation at Risk" and created a national discussion about the state of our schools. Awareness of "A Nation at Risk" went beyond those in education, in think tanks or among policy wonks in Washington. The media found it newsworthy and the report elevated education to the status "a national discussion," on par with the environment, public safety, military readiness, and taxes.

The trail of studies, think tank reports, legislative actions, government policies, teacher-group recommendations, and other proposals to improve education is long and wide. It is also full of potholes, reworks, U-turns and dead ends. Politicians believe innovation must come from the top. Teachers believe it must come from the bottom. Politicians believe any push-back from teacher groups, stymies innovation. Teachers believe that top-down dictation robs teachers of decision-making. And so, it goes.

Administrators must be superior project managers, pristine communicators, agile facilitators and authentic motivators. They must be guardians of state policy to assure school district compliance, get teachers to buy-in and implement, and at the same time explain the need for reform to parents. They must be inspirational evangelists and yet acknowledge that true faith in the system must live in the hearts and minds of teachers. At the local level, issues like school policy, how teachers treat students, the physical conditions of school buildings, and taxes are the issues closest to school parents.

While one will find an occasional protest by local taxpayers about course content or how students are doing overall, most parents only know how *their* kids are doing. These concerns are best addressed directly with teachers, with administrators or at the local school board level. But federal and state-funded studies reveal information about schools on a broader scale that cannot be obtained locally. Like all large studies, however, little is offered regarding possible solutions or efficient implementation. There is no basis to assume that those who gather data have any insight as to potential solutions. Only "those on the ground" can effectively find workable solutions and then implement. But as a means of identifying trends and broad concerns, large-scale studies are effective.

In recent years, states have legislated with increasing specificity. Like their national counterparts, they once set broad curriculum standards. But national reports of declining achievement rates, grade inflation, and lower scores on national tests have urged states to get more specific about not only *what* is taught, but *how* it is to be taught and more significantly, how learning is to be measured. While their intentions are noble, their directives encroach on school boards, administrators, and teachers, all of whom are better equipped to find solutions since they are closer to the students in their schools.

When a national study is released, it's usually accompanied by endless debate and opinion within education, broad speculation on the part of the media, and questions at school board meetings about "how we stack up." Out of all this comes the call that "something must be done." And so, feeling beholden to their constituents and believing that the solutions lie in the belly of legislation, state lawmakers put forth benchmarks, reporting standards and deadlines. They bring in specialists, consultants, and experts to testify. But in the end, they make decisions based on the political need to decide rather than the merits of the solution.

Still, it seems reasonable that national studies can reveal trends verifiable only by large collections of data. The federal government can frame the national vision for better schools. States can define broad objectives and direct school districts to reach solutions within target dates. Administrators can submit their plan of action to school boards for approval. And teachers can be charged with devising sound tactics to revise their curricula, improve the way they teach and change the way they measure. All concerned have the responsibility to report to tax-payers. Parents will see the results in their child's achievements.

Suffice it to say, government, special interest groups, think tanks, universities, foundations, teacher unions, societies, parent groups, nonprofits and even industry have all had an impact on our educational system since the beginning of the colonies. "Intrusion into the classroom" is uttered today as if it is something new. It is not. In the end, what we teach in the classroom is what our communities feel is important. But teaching ultimately exists in the professional knowledge of teachers themselves.

.

Testing in Schools

The Common Core Initiative, released in 2010, set in motion an explosion of ideas about how American schools should operate. The standards set educational goals and objectives for certain core subjects taught in K-12 schools. Music performance was not one of them.

Many of the principles were drawn from Achieve, an organization founded by the nation's governors and corporate leaders, to raise academic standards, strengthen graduation requirements, improve assessments, and establish benchmarks in all 50 states. (Achieve, 2017, March 29). The intention of Common Core was to make American high school graduates more competitive with their international peers. Language arts and math were the lightning rods. States were given the option to adopt Common Core. Today, forty-two have adopted the standard. Some currently have since taken actions to modify or abandon it. The use and implementation of Common Core is still a patchwork, at this time. Still, virtually every state has developed specific standards to raise the bar for the education of all children.

In the wake of Common Core, states set benchmarks for school districts, but the implementation is done by teachers and local school districts. States charged school districts with implementing their standards but offered little help to administrators on how to implement them in the classroom. States approved standardized tests to measure student achievement, but they subsequently dropped certain tests for others because some tests took away from key instruction time. Students failed to take the exams, and colleges were ignoring results. After many years of institutionalized state-wide testing, two practices have become commonplace in education.

"Teaching to the Test" - One is a tendency for teachers to "teach to the test," so say critics of the new testing demands. As a long-time teacher in high school and now in the college classroom, I find students focused more on what the answer is and less interested in how the answer was found. This is a change from my early days teaching in the 1970's. As a former CEO, I've always believed that the right answer is important. But the ability to problem-solve is more important. That's the "how." I always hired people that understood "how." In all my years teaching music, students were always concerned with the "how." It's what we teach.

"Data-driven Instruction" - The other Common-Practice is the use of what has become known as "data-driven instruction." Data-driven instruction comes out of the business management process referred to as "data-driven decision making." Faced with increasing accountability, school systems are implementing a variety of methods to gather data on their schools. The primary way is to issue a single test to an entire school district (targeting certain grade levels). It is this data that drives instructional change. One could stage a reasonable debate as to whether a business system, designed to measure productivity, efficiency, sales growth and market share, could teach education much about success in the classroom. But that is a debate outside the parameters of this book. Besides, empirical measurement has a longstanding history in education. In music, only performance drives instruction.

With the widespread use of testing today, it might be wise to, first, examine how testing works. To clarify our discussion, I'd like to propose definitions of three types of testing:

Common-Practice Testing is used in this book to refer to the variety of traditional paper testing used in classrooms for years. These tests are designed by the teacher, and questions are tied directly to specific course content and teacher-designed lesson plans. Tests of this kind use everything from true-false to essay questions which everyone has taken at some time during their school years. This form of testing is the dominant method used to assess in classrooms today.

Standardized Testing refers to the use of Common-Practice Testing on a broader scale, either district-wide, throughout an entire state, or across the country. These tests cover a broad spectrum of subject matter and are *not* designed by the teachers who instruct students taking the test. Standardized testing services hire high school teachers and college professors for insight as to what should be tested and how to craft questions. Teachers, called "item writers," actually write the questions. They are given rules to follow when writing the questions such as topics and phrases that avoid ethnic, gender, or regional bias.

Music Performance Testing refers to the assessment of a live performance of music by a student-musician. It is evaluated by the music director who has assigned the music to be performed. Performance Testing has very little in common with Common-Practice Testing.

The differences between Common-Practice Testing, Standardized Testing and Music Performance Testing are dramatic. Common-Practice Testing and Standardized Testing are very similar. They collect data in similar ways. Neither type measure application. They measure a student's understanding of concepts. Application comes in labs or well after graduation.

Music Performance Testing measures application. Application implies understanding in ways that Common-Practice and Standardized testing cannot. Music Performance not only implies understanding it demonstrates the discernment of elements nonexistent and thus unmeasurable using Common-Practice or Standardized Testing.

Since we contend that the **Inherent Nature** and **Desired Outcomes** of *Music Performance Subject Matter* are radically different from *Non-Performance Subject Matter*, it naturally holds true that the two are assessed in different ways. An examination of these differences can provide insight into the nature of music performance and how it is assessed.

Common-Practice Testing

1) Common-Practice Testing seldom, if ever, involves issuing the test in advance.

In preparation for a Common-Practice Test, teachers teach content and then review material to be tested in advance of the test. Teachers may even issue a practice test or issue what are called formative tests (or assessments, if you like) leading to what is called a summative test. Explain to students the structure and design of a given test is as important as reviewing the content that will be assessed. How a test is designed can impact how students prepare for tests. There is a perception by some students that one form is less demanding than another form (i.e., "fill in the blank" versus "multiple choice.). But students are never given the actual test in advance.

2) Common-Practice Testing, success requires memorization skills and strong recall.

Memorizing facts for regurgitation on tests does not always assure a grasp of subject matter and does not measure a student's ability to apply what he understands. Studies indicate that acquiring a good memory can be nurtured through training. (Klingberg, 2005) It also indicates that genetics plays a role in brain function and therefore memory. (Boag, 2016). Clearly, the ability to memorize has been part of education for some time. Some students are better at it than others.

3) Answering Common-Practice Test questions is a series of single independent acts.

Other than the connection questions have to course content, there is no relationship between one question and the next on a Common-Practice Test. While tests have unity around a topic, the experience for the student is often compartmentalized. In their mind, they execute the exam one question at a time. ("Ok, got that one...What's next?).

4) In Common-Practice Tests, a student's ability to decipher test questions is critical to their ability to reveal their knowledge of subject matter.

Students understand that a big part of testing success is navigating the design of the test itself. This has nothing to do with understanding content. It is about understanding "testing-code," negotiating through "trick questions," and, otherwise, navigating the tools used in testing. Additionally, students need to be able to read well in order to access the question. They then must marshal their analytical and writing abilities to respond to the question.

5) Data from Common-Practice Testing can tell you if there is a problem but will give you little information regarding a solution.

Tests collect data. Once tests are graded, testing services or teachers must then check the results. With objective tests, right and wrong answers are pretty clear, with an occasional faux pas when students misunderstand the question. Essay questions require more of a judgment call. But in the end, teachers must determine whether their students understood the content or whether test construction, invalid questions, or student testing capabilities could have skewed overall success. Still, with that, the test itself does not reveal why students made errors while testing. Teachers must deploy other analytical methods in the hopes of finding those answers. Students have to deal with the testing tool on the way in. Teachers have to deal with it on the way out.

Standardized Testing

Standardized Tests have been around since the beginning of the 20th Century They are designed by experts and are intended for use by more than one school. They can be taken using paper and pencil or by computer. Adaptive testing allows designers to present new questions based answers given to previous questions.

1) Standardized tests are convenient, easy to administrate and quantifiable.

One of the elements of Standardized Testing is its objectivity and ability to assess, void of teacher bias. Standardized Tests allow educators to compare students within the same school and in different schools. This provides data on an individual student's abilities but also on the school as a whole. It allows schools to identify weak areas and strong areas. It also gives them the data needed to track performance over time and compare schools.

2) Questions from standardized tests must be of a general nature.

They are not directly connected to the desired outcomes of specific classrooms nor are the data from these tests directly applicable to improving instruction. Furthermore, being general in nature, these tests are not used to assess higher levels of academic thinking. It is clear that music performance is not assessable using these tests, just as creative writing or an assignment to discuss different theories of personality would not be assessable with these tests.

3) The Standardized Test removes the possibility of teacher bias.

By contrast, Valid Music Performance Testing requires assessments that are filtered through the prism of a music teacher's background, experience, and their personal standard. The Music Performance Test requires teacher opinion. Therefore, any proposed method to assess Music Performance must have built-in protections against bias.

4) Performing well on Standardized Tests has as much to do with anticipating what a test will ask as it does with a student's understanding of the subject matter.

How frequent it is that students ask, "What's going to be on the test?" Practicing for a standardized test is not only viewed as advisable, but it is also considered crucial by some. Testing services such as SAT, ACT, and others, acknowledge this to be true. They not only advise the use of their "official practice tests," but recommend students take them under "test-like conditions." Schools, universities, College Board (SAT) and ACT testing services offer pre-test experiences. In addition, a sizable cottage industry has developed over the years to pre-test students in advance of required standardized tests. The stakes are high for students and also for schools.

5) Anticipating what's on a Standardized Test is equally important to teachers as it is to the students.

Standardized testing differs from teacher-created tests drawn from specific instruction and activities in the classroom. Teachers design tests around their *lectures* (specifics, emphasis), from the *text* (content, scope, and emphasis*), supplemental resources* used in the classroom (video, outside speakers, field trips, labs), and from discussion (counter positions, new ideas, and questions from students). Good teachers always reflect upon how to improve testing results. They will adjust how they teach, change text or resources, adjust lab experiences. They will also modify tests. In the case of national Standardized Testing, however, teachers have no control over test design. Therefore, have now become concerned with knowing "what's on the test."

6) Standardized Testing and Common-Practice Testing tools cannot be used to assess music performance.

This does not preclude using them for general music, music history or music theory. It also does not preclude band, orchestra and choir teachers from using these standard testing systems to measure non-performance musical knowledge in support of performance assessment (formative, perhaps). But they should not be the dominant method used to determine a music performance class's Desired Outcomes.

The Nature of Music Performance and Testing

Directors spend hours selecting and preparing music for performance. Yet, we spent too little time assessing individual students. While "lack of time" has always been an issue and still is to a degree, it's no longer a valid excuse. Large and small programs are doing it. They accomplish it with the help of technology. Your school will come to you with the assessment tools of non-performance class. They will ask you to institute their methods to assess your students. It's not enough to simply reply, "We don't do it that way." In short, it is our job to know how we asses, educate our administrators about how we do it and then work with them to arrive at a mutually agreed upon solution. This requires a keen understanding of how we assess and how it is different from non-performance classes. Here is how we are different:

Activities Prior to Assessment

Paper Tests versus Sheet Music

The printed piece of music handed to a music student in advance of their assessment is not analogous to an English teacher passing out an exam. The papers are different. One asks questions (Common-Practice Test). The other gives information (Sheet Music). If a student fully memorizes and retains facts for a Common-Practice Test, they will very likely have success - if they can decipher the test questions. Memorizing music in advance of a Performance Test is not the same as memorizing information for a Common-Practice Test (Matlin, 2014). Memorizing music in advance of a Performance Test provides no assurance that the desired outcomes will occur. Live performance is the Desired Outcome.

Issuing the test in advance

In Music Performance Classes students know exactly what will be on a Music Performance Assessment test (the questions). In fact, with the exception of a sight-reading exam, they have the test well in advance. Directors issue copies of auditions or playing tests to everyone, well before the exam. Students can seek help (the answers) from their teacher. They often work in collaboration with each other (copying), they execute the test a number of times before the actual music performance exam occurs (pre-assess).

Music students receive their test in advance. They perform it many times over. They have time to research their piece, ask questions regarding the printed copy of their piece. They can inquire as to how the piece is to be expressed and many other questions. With proper preparation and study, there is no need to decipher the music "questions" during the assessment. All this is done in advance of the test
.

A student taking a Common-Practice Test can study every element of content to be tested and still find the testing tool (how the test question is designed) to be an impediment to revealing their subject knowledge. This does not happen in Music-Performance assessment.

Students teaching students

During band sectionals, two clarinet students are seen playing the etude together, stopping regularly at times when things get "off." One student points out where an error occurred. She offers the other student a fingering and then demonstrates how to traverse a difficult passage. The two resume their duet, this time, to the end. When they conclude, there is an expression of delight. The more advanced student points out a note half-way down the page that was particularly out of tune. They test it. Student "A" points out an alternative fingering that will bring the note into pitch. They test it a second time with success. Both decide to play through the etude one more time. Again, they are delighted with the results. There are other duets and trios practicing together throughout the room at the same time.

About this time, the principal enters the band room while students are all playing in small groups. He requests that the band be present to perform at an upcoming school assembly. He quickly visits the director and confirms this. He thanks the director and before parting says humorously, "I don't know how you can stand all this racket." The director laughs and responds, "Oh, I don't even hear it anymore." The administrator departs never realizing that students were preparing for an assessment and they had the actual test in their hands. The director missed a chance to explain how "studying for a test" works in music performance.

Demonstrating the "right answers."

On the first day of school, he issues the material to all students. The students know exactly "what will be on the test." During the first three weeks of school, the band director spends some time on certain days practicing the etude in class with the students so that they know how it should sound. He calls on his more advanced students to play the etude for others in the section so they can hear a good model performance (almost like looking at another's test beforehand who received an "A").

Modeling

Teachers often play for their students or play recordings in order to demonstrate. Students then utilize their aural memory, striving, in practice, to match the standard heard in these examples. With familiarity, the visual memory (notes on the page) is enhanced and at some point dominated by the aural memory when musicians have played a piece many times over. At that point, pure expression can occur.

Activities During Assessment

The nature of a "right answer" in music

The musical "questions" and their "answers" run together. They are dependent on each other. Furthermore, there is no time for musicians to ponder a musical "question." They are instant events that must be answered immediately – before they are "gone" This concocted analogy between what Music-Performance Testing measures and what Common-Practice Testing measures (using the question-answer metaphor), should be enough to invalidate the use of Common-Practice Testing methodology in the area of music performance.

The Nature of Music Performance "Answers"

Music performance assessment requires that students multi-task. Notes on a page and phrases heard, as a result, are not independent questions with final answers. Were one to consider music as a series of questions (concocted, I agree), they would be interrelated and reliant on each other. They are "connected questions," with "reliant answers." To play horizontally (as in phrasing) and vertically (as in dynamics), musicians must successfully "answer many questions at once." Indeed, falling short when "answering" one musical "question" causes other "answers," correspondingly, to diminish in quality or disappear.

For example, if note accuracy in the upper range of a trumpet exam falters, it will invariably affect tempo as the musician struggles to recover. Should the conscious control of the diaphragm fail a young tenor as he sings a descending line at the bottom of his range, his pitch will wane, his tone will become uncharacteristic, and his required new breath will be late, affecting pulse, the start of the new phrase and his confidence going forward.

Recognizing correct music performance "answers."

No intermediary testing tool (paper exam) is used to assess music performance. The test results are demonstrated (applied) so teachers need not rely on a measurement tool (paper exam) that will hopefully reveal a student's understanding (testing validity). People who assume that the presence of musical qualities (i.e., tone, intonation, tempo, dynamic expression), are a series of independent "responses" to separate "questions" being "asked" in music, are significantly misinformed. Scoresheets with a list of qualities may present things this way, but they are never presented in performance in such a tidy manner.

In fact, one quality cannot be perceived in isolation from the other qualities present in a performance or listed on a scoresheet (tone, intonation, etc.). Success or failure in any given area such as tone must be considered in context and association with all other qualities occurring simultaneously to the "sampled" quality in question.

Furthermore, a passage formed with flawless intonation can be of greater value or made more significant by the demands of other qualities such as tempo, articulation, range, or dynamics. These are very complex perceptions that only a musician who has experienced them as a performer can comprehend and appreciate. This is the foundation for our premise that all assessment must be done in live performance assessed by a professional with the background and experience to perceive these subtle and continuous events in performance.

The elusive perfect "answer" in music

Music Directors have the responsibility to teach students that the ultimate performance is elusive. There is always someone better. This is due to the fact that music has an endless nature and is not finite. In math 1 + 1 = 2. In music 1 + 1 can equal 3, or 4, or more. Ultimate achievement is not the sum of all qualities present. The attempt to fully define desired outcomes in music performance curriculum falls short. They cannot be fully defined on paper. It is the teacher with their background, experience, and aural memory of their ultimate standard that determines the level of success attained by the student.

Recognizing Musical Expression

But there is more. Expressive music performance requires demonstrated abilities in imaging, emotional expression, symbolism, showmanship, communication, and mood-setting. Hours of practice cannot guarantee that these things will occur, but practice is required for them to occur. During performance, expression must be present in the soul of the performer first, then communicated strongly enough, so it is perceived by the audience. The music performance teacher-musician, with the background and experience to perceive it instantly, must then quantifying its merit against all previous performances he or she has witnessed in the past. Each time a teacher hears a better performance, the standard of quality is expanded. The musical "answers" can, therefore, exceed the expectations of the musical "questions," causing standards to increase and requiring future assessments encompass the "new possible." In subsequent assessments, the bar will naturally rise.

Forward Projection

Everyone who has ever played or sung music knows how the mind often reflects on "the next passage" while performing the current one. Musicians need to guard against reflecting on a "just played passage," at the risk of failing the next. Yet, they must mentally prepare for the next passage while playing the current message. This is a dramatic difference from the student in other classes who focuses on and answers one question at a time in isolation from all others. Thus, Music-Performance Assessment must be done live and by a musician-teacher who can sense how well students navigate the mental gyrations associated with music performance. It is observable only by a musician who has experienced it.

Physical Anticipation

Similarly, musicians anticipate and take inventory of physical changes required from one musical "question" to the next. Wind players must keep their body relaxed in order to breathe deeply. Percussionist must call on large body movement to express the musical phrase. Singers must control the mechanics of singing and yet express their song physically, with emotion. String players must harness the ability to control dramatic changes in physical energy in order to express dramatic and often sudden changes in musical intensity. All musicians must strive to master the unconscious and conscious physical requirements of the art to assure they remain "in the expressive moment" as they present an effortless, transparent performance.

When this occurs, we recognize it as "artistry." Athletes do this, also. It's called "being in the zone." Thus, trumpeter Arturo Sandoval and Michael Jordon are doing the same thing. This very important achievement cannot be measured with a written exam. It is perceived by the professional music teachers or sophisticated listeners who have experienced it themselves and recognize it when they hear and see it.

Memorization as it relates to Music Performance

Music Teachers do teach students to sing and play from memory. However, this is often done when performance conditions require it. Choirs will memorize to sing and present better without music in hand. Marching bands will memorize to focus on playing and moving. String players will similarly do so in certain venues. Cognitive memory is a valuable tool when taking Common-Practice Tests. In Music Performance, there are different types of memory required in addition to cognitive memory. They include:

Muscle Memory: Though it is not, technically, memory, it is most important in music performance. When musicians begin playing or singing, their body takes over. Some muscle memory is unconscious, similar to physical conditioning pursued by athletes. Much of it is "trained," beginning slowly, with "focus of mind" until the body moves as one desires. Baseball pitchers, drummers, and dancers use this method, continuously. Highly skilled and advanced student-musicians have highly developed muscle memory. Beginners have less. But muscle memory is central to all music performance.

Conceptual Memory: Science defines this as Short Term Conceptual Memory. It happens when "stimuli" (a note pattern that begins to climb) triggers information in one's long-term memory (a stepwise pattern beginning on the low G). The violinist, who understands the conceptual memory of a minor key with two flats, and suddenly sees this scale-wise pattern beginning on the open G string, will trigger the muscle memory of the G minor scale and ascend with barely a conscious thought of each note.

Visual Memory: Visual memory is the memory of the notes as they are arranged on the page. They are often patterns. Highly familiar sections of music, performed by advanced musicians, are often generated exclusively using muscle memory. If muscle memory breaks, a musician's visual memory kicks in. The musician pictures the next section of printed music in his head finds their place and then reverts back to muscle memory. Highly experienced musicians (most notably music performance directors) can tell instantly when this happens as they listen. (Imagine a Common-Practice Paper test determining this!)

Aural Memory: This is a vital component of Music Performance. Indeed, without it, musicians cannot recapture the sound, inflection or shape of the music they perform. Music instructors, professional musicians, and students have, as their life-blood, an entire history of performances in their aural memory bank. We all carry these memories around with us for our entire life. Students retain successful attempts they have made in the past. They also retain successful attempts by other students they've heard who are "better than they are." A fellow student's level of performing is often adopted as another student's standard of success. This is only possible with aural memory. You'll often hear a student in an audition make an error and instantly stop and say, "I'm sorry." They know how it is supposed to sound.

Activities After Assessment

Achievement includes "affecting the listener-evaluator"

No analysis sheds as much light on the need for a separate and distinctive means to measure music performance achievement than understanding the complexity of music expression and unforeseeable potential to affect the listener. Qualified and experienced teachers must be present during music performance assessments to weigh the merit of what is a very complex human expression, whose purpose is to impact all who listen. For, good music performance is not just a measure of tone regurgitation by the performer. It is equally measured by the impact that performance has on the listener.

Performance reveals solutions

Simply finding errors ("grading the paper") is not all that is being examined in a music performance test. Unlike Common-Practice Testing, Music Performance Testing instantly reveals the cause of errors at the same time the errors occur. Trained music-performance teachers can tell instantly the reason for performance problems in assessments (why the student errored). They also experience the performance itself, noting when a passage is expressed "from the heart" and when a second passage is merely presented – all be it "successfully."

Music Performance Contains Visual Information

Some music performance teachers believe in what is called the "blind audition." I do not. Blind auditions are playing tests where the director hears the audition but does not see the student. It's a method that has been around for years. While the musical performance can be perceived, the music teacher who performs blind auditions removes visual information that will reveal many of the causes for "error." Teachers must understand cause.

Achievement cannot be measured against a Rubric

The most important conclusion to be drawn from this discussion is that the scale for measuring success in music performance classes does not exist within a rubric. The number of elements present in music performance is too many, blended and subtle. Achievement in music performance is only measurable when weighed within the complex matrix of an experienced musician-teacher's background, experience, and artistic sense.

The Impression, Analysis, Comparison System replaces the Rubric

The core of this book is a full explanation of the Impression, Analysis, Comparison System and its accompanying Linear Scale. The first phase of any music-performance assessment is to first listen to the performance "as an audience would. The second phase is to process your impression of the performance from a subjective experience to an objective assessment. This methodology will be fully discussed in subsequent chapters

Conclusion

Sometimes, we in music education take too much for granted. That leads to missed opportunities to explain to administrators how we teach, how students learn and are assessed in music performance classes. The scenario above should give directors one way to explain how assessment must be designed differently for music performance classes. Our Desired Outcomes are dramatically different from all other classes and all other assessment methods. But we must recognize the difference first.

To even the casual observer, it should be obvious that something different occurs in advance of a Music Performance Assessment than in a Common-Practice Assessment. The fact that "Common-Practice Testing" and "Music Performance Testing" are different does not mean that they do not accomplish the same thing. They both are valid if they measure the desired outcomes of the discipline being taught. "Music Performance Testing" must be used to assess the Desired Outcomes of music performance and is not applicable to non-performance academics. Educators, administrators, and legislators much understand the difference.

Part 2

Music Performance Teaching

Music Performance in the Academic World

The earliest record of music performance being taught in American schools reveals that the curriculum, instructional methods and the teachers themselves came from outside education. There was never an institutionalized musical "schoolmaster" that came up through the ranks as a model student first, got older and then taught the younger ones, went off to teacher's college to learn the craft, and then returned to the one-room schoolhouse to teach. No, the story of music performance teaching in American schools does not read like "Little House on the Prairie." From the beginning, we were outsiders. In a number of ways, we still are, today.

We are artists ourselves but for whatever reason, found our way off stage and into the classroom. We have a passion for music and a magic ability to motivate. We speak about beauty and yet serve up commands like a drill master. We encourage a kid beyond their wildest dreams on one day and then scare them to death the next. We can fire off a dozen instructions in fifteen seconds at the beginning of rehearsal and then speak about one musical nuance for fifteen minutes, at the end.

Our curriculum is not determined by a committee or the school board. It comes from the entire musical landscape. Our job is to make good choices and select music beyond the range of our student's ability and then "get them there" by the end of the year. We don't use a textbook. Our textbook is sheet music, method books, and technique exercises scribbled on music manuscript.

Our students learn to model others around them – the older ones, the talented ones, the most determined ones, and most of all – those of us who teach them. Often they learn simply as a result of their own inspiration and understanding - attained only after doing something over and over again - until it's right.

Non-music performance teachers teach *understanding* with the hope young students can *apply* it someday. We teach young musicians how to *apply* it now, knowing that *understanding* will reveal itself in time. All things that are performed reveal *understanding* as they are *applied*. A good coach can hasten understanding. But a strong lecture on how the game of basketball works and how dribbling is achieved does nothing for the student wishing to play the game.

Non-music teachers teach the *whole class* at once in the hopes that each *individual* student will understand. We teach each student *individually* so that the entire group can perform *all at one time*. We give kids something to do immediately. We give them something they can do with each other. Like all teachers, we give them lifetime memories. Our memories are applied, real-life experiences. Those memories and their meanings last longer than the information gathering that goes on in most classrooms.

Music performance is not comparable to any other subject in the school – including general music. Our history is different. We came in three forms. We sang, we bowed strings, and we played wind instruments and drums.

Singing came first and was driven by an interest in improving pitch matching and harmonization in our churches. Schools readily accepted choirs since singing was clearly wholesome, universal, natural, and inexpensive. We made no pretense to duplicate the great composers of Europe. We sang sacred and secular songs of our land.

Our orchestras came to school with the sole purpose of replicating the great symphony orchestras of Europe. To this day, the standard in orchestra is to duplicate the masters. Playing a string instrument took patience, tolerance, and sensitivity. Students drawn to this art somehow matched the texture of the voice-like sound that can only emanate from the bow being drawn across a string – an art almost as ancient as the voice itself. It has the extra dynamic of being visual, thus pleasing to the eye and ear when done with grace.

Our bands were the most entrepreneurial and, to some degree, the most American of the lot. Vets who played in the military came home and "came-a-calling" at the school door - with an idea, a sales pitch and the promise of great things. At the time when would-be band directors arrived at schools, bands were already associated with Americana, town pride and a means to "stir the souls of men." Administrators perceived this to be a good thing, and they let the bandsmen in (as most were men in the beginning).

Bands and Orchestras came into schools much later than did choral music. School bands and orchestras existed only sporadically in the 19th Century when Lowell Mason was purposely establishing choral music in America's schools. Instrumental music was considered supplementary, usually met outside the school day, and was often taught by a regular teacher who just happened to be a musician on the side.

While much of early American culture had the mark of Europe, school music was an innovation of the United States. There was no legacy of instrumental music in the schools of Europe. And, choral music in American schools was more of an extension of the American church than the great Cathedrals of the old world. Not until the New York Philharmonic was founded in 1842, did European orchestras even begin touring American cities. So, emulating youth orchestras were minimal in the 1800's. But military, professional, and town bands were widespread in the 19th Century, particularly after the Civil War.

In 1830, Williams Channing Woodbridge, using a boys' choir, directed by Lowell Mason, himself, gave a speech in Boston to the American Institute of Instruction about the merits of choral music in American schools. In 1832, Lowell Mason founded the Boston Academy of Music. And in, 1838, the Boston School Board became the first school in America to include music in the school curriculum. Music then meant predominantly singing.

These three events, occurring so early in the history of our country and being choral in nature, give us ample evidence that singing has been in our schools for a very long time. Luther Whiting Mason's music series entitled, *"The National Music Course,"* first published in 1870, demonstrated that the genesis of choral instructional method in our schools was led by choral teachers well before bands and orchestras had entered the schoolyard.

Early interest in choral music education was primarily connected to church music. This religious interest in music would lead to the creation of schools to create more skillful choirs and more harmonious church services. From the beginning of America, choral music stemmed from the traditions of both folk and religious foundations. William Billings, the first American composer of choral music, laid an early foundation for singing and choral instruction during Colonial times.

During the 1800's, it was Lowell Mason who had the greatest impact on choral music education both through his compositions and his teaching practices. He was a significant factor in adding secular music to what had thus far been religious music in American schools.

In the 19th century, conventions and fairs helped promote choral singing in America. Patrick Sarsfield Gilmore produced Peace Jubilees that featured gigantic choirs of 10,000. The 1876 Philadelphia and the 1893 Chicago World's Fairs featured extensive singing as part of their daily events.

Social amusements were the initial reasons for the development of singing on college campuses. Glee clubs were formed, which performed local concerts for friends, and later they toured to sing for alumni. Eventually, more sophisticated groups developed. They performed the standard European favorites by Handel, Haydn, Mozart, and others. Probably the earliest official ensemble was the University Choral Union of the University of Michigan in 1879. Northwestern University, in 1906, was the first school to have an "a cappella" choir. But in 1902, Oberlin College was the first liberal arts college to offer courses in school music and in 1923 awarded the nation's first degree in music performance teaching.

The first instrumental program in a school was at Boston's Farm and Trade School in 1857. The growth of other instrumental programs was sporadic until the 20th Century. Instrumental music students received no credit for participation. There were no standard teaching methods, no standard instrumentation, or set curricula. The first school to offer academic credit for instrumental music was the orchestra at Richmond, Indiana in 1905.

Between 1880 and 1933 nearly all of the major orchestras in existence today in America were established. Much of this was due to the career of the first conductor of the Chicago Symphony, Theodore Thomas who was considered the first renowned American orchestra conductor.

In 1925, the end of the "Sousa Era," as it was called, gave rise to the popularity of the professional orchestra and the diminished number of professional touring bands. From 1900 to 1920, orchestras were far more present in schools than were bands. A survey in 1919 revealed that of the 359 cities surveyed, 278 had orchestras, and only 88 had bands.

But it was the infusion of former military musicians into civilian life the fueled the rise of school bands in America. At the same time, collegiate bands grew extensively, as well.

The Golden Age of Bands occurred between the Civil War to World War I, from Gilmore to Sousa. By 1920, nearly every town had a town band. They were used extensively at the local opera house or town hall in winter and the town square, city park or festive parade in summer. They were the pride of the community, and each band had their town name painted on the bass drum.

Austin Harding, the first director of bands at the University of Illinois once remarked to Edmund James, University President, that there were "more bands in Illinois than there were towns." He was accurate. Bands in the bigger cities were better than those in small towns, but each town had one. There were also fraternal bands, industrial bands and after 1919, American Legion Bands.

It was natural that bands would develop in the local school, particularly as school attendance increased due to compulsory attendance laws. From 1910 to 1940, the chance a child would attend high school went from 10% to 75%. But if one wonders why the high school band is as linked to the community as the football team, you only need look at the origins of the band movement. The music, instruments, and purpose came right out of the spirit of the times. It paralleled and mirrored the patriotic American identity that grew from the end of the Civil War to the triumph in Europe in 1918.

At the beginning of the 1920's, orchestras dominated school instrumental programs. By the end of the decade, bands dwarfed the number of orchestras in schools. At the famous 1923 National Band Festival, Edgar B. Gordon, president of the Music Supervisors National Conference, addressed a number of supervisors at a sectional meeting of the MSNC in 1923 in Cleveland proposed:

> *"The high school band is no longer an incidental school enterprise prompted largely by the volunteer services of a high school teacher who happens to have had some band experience, but rather an undertaking which is assigned to a definite place in the school schedule with a daily class period under a trained instructor and with credit allowed for satisfactory work done."*

The 1923 National Band Festival was pivotal to the acceptance of instrumental music in a school's curriculum. But the declaration by Edgar Gordon hardly set off a musical tsunami of academic credibility nationwide. In time, the notion that music performance would have a place in the school day took hold. But broad acceptance of academic credit did not. Music as a graduation requirement in high school is still spotty, today. And applying music grades to grade point average is even rarer.

In 1929, the American Bandmasters Association was formed. John Philip Sousa was elected first honorary life president. Just as the 1923 National Band Festival had served as a catalyst for acceptance of bands in American schools, the ABA provided a more universal foundation for the training of new directors. They did much to establish standardized and instrumentation, rehearsal techniques, and performance practices. They also encouraged new repertoire. The ABA encouraged noted composers to write original literature for band. This brought band music into its own. No longer would they simply play marches, reels, and transcriptions of orchestral works. Composers such as Holst (Hammersmith), Grainger (Lincolnshire Posey), Resphigi (Huntingtow Ballad) and Cowell (Shoonthree) wrote significant new works for band during the 1930's.

Through the depression and World War II, all music programs in schools were impacted. The most sustainable at that time was choral music, partially due to its established position in all schools and the relatively low cost of choral programs, as opposed to band and orchestra. The popularity of Swing bands seeped into school band programs, and dance bands began to appear in some high schools across the country. These were clearly something extra and optional, and they rehearsed outside the school day for the most part. This author's father played in a high school big band in the mid-forties. They played so many dances on weekends that they were forced to join the musicians union.

The periods following World War I and II brought tremendous change to the economic, social and cultural life of America once the GI's came home. In the 20's, colleges and universities grew by 84%. And the rise of the college band in America came following World War I, culminating in the formation of the College Band Director's Association in 1941. William D. Revelli, Director of Bands at the University of Michigan, led the group in its first year. The years following World War II created the baby boom and major expansion in high school bands. All programs expanded in our schools, particularly music performance programs. The huge growth in high school bands followed World War II at the beginnings of the baby boom filled programs throughout the country and saw the launch of the Band Clinic in 1946, later called the Midwest Band Clinic in 1947, the Midwest National Band Clinic in 1951, the Midwest International Band Clinic in 1968 and finally the Midwest International Band and Orchestra Clinic in 1986. Today, it is the world's largest instrumental music performance conference, annually drawing approximately 17,000 attendees to Chicago from all 50 states and as many as forty countries.

In the 50's and 60's healthy band programs, emulating the university bands, established high standards for literature and performance. Serious band literature was no longer limited to orchestra transcriptions and old "war horses" from the pre-war days. Bands came into their own establishing the wind ensemble and the large band idiom as an expressive art form on its own. New young composers and arrangers filled the demand for new and better literature for band – essentially, rewriting the national "textbook" for school band ensembles. In the 60's, the music played in school music performance began to change. Jazz band music entered the band world. Swing and Jazz Choir entered choral programs. Orchestra programs maintained their original character, that of preserving the classics. But band, orchestra and choir music, that had its roots in the lyricism of Western Europe, also began to make different sounds.

The African-American spiritual, along with authentic African rhythms and harmonic colors, entered standard repertoire in both choir and band music. The influence of rhythm in American music showed itself in standard literature for all three ensemble groups as the ostinato, and rhythmic puzzles of contemporary composers took their place in our "textbook of literature." Music moved away from lyricism and toward hard shifting parallel harmonic structures, expressing modern sounds present in commercial structures.

In the 70's and 80's, Orchestras followed their long-cherished role as standard-bearer of classical music. But contemporary harmonies and non-European-based music began to appear in published music. Pedagogy drove much of the literature designed to teach fundamentals within the context of performance. And, "watered down" versions of classical music, which had always existed, became more accepted as "standard literature." Still, state music associations held true to playing "the classics" at district and all-state conferences.

In a survey of 652 schools in 1998, Robert Gillespie of Ohio State reported that enrollment in school orchestras increased during the 1990s, although the number of orchestra teachers has remained relatively stable. Larger schools are more likely to offer orchestra instruction. With so many opportunities for both male and female students in high schools today, it takes a large school population to field a large number of choir, band and orchestra students. Of the three major performance ensembles, orchestras have fallen off more than band and choir.

Pop music entered choral music literature, and pop style singing became a student's model for the choral sound. Choral directors sought quality arrangements of pop material as best they could. But the prevalence of the recorded pop vocal sound often meant "un-teaching" the sound students possessed when they enter the classroom having listened to hundreds of hours of "improper vocal production." Here too, choral teachers, all trained in the operatic style of vocal production, worked to maintain the sound produced by their student singers by deploying sound vocal methods regardless of musical style.

The creation of pop vocal productions that started with groups like "Up with People" in the 60's and big stage vocal performances in the 70's, and contemporary group singing in the 80's had their impact on the prevalence on the show choir movement in American Schools. Critics point to show choirs as being pop in nature, dominated by choreography and driven by the element of competition. Resisted by a good number of traditionalists, show choir, swing choir and jazz choir style have a dominant place in school choral programs in the United States. Good programs are able to do all styles of vocal performance. Like Band, the solid teaching uses standard literature and established techniques to develop their high school musicians.

Band programs have experienced the highest degree of metamorphosis. High school marching bands and related ensembles look very different today than they did in the 60's. One must realize that nearly all high school marching bands prior to the 70's copied what the college bands did. Back in those days, college football game broadcasts used to show the halftime shows of each marching band. High school directors spent a number of Saturdays, watching television for new ideas that they could incorporate into their half-time shows.

Like the college bands back then, we changed our half-time show each week. Nearly all of us carried sheet music on the field. Our style of marching was either military or what was sometimes called, in the Midwest, "Big Ten Style." The marching band activity was different in each state. Ohio bands might adopt the style of Ohio State. Illinois Bands would look to the University of Illinois. Texas bands might copy Texas A &M. And, a good number of bands in California would model off of USC. We used baton twirlers, dancers, team mascots and marched in military formations. We made "picture shows." Drill amounted to a series of five or six "stops" that might project a stick figure man for one song, an airplane for the next song, the first letter of our school name during the school song and one for the opposing school facing their side for their school song. Our movement from one picture to the next looked like a group of ants all heading in different directions until the picture locked in.

The first change in marching band style was a result of Bill Moffit. Moffit was an innovator in both marching band style and music. His "Patterns of Motion," revolutionized bands and their halftime shows, moving away from the military style of marching. His style dominated both college and high school marching band shows and competitions from the late 1960s to the early 1990s, when drum corps began to become popular. His drill movement provided high school directors with a formula-based system for marching band drill. Moffit was the first to commercialize drill writing services for the high school band. His arrangements were also used extensively.But the most dramatic impact on marching band came from a musical tradition outside the classroom – Drum and Bugle Corps. Drum Corps are comprised of "G Bugles" and drums used in the military. While we discussed the extensive use of bands in the military, drum and bugle corps can be traced to the early days of the Marine Corps.

In the 18th and 19th centuries military musicians, provided a means of passing commands to soldiers in battle formations. The sound of various drum beats and bugle calls could be easily heard over the noise of the battlefield and signaled Marines to attack the enemy or retire for the evening. Military posts authorized a number of buglers and drummers to play the traditional calls. The United States Marine Drum & Bugle Corps was formed in 1934 to augment the United States Marine Band.

Beginning after World War I through the 1970s, corps, and competitions were often sponsored by the VFW, Scout troops, churches, the Royal Canadian Legion, and the American Legion. The roots of these organizations were in the military. The number of drum corps exploded beginning in the 1950's, and by 1972 there were nearly 2,000 active drum corps in the United States. The year the drum corps separated from their sponsoring organizations and formed their own organization called Drum Corps International.

This began a cross-pollination, or some might say "invasion," of drum corps music, marching method and show style different than any college or marching bands in the country. It began a swing away from college marching bands as a model. More and more band directors began to change to "drum corps style," as it was called. More than anything, drum corps brought a show format different from the typical half-time show. Shows followed a format – opener, presentation of colors, concert (standstill), drum solo, production number, and closer. College and high school bands present single songs connected only by P.A. announcements acting as the conduit to explain the show.

At the right moment, ex-Cavalier Drum Corps member noted drummer, instructor, inventor, and entrepreneur Larry McCormick and his wife started Marching Bands of America (MBA) in Whitewater, Wisconsin in 1976. MBA became Bands of America in 1984 and moved their national contest to Indianapolis where it is today. BOA holds regional competitions throughout the country for marching band. These contests plus the National Concert Band Festival, Honor Band of America and Summer Symposium and other programs brought marching band styles from around the country together. Though BOA is certainly not the only contest or even series of contests in the country they are and have been a driving force in the creation of what is now considered an art form on the football field. They were the vehicle to "nationalize" the band movement.

Today, Drum Corps utilize brass band instruments and instructors in the band world also teach drum corps in the summer. Offshoots of the competitive area of drum corps and bands include Winter Guard International which highlights color guard productions indoors during the winter months. Drum lines, complete with visual design compete in winter, as well. Like bands, color guard show-design and instructors that specialize in visual design, have infiltrated into the band world. The people involved in drum corps, color guard and competitive bands are essentially the same people. Competitive Pageantry Marching Band is now an industry.

Marching band is big business today as booster groups raise thousands of dollars for arrangements, drill design, outside instructors, equipment vehicles and hundreds of other necessities to compete in this artistic activity. Today, high school marching bands can range from a band that looks very much like a band of the 1930's all the way up to massive organizations that produce elaborate productions including electronic sounds, multiple keyboard instruments, dancers, guard, props and special effects.

Today, there are different types of band programs relative to marching band

> a. Bands that seldom march (usually, no football)
> b. Bands that perform for football games and local parades
> c. Bands the compete in local or college-sponsored band contests
> d. Bands that compete in regional shows, state-sponsored shows
> e. Bands that compete in BOA Regional Shows and other regional contests.
> f. Bands that compete in National Contests or BOA Grand Nationals

For the purposes of this book, the development of competitive marching band has only one significant element. That element is the development of judging systems used in the competitive arena. With the rise of competition in drum corps and bands, the need for valid, workable and accurate judging systems and highly trained judges to deploy them created training organizations for prospective judges.

Though band contests have been around since 1923, and colleges have sponsored innumerable contests over the years, none of these school band-related activities generated schools for judging. College directors, longtime high school directors, and others considered experts due to their years in the business, have always judged bands. In many cases, band directors judge bands directed by their friends.

It was the competitive drum corps activity that drove serious inquiries into how subjective art products could be ranked and rated objectively. Most certainly, the band, choir and orchestra world have some wonderful adjudicators who have a natural instinct for judging, highly respected reputations, a history of outstanding teaching and an understanding of how to rate a musical performance. No doubt, workshop, seminars, and symposia on how school musical groups should be judged have occurred over the years.

But no university, society, competitive festival, college-sponsored contest, state or city-wide event, has studied *and* tested the process of music performance evaluation as have the architects of competitive drum corps and band judging, established over sixty years ago. Their work reveals the craft of judging the subjective and arriving at an objective assessment so valued by schools today.

Our Grading Legacy

I can't think of a time when my music professors in undergrad school ever mentioned assessment in any of our classes. Oh, I do recall taking various education courses. And a few dealt with empirical measurement. My left brain enjoyed those classes. I found them interesting. But, in my mind, testing had little to do with my music classes. We all knew what the test was in music. You either "nailed it," or you didn't. We were young. It was our nature to make quick decisions. For us, it was either "thumbs up" or thumbs down."

Back then, education courses tended to teach the basic standard deviation material, bell-shaped curved concepts, and test validity. The professors were education specialists. We were music performance folks. They didn't understand what we did. They didn't understand our objective. They could not imagine a teaching system void of their time-tested tools to assess achievement. They just assumed we'd apply their science to our discipline – music performance. We didn't.

After attending a required education class, I'd venture across the quad, enter the music building and find music performance majors stuffed in practice rooms, rehearsal rooms, theory, and music history classes, and a number of fairly practical, but brief, pedagogy classes striving to give future band, orchestra choir directors "a little bit of everything." We were learning content, or what we in the trade call, "literature." It nearly comprised 100% of our curriculum - solo recitals, ensemble work, full ensemble concerts, private lessons, public performances, madrigals, half-time shows and on and on.

"You can't teach it if you can't play it," was a mantra frequently heard in my undergraduate days. The way to succeed as an ensemble director was to become the best ensemble performer you could be. In undergrad school, the mission was to provide us with the most intense performance regimen possible - supplemented with methods, theory, conducting and history. There were one or two classes available on "how to run a program." They usually were accented with stories about how our professors had done things for years. These people were our models. Learning to teach music is very much about watching the best do what they do and applying it.

The hope was that we'd acquire musical insight, learn what a quality ensemble sounded like, and take that same mission into our rehearsal rooms, as directors. Hopefully, we'd demand the same excellence of our students and pass performance standards on to the next generation. That formula is still active today and, for the most part, it works. It's proven to work for many years, well before the American public schools.

In 1975, I attended graduate school at the University of Illinois while continuing to teach. How fortunate I was to have some of the most influential minds in music performance at the time, as my teachers. Mary Hoffman, Richard Cowell, G. David Peters and Charles Leonhard widened my vision, challenged my thinking and gave us all a broader sense of music performance, its history, and importance in American public schools.

As brilliant as these pioneers were, the issue of how to assess student performance based solely on performance was not addressed. It was not, and still is not being addressed today within the music performance community. And yet, the reality is that music performance classes are designed to create musicians.

In graduate school, our focus was more on program management. Our professors stressed the value of music performance and how best to deploy it. Foundations and principles of music performance were covered. Conducting, arranging and compositional courses were options. There were informal "debate societies," that met in various educational and thirst-quenching settings, to discuss what music educators considered "good literature." There was plenty of talk about greatness we'd witnessed in our business but no discussion of grading, measurement or assessment. Opinions ruled the day. Discussions inevitably turned to how people "did things" and "what kind of programs" they had. This caused most graduate students to consider what type of program they had or wanted to have. Those in grad-school with teaching experience could not help but reflect on their school, their program, their administration and their community.

Depending on where you studied music performance, your experience might have varied from mine. But the "big stuff" was pretty much as described above for most of us. I've always had a love-hate relationship with schooling. I loved the reflective part of education. But I often chuckled at the "out of touch" nature of the university, charged with training musicians how to teach elementary, middle school or high school music. But this is not an indictment of our teachers. Their job was to instill the passion they had for music, and they did. They taught us what good music was and it seldom required us taking notes. We learned as we performed.

And so, I and thousands of other band directors, orchestra directors, and choir directors set off to develop the best performing groups possible. Most of us would move from our first job to a "better situation." A better situation meant a school that allowed us to execute the standards pressed upon us by our directors and college teachers.

When it came time to grading kids in our band, orchestra or choir for the first time, we almost had to create the criteria on the spot. As rookie teachers, we reflected, "Ok, let's think. What are the important things we expect the kids to do in order to contribute properly to the ensemble?"

Naturally, we reflected back on what our directors valued. A partial list included things like attendance, attitude, leadership, effort, a signed practice card from mom or dad and finally, performance. Performance did not mean how well one played, however. Back then it meant, "Did you show up for all the concerts" My old education professor at Illinois State University, Dr. William Zeller, would have been shocked by this method.

What's interesting about all this is that when it came to putting grades on a report card, we chose to rate behaviors – "Did he show up for everything?" "Is she excited about choir?" "Does John have a bad attitude?" "Does she practice?" In reality, although our schools used a five-level grading system – A thru F, we used three levels. They went something like this:

A "Everything is going fine."
B "You better start showing some effort."
C "This one needs to consider something else next year."

What's the old saying? "It's funny because it's true?"

The problem with this antiquated grading system is that it told us little about each student's achievement beyond simply "showing up." There are a whole lot of kids in between "consider something else next year" and "showing up." Furthermore, the majority of kids *do* show up –every single time. How in the world were we capable of distinguishing?

Did this mean that band, orchestra, and choir directors had no clue how to evaluate their student musicians? Did it mean that we were lost at sea in the ocean of student assessment with no guidance system, no rudder? Did it mean that we had no tool or capacity to make finite distinctions between the twenty clarinets in our clarinet section, or ten first sopranos in choir or the twenty-four violins in orchestra?

No, of course not!   Furthermore, did we care?

No. We spent little time grappling with how well our kids played. We heard it every day in rehearsal, in lessons, in performances, through practice room doors, and amid the pre-rehearsal discordant mixture of sounds that sounded like noise to others but provided us the chance to pick off errant missed accidental like a laser gun.

Did our administrators focus on music performance assessment? No. For years, administrators focused on traditional classroom assessment. We were viewed as extra-curricular activities and even clubs for years. In some states and school districts, we still are. If the kids and parents were happy, the director was positive and cooperative with school policy, and the band, orchestra, and choirs "sounded good," things were working fine.

Did our parents care? The most important thing to a parent is that their child is enjoying band, choir or orchestra. Most view it as a means to round out their child, teach them discipline and provide a place to be associated with "good kids." Parents usually asked about their child's grade when it was not an "A." The common phrase, "How do you get a "B" in choir?" (or band or orchestra), was not uncommon.

Point in fact, until very, very recently band, orchestra, and choir teachers were not called upon to submit detailed course outlines, lesson plans and assessments to their departments or administrators. For years, the extent of "administrative busy-work," as it was often called, was a course description for the annual course catalogue. That document included a broad general statement about the ensemble, entry requirements, requirements to own one's instrument if with band or orchestra and, most importantly, a commitment to "attend all outside practices and perform at all concerts and public events."

Commitment is big. It always has been. It's been part of our heritage for years. If you think about how the first directors brought bands into our schools, it makes sense that rules, regulations, and commitment are part of band DNA. The early pioneers of school bands were military veterans. They brought high standards to our industry.

During my years as Associate Executive Director for Bands of America, Revelli was active and involved in the creation of the National Concert Band Festival. I recall seeing him conduct the Honor Band of America in "The Stars and Stripes Forever" at Medina Temple in Chicago. After rehearsal, I got a chance to talk with him for a short time. I had spent time teaching at his old high school in Hobart, Indiana and he shared stories of how things were in Hobart before he moved on to Michigan. Revelli shared that in his first year at Hobart he started fifth graders and had selected four cornets to begin lessons. In that first lesson, he told the boys the following, "If any of your four are even considering not staying in band all the way through your senior year in high school, then quit now. Because I hate quitters!"

I mentioned this anecdotal tale to remind us all from whence we came. Is it not true that great band, choir and orchestra directors all seem to have a commanding presence? They may be aggressive like Revelli or in command due to their passion for music, personal intensity, artistic vision and love for their students. Revelli, by the way, was all of these. It's helpful to remember that we come from a different heritage than do non-music performance classroom teachers. For many decades we were often left alone as long as "things were working." Plus, as we've heard a number of times over the years, administrators were not too reticent to qualify their relationship with performing arts with the phrase, "I don't understand what you people do." Some of us more fortunate directors had thoughtful intelligent and interested administrators. I benefited from two great educators and mentors in my time. I also taught in a school where I was never formally evaluated once.

Do we assess?

There's something about band directors that's different from orchestra and choir people. I've taught in all three areas in my teaching career, but most of my time has been spent with bands. The band world has its share of intellectuals, artesian and prophets. But in the main, we're good musicians who understand entertainment as much as music. We perform in public more than our brethren in choir and orchestra, and we're part of sporting events. We're way more expensive for our school district than choir or orchestra, and our parents raise an ungodly amount of money to help us survive. We perform in the rain, snow, hot sweaty gyms, malls, and on bleachers in the end zone. We're also journeymen/women with backgrounds in logistics, fund-raising, clarinet repair using rubber bands, and barking commands from fifty yards away.

We're rather pragmatic about things. We make small decisions quickly and big decisions with confidence. Whether gregarious and outspoken or introspective and cerebral we all have opinions. We talk about and debate quality - all the time. We talk about how kids play. We also talk about kids being "hungry" which, of course, means motivated. When we hear kids that stand out, we point it out. We know what our standards are and we act on them. Performance quality is known to us, and it lives in our gut.

I remember sitting around a table at district festival a couple of years ago with a group of band directors. Our kids were auditioning and, as directors will do, we started to "chew the fat." The usual conversations came forth – "How's your band doing?" "What kind of marching band season did you have?" "How's your family?" As often happens, the conservation turned to issues in our schools like policy changes, scheduling issues and administrative demands that were "gumming up the works." On this particular Saturday, someone mentioned the word, "assessment" in the conversation. A collective moan rose up, and the group took inventory.

"My school's got us filling reams of paper with descriptions of what we do, how we teach and how we grade kids," said one director.

"They haven't bothered us yet," said another. "I think they're too busy fixing all the other departments first!" A laugh went up around the table.

One of the more experienced directors, who built one of the top band programs in the state, expressed his concern. "I've been doing this a long time. I've seen a lot of changes over the years, but for the most part, they left us alone. I've been at my school for twenty-five years. Last month, our curriculum director came down to see me and told me I had to start teaching composition in my wind ensemble."

"I know how my kids play," said one director. "Why do I have to explain it to them?"

"As long as we show up on Friday night, they're happy, right?" said a third. More laughter. Finally, one director added, "Well, if you're not assessing your kids, you have no basis for giving the kid a grade, and we *are* in the education business." He went on. "If we don't have a system to assess individual students in our band, then we can expect someone will come in and tell us we should. They're also liable to tell how to do it."

If you were not a band teacher and happened to overhear this casual conversation, you'd walk away thinking that band directors never evaluated students. You'd also likely conclude that they were opposed to doing so. But consider this:

- When an orchestra director walks into a violin sectional rehearsal with fifteen violins warming up, and one student suddenly plays "F#" in a piece written in Bb major, the director will stop before she gets to her desk and make a b-line to that violinist and point out the key. When she does this, she is assessing.

- Every time a choral conductor stops and corrects pitch in the alto section and explains to students why the problem occurred and what needs to be done to prevent the issue, he is assessing.

- When a band director hears the French horns enter well under pitch, and quickly turns to the section, raising his left hand in upward direction, while offering a lifting facial expression, he's reminding the horns that they need to take a full breath next time - as this important line signals a change of key. When he does this, he is assessing.

So, are music-performance teachers assessing their students? Of course, they are. They do it every minute of the day, every day. Assessing is how we teach kids to play. We don't teach and then assess. We assess, and then we teach. Assessing is *how* we teach.

Yet, here are a few other observations:

- Some administrators have the impression that music performance people do not assess.

- There are school districts that are requiring common-practice testing in their music performance classes.

- Some directors are so intuitive about what they do that they don't realize they assess every minute of the day. Yet they *too* will state that they don't assess.

- Some directors believe they should not be required to submit empirical evidence of assessment.

Let's discuss administrators issue first:

Administrators believe we do not assess.

No one should be surprised that administrators believe we do not assess. Unless they are former music performance teachers, they have no way of knowing that we *do* assess unless we show them. This is not a sign of their weakness as administrators. It is a sign that we have not explained 1) what we do, 2) how our assessment methods connect directly to our desired outcomes and 3) how our methods can be a valid alternative to common-practice testing. The music-performance community must develop a valid assessment tool that measures *our* desired outcomes and can be validated by school administrators. We must then actively participate in the curriculum change processes within our school and base our assessment methods on their superior ability to test the desired outcomes of our courses – namely performance. We should not base our proposals on external factors such as our lack of time, their lack of understanding of what we do, or the lack of the necessity to assess individual students since they perform in public.

Administrators want us to use common-practice testing

The preponderance of general music educators *has* been engaged. Common-practice testing, in the main, works for them. But a limited number of music-performance educators have developed assessment systems and those who have, often assess peripheral evidence that could easily be collected by a student teacher or an attendance clerk. Lacking an alternative to common-practice testing, administrators will press further demands for common-practice testing from their teachers, unless and until a valid alternative is presented.

Directors think we do not assess

Directors who believe that we do not assess have framed their definition of assessment in common-practice testing terms. They are missing the fact that assessment, reassessment, self-assessment and student growth are ingrained in our music-performance teaching process. The very act of teaching in our field is a continuous flow of assessment and reassessment action. It is what music-performance teaching means. Here are some examples:

> *When a private teacher teaches her fourth-grade piano student to play her first three notes with the right hand starting at middle "C" and ascending to "E," she demonstrates, and then says, "Now, you try." The student makes her first attempt (assessment). She stumbles with her third finger and winces in disappointment (self-assessment). "Try again," says the teacher. (reassessment). The student succeeds. "That's it, wonderful" the teacher responds. (assessment).*

When an orchestra director provides a downbeat for his string section to begin their first warm-up in rehearsal, he has a number of assessments in mind, but he is first looking for a uniformed attack. He gives his preparation and then provides a clear downbeat, only to stop when a number of the second violins enter early (assessment). He presses them to watch, tells a few to adjust their seating angle and music stands, so they are in his line of sight (individual assessment). He then gives a second downbeat (reassessment), and an anxious viola enters ahead of the ensemble. He stops, cuts of the ensemble, looks at the embarrassed viola and smiles (individual assessment). The viola student rolls her eyes, confirming her error (self-assessment). Saying nothing, he resumes and provides his third downbeat (reassessment). He is satisfied with the entrance and continues, shifting his ear immediately to other issues. He sees small bow movement from his first violins and hears the accompanying weak and thin tone associated with it (assessment). He also hears the bass section rushing tempo (assessment) as they move up the scale. His first cello is playing a dynamic well above the entire cello section (assessment) and the half the viola section has failed to properly shift as dictated by their three-octave scale (assessment).

He cuts off the orchestra and delivers a response:

> "Basses, you must hold tempo. You have the only pulse-notes in this section. You must watch me, not listen." (assessment).

> "Good job watching this time, 2nd violins, that was much better." (assessment) But 1st violins, you need to move the bow. Don't interpret the slow tempo and soft dynamic to mean slow movement of the bow. You still need to create a characteristic sound." (assessment)

> "Better that time, Jane" (viola) (assessment)

> "Eric, (cello) could you bring down your dynamic a bit." This section actually calls for a mezzo-piano" so you play under the violins." (assessment)

> "Violas, you need to begin in 1st position here. Then shift in the second octave, so you're in position for the 3rd octave. Mary, (to the first chair) could you show them?" (The first viola stands and turns to her section, demonstrating the entire 3-octave scale). (students teaching students) "Thank you, Mary. Let's try this, violas." (the violas run the 3-octave scale with success). (assessment). "Good," says the director.

Using the orchestra rehearsal as an example, is there any doubt that assessment is occurring here? Two questions come to mind:

"What might we say about this?

There are some assessments in the above orchestra rehearsal that are ensemble-based - the downbeat, for example. These ensemble issues cannot be used for individual assessment. Nor are they all a result of individual training only. There are group skills that are only teachable in rehearsal and only assessable in live performance. Nonetheless, they do not fulfill the need to assess students on an individual basis.

There are a number of assessments that are singular by nature – proper position for the 3-octave scale in the violas, for example. Each string voice has a different set of technical skill requirements unique from the others. Does that indicate that the violins are experiencing an entirely different subject in orchestra than the cellos? Yes and No.

Each instrument or voice has different technical *skills* to master (shifting), yet all voices and instruments have common musical *fundamentals* (scales) and *expressions* (crescendos) to demonstrate. These three desirable outcomes *can* be assessed in ensemble rehearsal but not on each student. Therefore, administrators and music-performance teachers must find opportunities for students to assess the desired outcomes on their own.

Ensemble rehearsal classes cannot be used to assess each student's *skill*, *fundamental* or *expression* level. It requires sacrificing ensemble instructional time for all students. When directors talk about "not enough time" to assess they are usually stating that they do not have the required individual or sectional contact time to individually assess students on desired outcomes.

Administrators cannot demand individualized assessment from music-performance classes on one hand while at the same time, provide fifty minutes of ensemble time as the only teacher-student contact each day. Individualized common-practice and standardized testing can be done in groups - all at once. Individualized music-performance assessment cannot be done in groups - all at once.

What might an administrator say about this?

An administrator would have to concede that assessment is certainly present. She would point out that individual assessment on each student is not present. We have discussed that issue above. But, should a solution be found to test students individually, she might point out that we are not assessing students using the *same material*. She would be correct on this, also.

Most non-performance classes test all students on the same material, in the same way. This assures that assessments are uniformed between all students. This, of course, is necessary to assure the integrity of scores across all students.

In music performance classes, all material is different depending on what voice you sing or instrument you play. But this would not invalidate the assessments, simply because students are assessing on different material. Here, we are not speaking of different musical selections. We are referring to the different skills, fundamentals, and expressions required within each part of the same piece.

The *skills* required to play the trombone are different from those of the alto saxophone, but the scope of those skills are equally wide with equal *demand*. The *fundamentals* of trombone and saxophone (for example scales) are the same but come with different levels of *demand* because of the construction and nature of their design.

Thus, a one octave concert "Bb" scale presents a lower level of *demand* for a trombone than it does for an alto sax. Conversely, alto saxes have a lower level of demand playing a one-octave "G" scale than do trombones. Much of this is driven by familiarity that trombones have played in concert "Bb" from the beginning while alto saxes play in concert "G," early on. Add the second octave to the alto sax "G" scale, and the demand increases due to the variation in second octave fingering. Add the second octave to the trombone and the demand does not increase so much due to the position changes (equitable to sax fingerings) but the embrasure support and technique needed to achieve the upper register.

The point here is that the demand assessed on each instrument or voice will be equal, relative to the particulars of the instrument or voice. Assessment of the *skills* and *fundamentals* within a music performance measures the *response to demands* not the *recall of specified information,* as is the case with non-performance classes. So what of *music expression?* The demonstrations of expression in musical performance vary, but the requirement to achieve expression is present in all parts at all times – thus equal demand.

One should mention that there are, of course, differences between like instruments in most ensembles. Clarinet parts will regularly be three different parts, each with a different level of demand. The violin section in an orchestra is comprised of 1st and 2nd violins each with two different parts. This is the same with 1st and 2nd sopranos in choir. How might this be explained to the school administrator? Though the 1st violin assessments will be different than the 2nds (two different parts), the weight or demand of all assessments given to the 1sts, compared to that of the 2nds, will be of relative equal demand for the players in each section, based on their starting abilities. The grade issued to each 1st and 2nd violin is a different matter that will be discussed later.

Assessments in a given grading period must be of equal *volume* (number of assessments) and *weight* (demand placed on each performer relative to their part which is assigned based on their starting ability.

Directors don't believe they should have to assess

To a degree, music performance directors want the best of both worlds. They desire and require the support of school institutions for, facilities, and support systems, but too many also want to function in isolation from the mandates that all school districts have regarding assessment. Schools must provide a relevant education that prepares students for life, do so fairly and equitably, provide the best possible teachers, and report student progress using an equal and valid system. Some directors, who make musical judgments all day, resist being asked to provide validation that they do so. There is ample evidence that many substitute behavior (all of which are important), for musical achievement (see next section).

Common-practice assessments for music performance have been called "busy work." They've been dismissed as "an academic exercise." They've been declared "irrelevant." And, they've has been moving through many school systems one department at a time. They are now arriving at the music rehearsal room door. The problem music-performance directors have is that their assessments occur too rapidly in the day and in great number to capture them all. Our challenge is not creating assessments. We have plenty. Our challenge is to determine which outcomes should be assessed individually, how best to assess them, when to assess them, and how to report these assessments to administrators satisfactorily.

The resistance many band, orchestra and choir directors express about new requirements in assessment is that administrations are not simply asking them to assess more, they are asking them to assess in the same way that all other subjects assess. I believe we've already demonstrated, here, how ludicrous that is. In some schools, directors are not only being asked to change how they assess but what they teach and how they teach. In the main, music-performance people have not been engaged in assessment discussions nationwide, thus far. They have let the question come to them rather than address the challenge head-on with valid systems that measure our desired outcomes, not hollow busywork disconnected from performance objectives. The result is that, to date, they have had "little voice" in the matter – to their detriment. But we should not sell ourselves or our students short.

Developing and reporting valid music-performance assessments is part of our job. Administrators have a job to do that is not only in their job description but, in many cases, is written in state law, tied to school funding, and tied to their compensation. Every school district takes a different approach to assessment accountability. Regardless of how your school addresses the process, accountability is now part of our job. Busy work is only such when it is irrelevant work. No one assesses more intently and more often than music performance teachers. Hopefully, this book will help you improve your assessment methods and better understand how to communicate what is one of the strengths of music performance teaching – assessment.

State of Music performance assessment today

Armed with only my own experience and anecdotal evidence drawn from hundreds of conversations about assessment with fellow music performance teachers, I felt obligated to do some research. My mission was to determine if music performance teachers around the country were assessing and if so, were they doing so in the same manner as the directors I have spoken with informally. Prior to my research, I had a good amount of data already. Being from Chicago, I was most familiar with bands in Illinois and surrounding states. Having spent forty years judging bands and drum corps in twenty-three states around the country, I became familiar with programs that competed in the marching band activity. My five years with Bands of America exposed me to bands in many sectors of the country. My exposure to orchestra and choirs was limited to the state of Illinois.

Nevertheless, I found a very low percentage of music directors assessing and those that *were*, used very few live music performance assessments as their primary basis for a student's grade. Most had auditions to place students in various ensembles. In this case, the majority of directors also used playing auditions as the means to seat students. Advanced students auditioned more frequently for various, conference, county, district and state auditions than they did for their director.

I first spent some time looking through a GIA publication entitled, "The Practice of Assessment in Music Education," (Editor Timothy S. Brophy, 2010). It is a substantial book which covers the proceedings of the Florida Symposium on Assessment in Music held at the University of Florida in 2009. The publication presented papers, speeches, panel discussions and keynote addresses by music educators, scholars, researchers, music administrators and students from 27 states and 13 nations. Attendees spent three days discussing what they called effective frameworks, models, and designs for assessment in the classroom, assessing on a large-scale basis, assessing music programs, and assessing data to improve teaching and learning. A good portion of the book covers general music, practices in different states, countries, higher education and K-12 classrooms. I focused my attention on three presentations, in particular:

- *"Student Assessment in the High School Band Ensemble Class,"* by John P. LaCognata of the University of Florida.

- *"Assessment 101: Basic Strategies Every Director Should Know for Teaching and Assessing,"* by Charles Hoffer of the University of Florida.

- *"Assessment Practices in the Choral Classroom,"* a panel discussion by Russell L. Robinson, University of Florida, Lynne Gackle, University of South Florida, William Renfroe, Largo High School, Penellas Count Schools, Florida, and Ann User, University of Akron.

In the first presentation, LaCognata presented a survey of 45 band directors (158 were polled). This, of course, struck me as a small sample. But the real "takeaway" from his report was that neither he nor any of the 45, who responded, spoke about *how* they arrive at a raw number when assessing. Admittedly, this was not the purpose of his survey but reading his report would be the first of many I would read with no discussion of the "how" – only the "what."

The other bit of information was how far music-performance classes needed to go before they are truly measuring music performance achievement. LaCognata surveyed how band directors assessed in their band class. Consider some of the data below (the parenthetical notes are mine) Of the 45 band directors who responded

- 43 used Participation (classroom attendance and engagement)
- 43 used Performances (making all performances)
- 27 used Attendance (like outside school practices)
- 30 used Conduct/Discipline
- 26 used Written Tests and Worksheets
- 25 used Attitude
- 41 used a Practice Log
- 5 used Student Self-Assessment
- 4 used Requirement checklists (likely valve oil etc.)
- 3 used Peer Assessment

There were other methods used that were more akin to actual performance abilities:

- 7 used Sight-Reading Tests
- 6 used Computer Assisted Programs
- 5 used SmartMusic

Even though this is a small sample, the use of behavioral assessments rather than music performance assessments was startling. The first thought that came to my mind was, "I wonder what these bands sound like?" They might be absolutely wonderful. They might be average. And, they could be, very well, poor. The point is, there is little on this list that assesses how kids play in these bands.

Assessments on 1) participation in the classroom, 2) perfect attendance for all performances and practices 3) pristine behavior, 4) a good attitude, or 5) high ratings from their fellow musicians, do not measure how a student is playing or advancing against a set of musical performance desired outcomes. Students could easily score high on all of the above attributes and leave school as average to below average musicians. My guess is that there are some fine musicians in these bands. But achieving superior rankings in these four would give no indication of their progress or achievement levels in music performance.

These same 45 survey respondents were asked to explain the purpose of these assessment methods. Their answers included:

- Provide feedback to students
- Identify student needs
- Determine future instructional direction
- Identify general class needs
- Demonstrate student accountability for learning
- Determine what concepts students are failing to understand
- Determine whether instruction has been successful
- Motivate students to practice their instruments
- Set or maintain class standards
- Determine the level of music performance for public performance
- Help students prepare for public performance
- Provide feedback to parents
- Establish or maintain credibility for the band program
- Determine whether students are practicing at home
- Rank students according to individual performance levels

These two lists, particularly when placed side-by-side, had me shaking my head. Is the second list truly a list of "desired outcomes" in these 45 band programs? If you look at the first list, do you honestly believe that these band directors are assessing students based on music performance achievement? Do you believe that first chair players are determined by 1) attendance, 2) conduct, or 3) submission of a portfolio? Hardly.

A key difference between a standard classroom teacher and a music performance teacher is that directors know how each student plays. As stated earlier, music performance teachers assess all day. It's how we teach. Knowing that, one can only conclude that criteria listed above are "window dressing" designed to either 1) meet the requirements of their school districts, 2) provide material for a band handbook or 3) submit data for a university study. But it is not a valid system for assessing music performance achievement and growth.

In his presentation *"Basic Strategies every Director Should Know for Teaching and Assessing,"* Charles Hoffer ties individual assessment to improved teaching. I believe he is correct in this. Since he does not clarify further, it is unclear whether Hoffer is proposing that assessment improves teaching strategy or teaching pedagogy.

But my experience is that while non-performance subjects can provide a teacher with cogent evidence, music performance assessment provides cogent evidence and corroborating evidence that directors can use to determine corrective action – on the spot. To that extent, the practice of assessing individuals in music performance fosters better teaching.

These assessments can be used as formative or summative assessments and applied to grading. But they should not be frivolous. They should be drawn from the literature currently in rehearsal or developmental skills set for each grade level. Armed with new understanding, directors can deal with similar issues proactively from the podium in the future. This would eliminate the need to assess the same material each time a piece is performed. Is it not true that master teachers are often those who have accumulated a large portfolio of solutions acquired through years of teaching and know how to communicate to students? I believe it can be said that younger teachers gain more from using individualized assessment than the highly experienced teacher. It is a fact that experienced professionals in any field have "seen more" than the apprentice or less experienced teacher.

Hoffer goes on to describe three benefits to individualized assessment: "1) It provides the teacher with the most accurate measure of how well their students have learned, which in turn contributes to improved teaching. 2) The results can be used in giving students grades. 3) Students are more motivated when they realize that the will be heard individually."

I disagree with point #1. Here, Hoffer accepts the notion that all that is to be learned in music ensemble class is demonstrated exclusively during individual assessment. I recall a cellist in my orchestra that could single-handedly play louder than the other twelve cellists in the section. It was certainly something both he and I were fully aware of. It was something I could only assess in ensemble rehearsal. It had to do with how he listened and what role dynamics played in his ability to express properly in any given piece.

Hoffer is correct about #2. Is it not the whole point of assessment? Yes, I understand assessment can teach students and even enlighten the teacher. But if there were no grades to be issued, individualized assessment would be on a "need-to-know" basis. And, that is how most ensemble directors view assessment. Knowing each piece of music reveals its demands and every group of students arrives with their abilities and limitations. Thus, the notion of a traditional lesson plan goes out the window. This is why music performance teachers cringe when lesson plans are required. Writing lessons plans is about as fruitless as writing assessments prior to ensemble class. Proper instructional method calls for a forecast of the agenda at the beginning of class and summarization at the end. But unlike most non-performing subjects, a rehearsal takes many twists and turns.

But have we not all gone into rehearsals with our list of notes for rehearsal? Of course, we have. But this occurs toward the end of the learning unit (after the piece has been "worked" awhile) not at the beginning. Even if we are most familiar with a piece of music, the first few rehearsals are discovery sessions. What will our kids do with this new piece of music? We do not know until we try. However, experienced teachers in districts for some time and "know their kids," can predict with a high degree of accuracy. Where this plays out to the positive is in the selection of literature.

It is not enough for teachers, however, to plan the same way a non-performance class teacher does. Procedures in music rehearsals are (and certainly should be) rather predictable (tuning, warm-up, announcements, etc.) But once the students and teachers begin their journey through the piece, assessment takes over. It is our teaching process. This has great implications for how and when teachers should be observed by administrators.

I fully agree with Hoffer's final point #3 and anyone that has spent time with students today, knows how motivated they get when individualized assessment occurs. That motivation dissipates significantly when no grade is attached. Talented directors will always inspire students to practice and learn. Assessment probably inspires the student to practice.

Hoffer spends sometime proposing that the "entertainment" element of school ensembles detracts and is in direct conflict with learning. He sets up a false dichotomy of "teacher versus director." He talks about how education diminishes due to the performance demands of all school ensembles. I couldn't disagree more with him on this point. He's been influenced by the general music crowd on this one. I will always defend the notion that learning to perform and performing is the best way to understand, execute and realize music fully.

It is the choice of literature and the depth of the music selection that matters. It is also the breadth of music selected. An orchestra conductor that only plays the classics does just as much of an injustice to his students as does the conductor that never plays a classic. In the band world, we heard (and still do in some places) the same argument about marching band. Band directors who spend two or three months playing different pop songs, using flip-folders in order to present what they claim is a "wider breadth of experience," simply due to the *number* of songs learned in one season, ignore the fact that pop tunes adapted for wind bands are heavily repetitive, regularly full of rhythmic ostinatos and significantly lacking lyrical expression. These directors criticize bands that perfect one show per season and generally play more expressive material, often with a depth equal to concert band literature. I have done both. There is no doubt in my mind that an in-depth, single show with three, four or five pieces teaches much more than the first approach. In addition, assessment, students teaching students, and peer evaluation are much more present using the "single show" concept.

Hoffer also states that "very few band directors have a planned curriculum, which means it's unlikely that they do much planning, at least in the sense that they prepare written lesson plans." The reader can likely perceive my reaction to *this* statement. Could I say, once again, that music performance directors *do* construct a curriculum, and they *do* plan instruction, and they *do* assess? It totally revolves around the literature we chose to perform.

The music we plan to perform should be 1) music with expressive depth and intrigue 2) music that is written to challenge of our students yet is achievable within the time allowed 3) music that teaches students the wide range of musical style 4) music that is enjoyable to play, and 5) music capable of setting new standards if achieved in performance.

I dare say that planning by music performance teachers includes 1) course content selection (picking music), 2) scheduling music to be played throughout the year, 3) anticipating and reacting to rehearsal achievement (assessment) and 4) analyzing performances (reflecting and pre-planning) It is a much deeper process and requires a more intense analysis on the part of music directors than teachers of non-performance classes.

Hoffer further states that "Because some sections in bands, orchestras, and almost all choral groups have several members, assessing student learning will take place in smaller groups, which of course is better than assessing only the entire group. I might suggest that the term "better" be replaced by the word "different" in this case.

Hoffer accurately describes some ways to assess individually in large ensembles. We've all used the method of hearing students "down the row" to see who knows and does not know a part. I've seen conductors change the seating arrangements and part assignments "on the spot," after assessing this way – particularly if the section is critical to the arrangement. He discusses openly the need to play in front of others and learn not to be nervous. In time, students get used to it. I've always stressed that music will always be beyond our reach regardless of how well we play. Admittedly, I've asked students from the clarinet section to play if I perceive any reaction to a struggling 3rd cornet. It only takes a few times, and soon everyone learns to be respectful of the others.

I fully support Hoffer's final statement about assessment:

"Although conducting assessment procedures requires extra organization and planning, as well as a small amount of additional effort, it is well worth doing. In short, it is a necessary practice to improved teaching and increased student learning."

The final report I found important was the panel discussion involving Robinson, Gackle, Renfroe, and Usher entitled, *"Assessment Practices in the Choral Classroom."* Might I say at the outset that reports on the "current practice of assessment" are not that helpful? Researchers are discovering that written assessments and other processes used by non-performance classes in the past seem are what many music-performance teachers are using today. Certainly, directors should not read the results of such surveys and feel incompetent in regards to student assessment. As I have stated heretofore, I contend that directors assess all the time.

Most of what the panel suggested included comments on 1) rehearsal procedures 2) the importance of procedures and handbooks to communicate them 3) the importance of vocal part and sight-singing tests 4) the use of non-musical assessments (checklists) such as attendance, punctuality, attitude, etc., and 5) a document to explain to students and parents how grades are determined. As you can see, their discussion followed what we most often see when music-performance people get together and "talk assessment."

But the panel presented a worthwhile approach to studying music performance assessment going forward. They posed six questions that future researchers should include:

> 1) How are students graded in the choral classroom compared to other areas of non-performance classes?
>
> 2. How are students graded in the choral classroom compared to other areas of music?
>
> 3. What does the research suggest for assessing the choral classroom?
>
> 4. What do teachers say about assessing the choral classroom?
>
> 5. What systems do veteran choral teachers use?
>
> 6. Is there a gap between what teachers are doing and what research suggests?

These statements align with other empirical methodology but have flaws. Here's my response:

> 1) I contend non-performance classes are inherently different and invalid as a model for assessment in performance classes so what further comparison is needed?
>
> 2. If a large percentage of teachers in all three areas of music (band, orchestra, and choir) are not assessing, doing it incorrectly or measuring things that are not valid (which all studies indicate) would it matter how students graded in the choral classroom compared to other areas of music?
>
> 3. Since most of the research in music assessment reports are about what everyone is doing now, then why would it matter what research suggests for assessing the choral classroom?
>
> 4. What teachers say about assessing the choral classroom is a worthwhile investigation. What is needed here, however, is an opinion, not another report on what teachers are doing. It's time to ask music performance teachers about their opinions on this matter.

5. What veteran choral teachers use can only be valuable as a comparison to what lesser experienced teachers use. The opinions of veteran teachers may be more valuable and likely more forthcoming.

6. Regarding the question, "Is there a gap between what teachers are doing and what research suggests," my review of what constitutes research in this area to date would put this question quite low in importance.

In addition to a number of books I reviewed in preparation for this work, I spent a good amount of time reading numerous dissertations on the matter, hoping I might find some revealing new ideas in the area of music performance assessment. I found most of them to be constipated with process, heavily ladened with reports on the status quo (easier to quantify) and sadly short of any new ideas on the level of Cowell, Green or Langer or other philosophers of teaching that might shed light on the topic.

At the risk of sounding sacrilegious, might I say that I find a lot of university research to be tedious? After reviewing various doctoral dissertations in education, one comes away wondering if there are any new ideas out there or even an original thought. Dissertations in education today are often a report on all other reports that have been created previously – about *other* earlier reports.

Doctoral candidates spend hours researching, formatting and revising reports for committees to approve. The reader is left with the challenge of working through all the parochial language in an attempt to find "the point." I understand doing scholarly research requires a good amount of evidence and empirical methodology. But, from a practical point of view, most of it is worthless.

Consider this nugget of information:

> *"Measurement is concerned with the systematic collection, quantification, and ordering of information. It implies both the process or quantification and the result." In contrast, educational assessment is "the interpretive integration of application tasks (procedures) to collect objectives-relevant information for educational decision making and communication about the impact of the teaching-learning process."*

I don't know about you, but by the time I process this paragraph through the left side of my brain, I have a hard time finding any of it relevant to what happens when a student cellist enters my office to audition for advanced orchestra.

I sought out publications and doctoral work that surveyed assessment practices by music performance teachers across the country. Some surveys were limited to a state. Others surveyed directors in a number of states but often within one region of the country. Regardless, I found the data very similar whether collected recently or ten years ago.

Phillip Matthew Kancianic, in his doctoral thesis entitled, *"Classroom Assessment in U.S. High School Band Programs: Methods, Purposes, and Influences"* (2006), surveyed 2000 band directors drawn from an MENC list and received 634 usable responses.

In one section he described factors that were impacting the director's ability to assess individually. Time was clearly the #1 factor but realizing that this thesis was done in 2006 (data likely collected over two years), the use of technology as a solution relative to the time needed to collect data, changes this. When directors indicate that they have no time to assess, they are actually talking about no time to collect the data. With the advent of more quality recordings on smartphones and the development of SmartMusic and other resources, data collection time has been significantly reduced. Those using these new data-collection systems require less time to complete the process and can assess when students are not scheduled or present.

Synopsis of responses other than time restrictions reveals the lack of continuity among band directors regarding assessment. It also reveals how many of the practices being used at this time, lack rationale or foundation. Frankly, if this particular survey is any representation of what is happening in music performance assessment in our schools, then not only haven't we "put our toe in the water," we haven't even found the beach!

While this survey is ten years old, other studies I've read have *"time limitations"* as the top impairment. But the list below is a partial list of the 194 different responses received by Kancianic. There are some valid methods here and also some "real gems" on this list.

When asked how directors assessed band students, responses included the following:

1. Nine-weeks written test on musical terms, plus two scales
2. Scales, arpeggios in all 15 keys and play "Happy Birthday" from memory
3. Articulations, rhythms, and fingerings
4. Attendance at required after-school practices, performances and events
5. Audience acceptance of performances
6. Casual conversation as a non-graded assessment
7. CD Listening projects
8. CD/MP3's and Videos of concerts for self-evaluation
9. Challenges for chair - contests/festivals
10. Classroom behavior & concert attendance
11. Comments of audience and administration

12. Common sense - Can you play this part? Why not? Correct it. Now go practice it.
13. Participation in marching band, district band contest, solo and ensemble contest
14. Students are given a band arrangement and must prepare it for a concert without the help of conductor/director, the in-class performance is used as an exam grade.
15. Constant teacher/student interaction and feedback during rehearsals.
16. Criterion-referenced district-devised test
17. Daily observation of students' efforts to attain my expectations as listed in the band handbook.
18. Daily recollection
19. Give students the chance to challenge a chair if they think they are better than the placement I gave them.
20. I don't. There is no time. Rehearsal for the next performance takes all available time.
21. I grade 5 students at random every day
22. I use my ears!
23. Attitude
24. Audience and Administration reaction
25. The class assesses itself on an irregular basis

Part 3

Measuring the Aesthetic

Musical Meaning

Reflecting on *"Philosophy in a New Key, A Study in the Symbolism of Reason, Rite, and Art"*
Suzanne Langer (Harvard University Press, 1941)

What music teaches

There are critics. There are philosophers. There are savants and great historians…the artful genius, virtuoso, maestro, and prodigy. They have all tried to define the meaning of music at some time. Why is this difficult? We all enjoy it, some of us love it. Is it simply that the meaning of music is best defined by what it means to you…to me…or any other person whether genius or an innocent child. Is it personal, then? As we have stated, the musical experience is different for each person, even if present in the same concert hall. Should it be said that music simply means something different to each person and leave it at that?

Let's assume for a moment that music *has* no distinct universal meaning. Let's assume meaning in music only refers to what it means to the individual. At the risk of sounding like that famous quote, "what is…is," might I ask, "What is the meaning of meaning in this case?"

Imagine an elderly lady in Tennessee sitting on her porch in a rocker on a hot July day. Her grandson picks an old valley-tune passed down to him by his deceased grandfather. As he picks and sings in a soft falsetto - lyrics with a hint of brogue, the old woman casts her eyes out over the trees in the bright sun, then to the small goat grazing along an old stone barn that she and her husband built together when they were newlyweds, starting their lives together.

Lots of visions come to her mind. There is a comfort and warmth that embraces her spirit, and for these moments, she's lifted up in thoughts of her life and her short remaining time on this hard earth. She alternates her gaze between the smoky glaze over the tops of the green pines that surround her and the young fresh hands of her grandson, pulling and strumming that old familiar banjo with a lilt in his voice that echoed all the memories, experiences and feelings of her life. For the first time, she could finally consolidate all this into one. The unity of her simple home, her land, the trees, her presence on the old front porch and new life sitting at her feet had substance. The meaning that came to her at this moment was "information" about her life that was only obtainable in this setting where everything she could see before her was synergized in the sound of the old banjo.

And so, is this the meaning of music or is it its purpose? Is there anything new about the old woman's thoughts that could not have been obtained were her grandson off to school that day? Was the banjo lament simply present as she, through her own fruition, came to the realization that her life has been, long, hard and productive and that she was ready to pass on to a new life with her deceased husband? Is music a bystander in this case?

Was it the catalyst? Did it simply relax her and allow her to perceive perspective all on her own? Or was the banjo-tune the messenger-cantata that disclosed connections, time distances, events, meanings and perspectives never perceived as life transitioned, until now.

Project our story forwards another twenty years when the grandmother is gone, and her grandson now listens to his younger daughter play that same old song. He looks about at the same land and thinks about the day on the porch with his grandmother. Similar visions come to his mind, but mostly he is transformed back to that day when grandmother sat with him on the porch. His story is revealed too but is comprised mostly of that day on the porch when he was ten. He brings fewer years and less perspective to the old banjo-tune than did his grandmother. But more is revealed this time around then twenty years previous. Like an old tale passed down, the simple country tune speaks to generations, but a little piece falls off each time it is revealed.

Is this what music means? Is this its purpose? Is it simply a means to capture the past, remember the feeling? In both of these cases, we have described musical meaning as "discovered reality" in the case of the grandmother and "reflective memory" by her grandson. Music in a setting such as this is, in fact, very common today. Nearly all music today is set in some visual format. Film, television, video, advertising, gaming, and even live concerts with huge video screens, lighting, and special effects, all take the prominent position in the activity of storytelling. In the view of most people today, music just helps. It's secondary. It's supplemental.

But is music just window dressing? If it is, then should we be surprised when school districts view it as an expendable item?

My father, who played in hundreds of dance halls, clubs and other venues from the 40's to the 70's had a second quote that applies here. Referring to the indifference of most people who hire musicians he said, "Music is like art on the wall. If it's there, nobody notices but people walk into a room with nothing on the wall, they notice something is missing." It's rather like shrubbery in the front of the house, is it not?

Then is music entertainment? Certainly, the thousands of dancers and revelers my father played to for years were there for entertainment and got it. Having played hundreds of jobs myself over the years, I can confirm that little changed during my playing days. It's clear that the meaning of music to dancers in a dance hall, the grandson remembering his grandmother, and the grandmother realizing the profound convergence of life's mundane events, all have meaning. In all three cases, music was the catalyst in these examples. But these common definitions do more to define human behavior in response to music rather than music itself. Were one to pose the question, "What does math mean to you?" the absurdity of defining music or any other discipline only in terms of how it makes people "feel" or what thoughts come to their mind when they experience it, explains little.

To discover a clearer definition, one might ask: What does music do? How does it do it? And, what is the result of its doing so? These basic, rather heady questions are, in fact, helpful if not important to answer. They become foundations for our belief in the significance of music-performance in our schools, define our desired outcomes and therefore establish our means of assessment.

If we cannot define it, how are we able to rationalize it as a significant offering in American schools? Secondly, being able to articulate a clear definition of music provides us with more support for our rationale for assessing music performance in our terms, using our definition – measuring our desired outcomes.

How have the great thinkers over time defined music? Attempts to define music have been occurring for a very long time. What began as a purely tribal rant to stir ancient man to battle or a rhythmic pattern to facilitate a dance of celebration, has evolved to an expression of sound that can capture man's most profound thoughts and inspire new ones. Surely, there have been explanations over centuries of music making that can help us.

None other than Plato (428 BC to 348 BC) put forth the thought that music stirred both good and bad emotions and caused humans to act on those emotions. Though no study has ever demonstrated the notion of the physical power of music, the notion has not fully left Western culture. Still, Plato's notion does not provide us with a definitive explanation nor would we ever consider using it as a foundation for our rationale for music in our schools or as a basis for testing.

Immanuel Kant (1700's) proposed music as an agent of intellectual progress and therefore worthy of a place in cultural society. With acceptance determined by the many royal and religious employers of musicians in Kant's day, it's not surprising that acceptance of music was viewed as a necessary cultural amenity during the classical period. Not only would this fail as a rationale for music in American schools, one can easily see how cultural enhancement makes music even more disposable in our schools under this rationale.

Wilhelm Wundt and Charles Darwin (1800's) offered their definition for music, but they had limited visions and clung closely to the fashionable psychology of the day. Wundt described music as a collection of "pleasurable sensations," and Darwin felt music could be considered serious if it could be traced to man's origins. There are many in today's world, I'm afraid, that possess this thought. But again, it makes our discipline vulnerable, and I can only imagine the difficulty in assessing based on these two notions, alone.

Charles Avison (1700's) offers a significant break from the parochial notions of Wundt and Darwin and discards them. Regarding Plato, he not only adds nuance to Plato's emotional component, but he also transforms it and gives us the first real insight into what actually occurs in the minds of humans when music occurs.

Avison was an English composer during the Baroque and Classical periods. He was a church organist at St. John the Baptist Church in Newcastle, England and at St. Nicholas's Church (later Newcastle Cathedral). He is most known for his 12 Concerti Grossi after Scarlatti and his *Essay on Musical Expression*, the first music criticism published in English.

Avison lived in a time when most musicians were the composers of their works. He suggested that music stirs the emotions as Plato had contended, but he does not assign those emotions as belonging to the listener but to the musician.

He suggests that the listener's emotions are not his but, in fact, sympathetic emotions to the musician who actually possesses the emotions and displays them in performance. In Avison's definition, we start to get a sense of the communicative nature of music. Communicating implies the use of signs, signals or codes that are used to communicate ideas just as language and mathematics in order to communicate ideas. This was a dramatic shift in thinking. But the next question, of course, is *what* types of ideas. But let's examine the actual mechanics of this communication first.

Langer suggests that "If music really grieves or frightens us why do we listen to it?" Indeed. Never before Avison and few since but Langer, have ruminated on this or have they acknowledged the need to do so. Avison states, "There are certain sounds natural to joy, others to grief or despondency, others to tenderness and love, and by hearing *these*, we naturally sympathize with those who either enjoy or suffer."

Armed with the perspective of a musician, Avison understood that the emotional reactions of listeners were real, but they were epithetical, temporary and only as deep as the musician could portray. Today, we call this musicianship. Expression projects these emotions, and good execution keeps them clear, unencumbered and transparent.

Bach puts it another way...

"Since a musician cannot otherwise move people, but he is moved himself, so he must necessarily be able to induce in himself all those affects (effects) which he would arouse in his auditors (listeners); he conveys his feeling to them, and thus most readily moves to sympathetic emotions."

But, what of the composer? Here Langer clarifies and builds on Bach's and Avison's enlightened views.

Langer proposes that as composers and performers became increasingly two different people, it was the composer who possessed the original emotions and expressed them in his composition. The musician performed in a noble effort to present the composer's initial expression. Langer explains: "The composer is, indeed, the original subject of the emotions depicted, but the performer becomes at once his confidant and his mouthpiece. He transmits the feelings of the master to a sympathetic audience.

This is why great conductors and performers must study and understand a piece before they can successfully perform it. Furthermore, the musician and conductor will have their own emotional reactions to the composer's output, be moved, inspired and informed by it. The listener will benefit from these "additions."

In the case of jazz and its improvisational core, the notion of a musician's "additions" *explodes* off the end of Louis Armstrong's trumpet, and takes the dominant position over the thoughts of the composer of the original tune. Great jazz improvisation relegates a composer's work to his original set of "changes" (chord progressions) and builds an entirely new communication with the audience from the musician, single-handedly. With a dynamic "new statement" every time a soloist "takes one," the audience applauds at the end of the solo, mid-piece, and awaits the next. Is it not fitting and, indeed inspirational, that the dominance of the individual performer would foster itself in the culture of slavery and the quest for freedom, that accompanies the development of jazz in America?

But music as self-expression, the common man's definition, does not tell our whole story either. Langer states that the history of music, like that of language, "has been one of more and more integrated, disciplined, and articulated *forms.*" She goes on to explain that "the laws of emotional catharsis are natural laws, not artistic." Does this invalidate or negate music as a means of personal and emotional expression? Of course, not. Anyone who has ever performed can verify the emotional relief experienced during and following an intense performance. Langer also confirms that "we can *use* music to work off our subjective experiences and restore our personal balance. But this is not its primary function."

The key to Langer's thinking is best described in her own words:

> *"If music has any significance, it is semantic, not symptomatic. It's "meaning" is evidently not that of a stimulus to evoke emotions, nor that of a signal to announce them: if it has an emotional content it "has" it in the same sense that language "has" its conceptual content – symbolically. It is not usually derived from affects nor intended for them; but we may say, with certain reservations, that it is about them. Music is not the cause or cure of feelings, but their logical expression; though even in this capacity it has its special ways of functioning, that make it incommensurable with language, and even with presentational symbols like images, gestures, and rites."*

Langer also identifies those with the notion that music is a kind of language. Though not as prevalent as the "emotions" theory, it is held by many. Few have successfully explained what such language is communicating, but those on the fringe of this theory often point to "program music" which deliberately mimics natural sounds around us. Langer humorously refers to a New York Times critic who, following a performance of Strauss, during the heyday of his programmatic frenzy, that the day would come when "the composer could compose the silverware on the table so that the listener could distinguish the knives from the folks!"

She points to the similar notion that music is a language of feeling, designed to communicate such things as love, longing, hope or fear. While all of this is true, it is not an *expression* of the composer's feelings but an *exposition* of them, attributable to a character on stage, a grandiose scene in a film or a cataclysmic event in a video game. Her music becomes a "source of insight, not a plea for sympathy."

She goes on…

"Just as words can describe events we have not witnessed, places and things we have not seen, so music can present emotions and moods we have not felt."

Ah, now a glimmer of the true significance, the true weight and the necessity of music in our schools take hold."

Langer's contributions to understanding the meaning of music are immense and far too robust for ample treatment here. But her contribution is that music has its own symbolic forms with the capacity to teach meaning and information that is unattainable using other symbolic systems such as math or language. Essentially, language uses words. Mathematics uses numbers. And music uses sounds. All three communicate different things, and each one is equally inept to explain the other. There is no better symbolic code (words) to communicate information or denote specificity than language. There is no better symbolic code (numbers) to communicate information, size or distance than mathematics. And, there is no better symbolic code (sound) to communicate information about implication, profundity, intimacy, power, action, confusion, happiness, love, humor, delicacy or what it means to be human than music – in our time or in the days of Beethoven.

I have often cringed when I hear music educators justifying music in the classroom based on its ability to teach math, teamwork, time management, coordination, discipline. Even our national organization, the National Association for Music Education (NAfME) rationalizes the need for music in our schools by purporting that it gives students "a sense of achievement," teaches them "responsible risk-taking," and, even, "better SAT scores."

Good Lord! Is that all we've got?

There isn't one course in the high school curriculum that *doesn't* teach the same twenty benefits that the NAfME lists as their rationale for keeping music in the curriculum. Music in schools must be justified on its own terms. There's no doubt that music provides all the benefits listed by NAfME but so do other subjects. Math establishes its credibility on its own merits. Indeed, math teaches things to kids that music cannot. Language arts teach things to students that music cannot. Indeed, driver's education teaches things to students that music cannot. But the experience of playing music teaches things about the human experience that no other subject can address.

I understood patriotism the first time at the age of ten when a powerful marching band passed in a parade. I understood the loyalty Americans owed Abraham Lincoln when I could not play due to emotion, as we came upon the finale of Harold Walters' "Civil War Suite" at band camp when I was fourteen. And, I understood the long arc of life upon hearing once again, Copland's 'The Promise of Living' at age 65.

These meanings and these experiences are why music belongs in the curriculum. There is no better system to aid in the building of a bridge than mathematics. Music brings nothing to that process. But ask Copland to tell the story of the might, men, lost lives, vision and grandeur of the finished product - and music surely is the finest way. As helpless as music is at building bridges, so is math at explaining love.

Musical Context

Reflecting on *"A Kid from Momence...Growing up after the War,"* Kevin McNulty, Sr. (KMC Publishing, 2016)

Teaching music our students can perceive

I will confess that after all these years I have truly become a musical bigot. Allow me to explain. Given the time to attend a concert, listen to a recording or catch a club performance, I really only want to hear the best. This is no slight on all the thousands of musicians working their way up to their musical potential. Nor is it due to any limitations of my time. It's impatience. I get that way when I listen to developing performers making failed attempts at a composer's intentions.

For a musician, listening to a "professional band" in a club with a bass player that drags, a singer that tries to sing beyond her range or a band that is simply out of balance, negates the experience. Similarly, an orchestra with a conductor whose career-long specialty has been Shostakovich or Wagner can miss the subtle expressions of Debussy or Ravel.

You might find this impatience odd since I spent years teaching young people how to play music. In my first go around right out of college, I will admit that I did experience frustration with my student's limitations, despite my valiant efforts. But that was no fault of theirs. Once a kid gets good, they graduate from high school and in comes another batch of neophytes searching for the upper register fingerings of their clarinet. Today, despite years of listening, performing and judging music, I teach free of any level of frustration over these matters. You would think that my level of frustration would be much more intense at sixty-five than it ever was in my mid-twenties. But it is not. I have acquired another skill along the way, the ability to understand context.

Perhaps I've learned to compartmentalize, you might say. But teaching is teaching. Listening to music is something different. The joy of teaching is being a witness to the student's journey regardless of the end result. The joy of music is hearing a fully transparent performance played by musicians capable of understanding and enhancing a composer's intentions. Thus, my musical bigotry is not directed at a particular style of music but at a bad performance of any style of music. Good is good and bad is bad, whether one is listening to the Chicago Symphony Orchestra or catching a blues band at Buddy Guy's Legends. Good teachers teach to the professional standard. But teachers must also give the kids their time to learn just as we were given. Thus, the desire to hear the best is not about avoiding "wrong notes." It's an assurance that the performers and, in the case of serious music, the conductor, have grown well past the mechanical requirements of the piece and have a depth of experience necessary to bring forth and add to the intentions of the composer.

What fully satisfies me has changed over time. This is because listeners and, in particular musicians, bring their own history to every performance. My earliest recollection of music had few expectations. It was all new to me. Today, in my "musically bigoted years," I bring my history and expectations to the performance along with the thousands of performances I have witnessed and given for over sixty years. Consider these two musical events in my life.

In 1953, I sat on a concrete curb with my family, awaiting the arrival of a rumbling off in the distance that was at least four blocks away but immensely present. It was an undivided sound but dense and weighted, created by sixteen, maybe twenty-four cadets all looking seven feet tall even at such a distance.

Like the sound, a wall of pulsing knees popped forward flashing a folding and unfolding of legs in perfect sequence to a growing volume of drums. I looked at their stride then raised my eyes up to see each flag overhead stiffened in the wind, participating in a portrayal of what looked like a mighty ship coming to port, oars churning underneath and sails stretched taut against the wind.

The sound grew as they came closer, now two blocks away revealing twenty to twenty-five brass horns meticulously anchored against green silk tops worn by equally tall men, held down with a wide cross belt that descended down to an equally wide waist belt and sash.

One block away now, the cadence broke into a heralding roll-off that brought horns up in a snap followed by a full brass wail that actually overcame the pulsing drum sound and caused me to raise my eyebrows in surprise. The sound and the vision came, pushed forward and increased until the first wave of rifles and flags passed no more than three feet from my seat.

"Sit back, Kevin," my father said to me. I pushed back a bit but leaned forward as the last line of silks passed, revealing eight snare drums all in a row all churning like a steam engine and pushing the ship past the gaping jaws of kids and thrilled adults.

This captured my undivided attention. White buck shoes kicked forward, drums, resting on the thigh of each drummer, rose and fell in perfect sequence. A high, alternating and rapid flow of arms drove large drumsticks into the center of each drum and each silk sleeve rustled in the wind. Then stern faces looking directly into the sun, oblivious to any of us, looking like figureheads on the bow of the ship. Then blaring sopranos played by deep breathing boys, sweating profusely as they marched into the late afternoon sun. Then, larger horns and big horns. The timbre of the brass changing as it passed in front of me, each section presenting its sound clearly but the whole of them bursting forth with a sound that slammed up against the storefronts on both sides of the street and went aloft, filling the air with open chords, punctuated by an ever insistent drumline.

My eyes followed them past and watched as they marched away, heals all lifting off the street's surface in perfect time like gaping rattlesnakes being dragged away to their death. I had just seen my first drum and bugle corps. I was three. I hardly took a breath the whole time.

In April of 2015, I sat listening to the Mahler 7th performed by the Chicago Symphony Orchestra at Orchestra Hall in Chicago. The conductor that evening was the leading Mahler expert living today, Bernard Haitink from Holland. For those non-musical people who may be unfamiliar with Gustav Mahler, he is, in my opinion, the deepest and most complex composer to have ever lived. I've been listening to him for over forty-five years, and I'm just now starting to understand his work.

He is simple and at the same time astoundingly complex. He can be bombastic and then as light as a single cottonwood seed in flight, all within the span of two measures. In his day, much of his music was declared crass, commercial and excessive by critics. But they too brought their history to the performance. They already knew the oozing, gut-wrenching emotion of Beethoven that, among other things, solicited throngs of panting female admirers to stalk him through the streets of Vienna. This music of Mahler was, in their minds, overindulgent and unnecessary at the peak of the great Romantic period.

But Mahler is the final coda of the Romantic period and stands atop all the "greats" before him that offered Mahler a foundation to create the ultimate expression of emotion and life through music. During the performance, I sat alone amid a fully occupied concert hall, and I hardly took a breath the whole time. There was no one present except me, the CSO, and Mahler, all participating in that same transparent vision of life at its extremes. Mahler is all about extremes. The portrayal was nearly flawless. The level of expression had its peaks and valleys, but on the whole, I came away more than satisfied.

No doubt, were I to sit on that curb today and watch the same drum corps come down the street, I'd still feel a certain level of spark, but it would be muted by my years of listening, playing and judging music. I would find flaws in the intonation, see men slightly out of synch as they marched by, notice a slight variation in the angle of the flags and filter the entire experience through the thousands of drum corps and bands I have witnessed in my sixty plus years. I would still smile as they passed and perhaps bring forward my memory of that first time and relive it, on purpose, as we so often do later in our life. It is one of the great celebrations of the cycle of life. I'd confirm that it was good, but I would place it in context...my context, my musical history and my understanding of performance and art.

Conversely, were my folks able to place me in Orchestra Hall for the Mahler performance at age three, I likely would have fallen asleep in my chair, awakened only during Mahler's bombastic moments. I'm sure my father would have looked down at me and said, "Kevin's not there yet."

These two very vivid and contrasting musical memories were clear indications to me that while Mahler was always there, and I could have listened to him at age three, I would have had no idea of what his sounds meant. Only the sixty-some years of experience between that parade and Mahler 7 could allow me to understand what I heard, listening to the Chicago Symphony Orchestra performance at age 65. As we learn to play, we acquire the building blocks to master increasingly more complex music – leading to our ultimate understanding. Full understand is always elusive in music.

There is no better path to understanding music than playing it. For this reason, music-performance classes take a superior position over general music classes in the teaching of musical understanding. Music theory classes in high schools, highly dominated by student performers, support improved music performance. General music classes enhance and support the development of "good listeners," and are usually dominated by the non-performing student. Elementary general music classes can spur interest in music performance. Just as child development specialists understand how kids grow and learn in school, music performance teachers need to understand how young musicians grow and learn musically.

My earliest recollection of music was one of curiosity. I'm certain that the very first bit of musical curiosity was stimulated by the *sound* itself. Is this not the first thing that music presents to us, even to this day? From there, my memory is a blur of harmonized singing, doo-wop songs on the radio, the sound of my father's bass, early 60's pop music scratching through a small radio, and my father's 78 rpm jazz records played on a booming stereo system, the size of a small coffin.

The first time I picked up a pair of sticks and struck my soon-to-be nicked-up dresser, the *physical* part of playing took dominance. Sound was not replaced by the physical dimension, my experience was now a blend of both. Whether playing my drums, matching pitch on my tuba in 5th-grade band or banging out chords on our family piano while mom sang, all music had an aural and physical component.

Band music in school and garage band "practice" on weekends, added another element to the sound and physical experience. Listening took hold. To a musician, this means *listening* to the musicians playing with you. Audiences listen in one direction. Ensemble members listen in two directions. They listen to themselves, and the listen to those around them – back and forth it goes – in an aural partnership the molds many instruments or voices into one.

Once I began to play in ensembles, musical *form* took a dominant presence in my mind. It brought with it a shifting of sounds, textures, and ideas. Form framed moods. Even as a thirteen-year-old musician, I understood form and also understood that its purpose was to present moods – contrasting moods – differences. These are the elements of storytelling.

It was not until I tried my hand at writing in college that *ideas* began to surface in my mind as a result of music. I had the fortune (and financial need) to play in clubs while in undergrad school where I met a keyboard player named Phil Tolatta. Phil was a writer and had written a number of tunes played by his former pop band called "The Winstons." They were a funk-soul band from Washington D.C. and had come to Peoria, Illinois work the kinks out for their next tour. The only tune that hit the charts was a song called, "Color Him Father." When Phil told me he was a writer, I told him I was starting to write too. He quickly asked me, "What are you writing about?" I went blank. I gave him a made up answer, but at that instant, I realized I had not been composing at all. I was simply tinkering. I had no ideas. I was learning the process of composing but had nothing to say.

It is very important for all of us as music teachers to remember where we were as kids and what we understood about music then. As music performance teachers we must understand what music means to the students we teach. The *physical* experience of playing or singing is primary to our young students, and we must understand *their* physical challenges, show them how, and guide their hands, their posture and breathing. Intonation may be our first priority, but for them, it is sound and the physical ability to execute. Once our ensembles have general control of sound, intonation, technique and listening, we broaden their perspective to include expression, a requirement of *mood* setting.

As student-musicians mature, the meaning of sounds, technical prowess, listening, and mood setting takes hold. Suddenly, literature and its internal demands are the focus. But to traverse up the ladder of band, orchestra, and choral literature, students must master the increasing demands of advanced music. Only when this happens does musical understanding occur. This is where the composer's *ideas* get realized. As our students get past the formative stages of performance, it's our job to lead them to the <u>*discussions*</u> similar to those that we have as mature, advanced and passionate music lovers. It's our job to not only teach our students *how* to play, but it is also vital that we teach them *what* they are playing and how to engage in the conversation about what it *means*. Music has meaning. Teaching *meaning* is how we lead them to a life that includes lessons only learned through the arts.

Certainly, standards, requirements, assessments, challenges, and your professional goals are important. But all of us must take our students on their musical journey beginning with where they are. Our personal standards have been honed over time. They are just beginning their journey. Just as that learned group of directors at Mid-West Band and Orchestra Clinic demonstrated widely different perspectives, our students have theirs too. It's not enough to simply be the pied piper, waving our baton for the masses with the hopes that they will all, someday, understand as we do. We must discover where each student is and provide a roadmap and means to discover how dramatic and important it can be in their lives. This requires assessment. What do our students know? Where are they on their journey?

Musical Judgement

Reflecting on *"The Activities of Teaching,"* Thomas E. Green, (1971, McGraw-Hill, Inc.)

Assessment requires a judgment call

During my years in business, I hired a lot of people. As you might expect, in order to find those employees, it required that I interview hundreds more. I had some great interviews and hired some wonderful people. I also rejected a whole lot of folks that were mostly good qualified people with wonderful qualifications but didn't have the qualifications that fit my job offer. I'd usually get a stack of one-hundred resumes. The first thing all executives do when hiring is to divide the first stack into two piles – "A's" on the right (possible) and "B's" on the left (rejected).

I got pretty quick at this process and eliminated the first 70% in a mere 15 to 20 minutes. On the first pass, I looked at one thing – background and experience. If I was hiring for a marketing person and they had a degree in sociology they went in the "B" pile. I'd receive resumes from history majors for accounting jobs, mail carriers for jobs in human resources and former executives for entry-level sales. Once I was hiring for an assistant and received a resume from an ironworker. This happens a lot in business. Too often, particularly in bad times, people want a job…any job.

Naturally, I had very specific qualifications in mind. I would make my decision based on the criteria I established going in. But there was no fool-proof test I could issue to candidates that would guarantee me that they could do the job. When the job description was designed, I thought very carefully about the qualities and skills I'd be looking for. The job description and the accompanying job ad highlighted the categories that would be factors in my decision, but they would not be the deciding factor.

Did I expect my winning candidate to match all criteria 100%? Of course not. That person doesn't exist. And even if I did find such a candidate, it would be my "gut" that would decide whether or not a person could actually "deliver" what I needed in the new hire. After all, interviews are a prospectus. Only on-the-job performance will tell me if I'd made the right choice. As anyone who has hired before knows, each candidate has pros and cons. To give me the best assurance I would make the right decision, I would have to lean very heavily on my experience in hiring and firing employees over the years. Sure, I had a list of questions, but I sought more than "yes or no answers." My questions were to elicited clues, evidence and other indications that my candidate would be successful in the job.

Would I use some sort of rubric? Not exactly. Rubrics might contain some criteria I seek, but I don't need a sheet of paper to tell me, "average amount of sales experience, "above average amount of experience," or "excellent amount of experience."

Would I issue all candidates a written test on the qualities I sought? Hardly. An interview is a performance, and although I'd have criteria, I would not use a test to make my decision because a written test could possibly capture a huge number of "clues" I could receive by actually interviewing each candidate and hearing their answers and passing that information subconsciously through my background and experience hiring salespeople. Once my final three were selected, I would double check my criteria and *still* have final interviews before making my choice. In the end, if you asked me to rank all candidates, I could do that.

I had to use my best judgment. And judgment draws on one's background and experience *always* infers criteria. I would never hire a candidate by simply guessing which one is better. That requires no judgment. I could never hire a candidate, "blind," if their resume matched all the qualifications listed in my job notice. That's tantamount to using a "marching test" to pick a candidate. There are no pre-designed "right answers." There are only appropriate answers. Weak candidates will often give you "right answers" but their presentation is not authentic, and you doubt the sincerity of their answer. Other candidates give you an answer you did not expect, and their answer expands the nature of the question. Those types of candidates are the type you want on your team.

Though I never thought of Thomas E. Green during my entire time in business, I understood him so much better on the second read some fifty years after my first reading in undergrad school and after making hundreds of judgments in my business career and in the competitive band and drum corps arena. His book, "The Activities of Teaching," was required reading in our educational methods class. It included an understanding of the philosophy behind teaching, learning and, most relevant here, testing. Or as Green called it, "judging."

It pleased me greatly to discover that after all those years, I had come to a system of evaluation that aligned fully with Green's contentions. I was also gratified to discover that Green would have agreed with my process for hiring and all the training I had ever received from the Central States Judges Association.

Solid principles that have been vetted and tested or conceived by great minds like Green's stand the test of time because they are based on what works. What works can be something as simple as chopping a tree down with an ax or as complex as fabricating that tree into a canoe? Green begins by defining judgment and distinguishing it from "guessing" and "knowing."

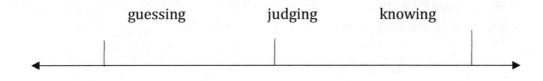

> *"If the exercise of judgment is opposed to guessing by its stronger relation to grounds or reasons, then what shall we say when the grounds or reasons are decisive? When we are wholly without any grounds for ranking, estimating or predicting, then we cannot be said to be in a position to render a judgment. But conversely, when our grounds or evidence are conclusive, then we do not need to render a judgment. In short, if the exercise of judgment is opposed to guessing in one respect, then it is opposed to a state of certitude or knowledge in another respect.*

The significant "take-away" from Green's work is important for music-performance teachers and administrators. Green presents clear evidence that judging or assessing is not based on your opinion. A student, parent or administrator may believe this, but that is only because they do not understand the nature of making judgments. Judging student performers is not a subjective act void of any criteria or past experience to reference. That's guessing. Nor is it something you can determine by issuing a one-hundred question written test. No written exam can measure performance. It can only assess memorization which may or may not be an indication of understanding.

Most people believe that Olympic Ice Skating officials judge by "opinion." Stage moms believe that auditioners pick their cast based on "opinion." And, from time to time students, parents and an occasionally administrators believe we do this too. This makes it important for music-performance teachers to assess using their judgment occurs by using criteria and filtering performance through their background and experience while checking your bias.

Green states, "Good judgment is the capacity to maximize the accuracy of one's estimates, rankings or predictions under conditions where knowledge is either unattainable or inaccessible." He makes the point that judgments are *not* subjective as might be feelings, opinions or preferences:

"They are always objective in the sense that they rest upon reasons, grounds, rules or principles. But the grounds of judgments are never conclusive, and therefore it is perfectly possible for different men to give different judgments on the same matter and even in relation to the same grounds, and it may also be the case that such different judgments are equally reasonable.

Langer, Green and the others set the logical foundation for the system of assessment that follows. Music performance assessment is a judgment call, requiring an actual live performance before a qualified director who has the background and experience to assess his students using a valid and tested system that can be adapted to any school district's grading system.

Section Two

Toward Credible and Authentic Judging

Part 4 - Foundations of Performance Adjudication

Judging music has been around for a long time. The inspired reactions, criticisms, and values placed on a music performance go back to Plato. But in the 20th Century, the science of adjudication was developed in an unexpected place – competitive drum and bugle corps. Borrowing from the systems developed in the competitive area of Drum Corps, music directors can institute a means to measure our desired outcomes - music performance. The proposed system can be applied to any school grading system.

Part V – Methodology

The techniques of professional adjudication are explained in detail. Directors will learn about applied science in the judging industry and its key element of– The Linear Scale. The Linear Scale, Impression-Analysis-Impression, and other techniques used in adjudication serve as a foundation for our assessment system. An actual timpani audition for the 8th-grade orchestra is used as an example of how the system is used with audition score sheets, or any contest sheet is an effective means of assessing.

Part VI - Scoring

Take a look inside the mind of a professional judge and learn how the Linear Scale works in a real situation. This unique section shows the reader what judges "say to themselves" when executing the delicate process of turning a subjective performance into an objective number. Three virtual performances are described, and the judge talks through his process of Impression-Analysis-Comparison to put the three in the right order and with the right rating.

Part IV

Foundations of Performance Adjudication

Genesis of Judging Technique

Drum and Bugle Corps had different roots than did school bands and emerged as a youth activity outside the school environment. They descended from military bugle and drum units returning from World War I and, later, World War II. Traditionally, drum and bugle corps served as signaling beginning prior to the American Civil War. But with the use of the field radios during World War I, obsolete and surplus bugles, drums, and equipment were sold to veteran organizations such as the American Legion and the Veterans of Foreign Wars. These groups and others formed drum and bugle corps comprised of civilians and veterans. Corps performed in community events and local celebrations.

Standards for drum corps were drawn from military practices like the *"Army Field Manual on Drill and Ceremony"* and from rudimental drumming patterns that went back to the Colonial Army. The story of bugling is a tale of efforts to extend basic bugle calls to more melodic settings and expanding the bugle's size to provide the middle and lower ranges. It was not until the modern bugle (rotors, then valves and eventually the adoption of the trumpet) that the full range of literature and expressions could be explored. Over time, rivalries between corps emerged, and competitive drum and bugle corps circuits developed all over the country. While parades and a few "stand-still" concerts were performed, the activity *was* competition not just performance. Drum corps participated in one, two or three contests each weekend during the summer. In the final weeks of the season, they would go on tour and perform four or five times in a week. This required a constant supply of judges for these contests. Judges associations spawned throughout the United States.

This history of drum corps judging is one of the rules established by the American Legion and VFW who ran the shows and held down drum corps attempting to express and be entertaining. This frustrated the drum corps increasingly at the 1960's began The restrictions placed on creativity in the activity, along with inconsistencies in judging and the general desire by drum corps to control their activity (and finances) came to a head in the late 60's and early 70's. Drum corps would meet at their annual congress and proposed changes in rules only to be snubbed by the American Legion and VFW who controlled contests and the rules. In the main, those changes were to allow drum corps to be more creative and entertaining. The VFW hung on to the old Field Manual from the military that required all tempos be restricted to 128 to 132 beats per minutes.

But in 1969, a group of corps managers, directors and instructors walked out of a VFW rules committee when their requests for changes were denied. In 1970, a group of corps held their own, yet short-lived, contest called The Midwest Combine." And in 1972, Drum Corps International (DCI) was founded and was designed to create one uniform, corps-governed competitive circuit for junior drum and bugle corps. But Drum Corps had not yet been nationalized, let alone internationalized. Different parts of the United States had regional associations that managed local shows.

There also existed a number of judging associations whose mission was to train and supply qualified judges to the drum corps activity. Drum corps judging associations sprouted up all over the United States but particularly in the East and Mid-West. There was the Pennsylvania Federation of Contest Judges, Massachusetts Judge's Association, National Judges Association, Canadian Judges Association, Northeast Judges Association, Mid-Atlantic Association, All American Judges Association and many more.

With the unshackling of the Legion and VFW and their restrictive rules, the creative juices of drum corps arrangers, designers and instructors were turned loose as the 70's ensued. And yet, despite what might appear to the reader that drum corps did not adhere to old standards, the history of the activity to this day is a compulsion to be innovative and creative and yet maintain the standards of execution and what new generations considered core to the identity of the activity.

In the beginning, judging was done by experienced performers, instructors, arrangers and drill designers. They were practitioners with an exceptional understanding of method. They studied the rules and guidelines of drum corps contests and developed techniques to adjudicate the events. The competitive edge of drum corps dictated refinement in judging techniques. It took years to create valid and practical methods of evaluation. The constant evolvement and creative expansion of drum corps from the 1950's forward required on-going improvements and innovations to judging methods. But it was a long road, and in a few cases, some wacky ideas were deployed.

The job of the judging community was burdened with the question, "How do we adjudicate these new formats, new styles, and new expressions while maintaining quality according to our standards for excellence?" Each judging association addressed new issues separately as dramatic innovations in show design, concept and expression expanded each year.

In January of 1970, the first national meeting of judging associations occurred to address the uniformity of judging across the country. Drum corps were beginning to travel more extensively. This brought out how different judges and different judging associations around the country were judging the activity. It was at this first meeting that Don Pesceone, an early pioneer of the activity, asked Paul Litteau of the Central States Judges Association, to articulate a concept of what was called, "The National Linear Scale." While a hand full of judges was using the concept, it had not been documented or framed as a principle of judging. This scale became the cornerstone of the judging system, but its use would still need to be explained, tested and confirmed over time. Today, nearly every drum corps and band contest scoresheet has the scale printed atop or on the back.

Paul Litteau was a very active and engaged judge at the time. Philosophies of judging were not just going through growing pains, they were all over the place. The judging community was full of men and women with ideas that were untested, illogical and baseless. Paul, being a man of logic and candid assessment, would usually sit in the back of a room, ponder a presentation of "the latest vision" and then either articulate its merit or attack its credibility. His articulate and methodical delivery disarmed many a wacky idea. His affirmation of a concept would find its way into the collective thinking of the group. In recent years, he made a few observations:

"Much of the synthesis (on how to judge) came about as a result of considering and refuting what was being passed off as philosophy and methodology."

Paul makes the point that descriptive words on the front or back of a score sheet are guidelines, checkpoints for a judge as they analyze. It is not a "punch list" of "gots" and "don't gots," As Langer states, art is not an artist's presentation of all qualities but the proportional presence of such qualities in performance resulting in an inspired and aesthetic experience for the listener. The performance should be experienced first. Upon analysis, a judge will discover that qualities were or were not presented in appropriate proportions to produces a meritorious or failed art.

The reasons for a good or bad performance can be explained on a list, but the list should not be the point of entry to that decision. A judge who skips the listener-experience and jumps immediately to a checklist of each quality in a performance misses the point.

A judge in the mid-60's once proposed that each sub-caption on the sheet could be divided into qualities to be considered. Hence, if "Musicality" appeared on a score sheet worth 20 points and it had ten descriptive terms below, then the descriptive terms would be worth 2 points each and should be separately evaluated with the result being the sum of ten unique evaluations. Of course, this is utter stupidity. Now, instead of asking a judge to make one decision, the judge is being asked to make ten! Indeed, there were many misguided systems proposed in the early days of drum corps judging. While it is not rocket science, many have attempted to make it so. Paul recalls one color guard general effect judge sitting in the back sideline stands because "he wanted to see different things." He probably did see new things, but it wasn't what the performance was designed to show.

Paul elaborates further. If a judge were to "focus on one quality (theme, for example), he might limit the opportunity in another (such as variety)" He is correct. The first job of any judge or a director doing a performance assessment is to listen first (or watch and listen as in the case of marching band or drum corps). He must let the performance occur. Keep his eyes off the score sheet and let his musical instincts guide him first. The synergistic nature of music performance can only be experienced when judges are in this impressionable state – before analysis.

No group did more to study, test, evaluate and apply judging methodology than the Central States Judges Association (CSJA) based in Chicago. For a number of years, it was commonplace to view East Coast corps as the leaders in drumming and Midwestern corps having particular expertise in marching. Similar opinions existed in those judging captions. There's plenty of evidence that both notions had their exceptions.

Within the "Central States" organization, each caption held a slightly different view of how judging should approach the changes that were occurring and anticipated the activity. The percussion caption tended to favor the use of the original "tic system" where errors were deducted from a drumline performance. It addressed the specificity and detail at the core of drumming. Of all the captions going back to the beginning of drum corps, it was drumming that always had uniformity as its core mission first. Indeed, though band directors attacked drum corps for their musicality, it was bugling they attacked. Back in those times, no director in his right mind would attack the drumming prowess of drum and bugle corps.

The brass caption felt particularly shackled by the old rules and believed that more subjective methods we used for evaluation. It was this capture that lived with the shackles of not only the old rules but a flawed instrument, never intended to play music of a subtle nature. It was a signaling horn and could not even play every note required of many popular songs being adopted in the 1950's to please audiences. Though I never heard it spoken by anyone, I often thought that brass caption people must have had thoughts about the obsession drum people had with perfection – "You guys are all concerned with measuring accuracy, and we don't even have instruments capable of achieving accuracy let alone measuring it." For this reason, I believe, the brass caption was the first to call for a lessening of the "tic system" and the further development of "build-up" system.

The marching caption was a mix of traditionalists and innovators. The particular group of people in the CSJA caption at the time had its share of great minds. Men and women of business, sales, industry, finance, manufacturing, public relations, marketing, management, science and the trades all comprise the visual caption of CSJA. There were notable artisans in the group, as well, from within and outside the drum corps activity. There were a few former brass instructors to my knowledge no music teachers in the caption until I entered the group in 1977. This was the logical place for debate to occur. And it did. Despite the varying backgrounds and experiences of the visual caption each person had a passion to "figure this thing out."

The marching caption fashioned many of principles of judging performance that are still in use today in both drum corps and bands. They addressed subjective judging in the areas of general effect, along with the objective (error deduction) nature of marching execution. When standard "tic" judging evolved into a more evaluative methodology, CSJA helped the judging activity navigate that transition to what we use today.

As each summer season ended, CSJA would go into self-evaluation mode. What works? What doesn't work? What are the drum corps doing new that we have no method to assess. What new system can address these innovations but adhere to other execution standards of uniformity? What are the universal qualities of entertainment and expression that provide guidelines to judge the effect of any drum corps show regardless of style? Committees met through the winter to craft new methods. Experienced judges reviewed preliminary reports and added their commentary. Ideas were reworked further. In winter the entire organization would meet to review proposals. Open discussions, debates and, indeed, arguments ensued until most everyone was satisfied. It was a study in building consensus.

In the spring, training on new and existing methodology occurred. The overriding goal was to leave the spring seminar unified, with a full understanding of how new creative elements would be judged through the summer. Following the summer season, the process began all over again.

An excerpt from my book entitled, *"A Kid from Momence...Growing up after the War"* (2015) gives an account of how a typical caption meeting ensued in the visual caption of CSJA. I was a young intern at the time, and our debate was whether or not a general effect judge should evaluate a corps strictly through the prism of his own instincts, background, and experience, or whether he should have a list of criteria to guide him in his subjective decision.

> *I remember a particular Saturday morning meeting where advocates for one position were battling back and forth over a sensitive topic. The conversation was sophisticated, passionate and acrimonious on all sides.*
>
> *The debate was over whether or not General Effect judges should strictly use their "gut" in arriving at their numbers or if certain criteria, perhaps on a list, could be added to the sheet to remind the judge of what should be considered. The debate raged on.*
>
> *"A judge has to make a decision based on his own experience, not something we dictate to him," stated one advocate.*
>
> *"But a judge's background and experience may be biased toward the style he is most comfortable with, and he could miss elements that he should consider," said another.*
>
> *Still, another interrupted, "I'll be damned if I'm going to read a list of qualities that are supposed to be in "good shows," and then sit there waiting for them to appear before I can arrive at my number. I know good drum corps when I see it. I don't need a committee telling me when a show is exciting."*

And finally, "Who's to say that we or any other group of judges know exactly what should be on a checklist, anyway. We can't legislate such things. After all, that's the point of the GE sheet. We are supposed to react and reward. That's all that is required."

[Following two hours of debate, a senior judge named Rick Maass spoke up]

....a deep voice spoke up from the back of the room. It was Rick Maass, one of the founders of CSJA. Rick was a judge of national stature and not only shaped CSJA but impacted the activity nationwide. He summed things up this way,

"As you know I do a lot of flying around the country. Like all of you, I must trust the competency of the pilot to get me where I'm going, safely. I never want a pilot that does not have a checklist." And then Rick paused for effect as he could do so effectively. Then he added. "At the same time, I also don't want a pilot that needs a checklist."

The debate was over. Rick had spoken. Rick had led. But Rick spoke last and let the troops voice their thoughts - not in a patronizing way as so often happens within project teams but in a deliberate way - knowing that the debate was important for all to "buy-in." He was wise enough to understand that decisions are so much more powerful and execution much more guaranteed if consensus is built from the ground up rather than out of the mouths of the "Grand Dukes" who have been there for a long time.

CSJA was more than a training organization. It was essentially a large debating society, committed to convince, cajole, advocate and persuade most to agree how to do our craft. Everyone knew we were breaking new ground and what was decided in these meetings would impact the entire activity. The sense of mission was overwhelming and obvious to all. It was wonderful.

Few judges in CSJA had a more senior status than did Rick Maass. Rick was an "Eisenhower," waiting in the back row, listening and letting others "hash things out." There were others too, but this day, Rick would articulate the right decision. Interestingly enough, his final solution encompassed the strongly held positions of both sides of the issue. He had the vision and the wisdom to see the merits of each opinion. The advocates had debated for nearly an hour. He brought it to a conclusion with the most obvious solution. Two things stand out relative to our discussion, here.

- Assessment methods must be connected to, be reflective of, and derived from the very activity it proposed to measure.
- Rick Maass confirmed in practice what Green deduced as a philosophical principle. "Valid performance assessment requires a knowledgeable and experienced judge with a background as a performer and list of criteria to guide his decision."

Many great minds across the country have contributed to the art of judging. I have related my direct experiences with the Central States Judges Association because it is my best reference. During the decades of drum corps, judges, corps directors, instructors, designers, and arrangers all contributed. But the core principles of performance adjudication were applied and tested more often and more extensively than any symposium, dissertation, or studies generated by universities or expert panels established by government. There are some very brilliant concepts that have been put forth by smart people in the area of assessment. The work of competitive music contest judges should be dealt with seriously for I believe it comes closer to valid assessment than any being used today.

In CSJA, there was no conversion process. This does not infer that judges did not make grand attempts to convert others to their point of view. For, they often did. But it was done in the context of a caucus. Advocates for one position or another would form small groups. They would hash out their position behind the scene and appoint a spokesperson to present to the body. In the end, the entire caption (visual or music) would articulate the consensus. Once agreed, judges would enter the competitive season with a defined and agreed-upon procedure.

It often occurred that alternative methods discussed in debate had enough merit to test in the field. From time to time, judges would be assigned to try these alternatives during the season and bring test results back to the group the following winter. It was not unusual for a proposed technique to fail one year, be tested during the season and approved the following year based on applied data collected during field trials.

No doubt, many in the scholarly community have not heard of the Central States Judges Association nor would they consider it 'mainstream" in terms of educational research. Yet the people who comprised this group ranged from practitioners to scholars in their professional field and masters of adjudication methodology. As was stated earlier, there is no research done at the university level more tested and formulated regarding music performance assessment than the work done by CSJA over three decades.

What is important for administrators, department heads, and directors to grasp is the process by which the judging method was developed. While some schools foster and encourage vigorous debate. Others do not. In business, companies that encourage discussion and welcome different points of view from all members of their team, are more successful. No doubt, they too have their "Ricks" who articulate conclusions only after employees, managers and department heads all have an equal say in the final resolution.

Assessment is an applied science. It, therefore, must be developed through trial and error, vigorous debate and group consensus so all school faculty "buy-in." It is, after all, a process that is applied in the classroom. Teachers must believe in whatever system is deployed in their school, or it does not work.

School Music Contest Judging

Bands, orchestras, and choirs go to music contests. With the exception of some states, they are usually annual events where groups are given ratings almost exclusively, without rankings. When attending "non-competitive" events, the goal is to achieve what is generally called a "First Division Rating." Twenty bands can attend a non-competitive state contest, and fifteen of them can all obtain a first division rating. There could be five first division ratings. There could be none. There is no distinction (ranking) in the event other than getting a first, a second, a third or, God forbid, a fourth. It's an "individualized assessment" of each group against accepted musical standards and descriptions of basic musical qualities such as tone, rhythm, intonation, and balance, printed on a single score sheet.

Some states such as Indiana and Texas have qualifying events and declare state champions. Other states combine large group, ensemble and solo events to declare class rankings in their state. Directors can also choose to participate in University or non-state sponsored contests and festivals, as well. Some of these are competitive.

But in most states, the contest host, who is generally the local or university music director, does the hiring of judges. A university will select a notable conductor from another university to draw high school groups to their events. A school that hosts a solo & ensemble contest for their state organization may choose from a state-wide list or in many cases hire other directors or retired directors to judge their contest. Independently sponsored contests will hire judges that have reputations in the activity. Active Band, Orchestra and Choir directors with reputations as great directors are often hired to judge contests.

Other than the winter guard contests and other competitive circuits which are run by Winter Guard International (WGI) and other organizations, judges for contests are chosen by contest directors sometimes off an approved list other times ad hoc. The good ones use their instincts and their years of conducting and teaching groups to judge others. But these directors are teachers first and judges second. Few have ever had any formal training in judging. Many of these judge-directors will judge once a year. School, university, and state organizations might only hire judges once or twice a year.

Judges meet before each contest and are given, on average, a fifteen to twenty-minute orientation. I have found that most contest directors open judges meetings with a comment that goes something like this:

> "You are all good teachers. You know how to do this. Just be fair and make good comments. We want this to be an educational experience for the kids."

Little is said about how sponsors want their contest adjudicated. But here's the significant point.

In casual conversation, at contests, in grad school or undergrad school, there is rarely a conversation about *"how to turn a listening experience into a raw numerical score."* Because of their experience in the business, most good directors "get it right" most of the time. But it often takes music directors years to learn their own system – whatever that might be. What might that learning curve be if universities taught undergraduate and graduate students how to rank, rate and grade? Our point is not to create more and better judges, though that would be welcomed. It is to train teachers how to assess music performance.

With the exception of a number of marching band events where judges might judge eight or ten times in one season, there is little opportunity for most school music judges to practice their craft. Most directors do not judge that often. If they also do not use assessment systems based on music performance in their schools (and as we have demonstrated many do not), they do not have the opportunity to fine-tune or find distinction between one student's ability and the next.

Methods of judging in school performance contests and festivals have not provided any practical assistance either. Judging at music contests across the country is all over the board. The competitive marching band activity has a bit more "unity" to it. But a very high percentage of marching band judging today is "off a script." The script is "a list of words on the back of a sheet." That is not a process. A process is absent from most judging practices today. As more and more "national judges" are chosen from the ranks of "good directors," the fewer judges know about the actual craft of judging. Armed with their musical instincts, most judges can come close to agreeing on the top few bands and those lagging at the bottom. But they have a much tougher time determining scores for the bands in the middle.

But outside of marching band, all other judging of music contests lacks any formalized systems beyond the score sheet and a director-judge's reaction to a performance. Texas has an approved list of judges for their contests such as the Texas Music Adjudicators Association (TMAA). Here, judges are approved based on their record of achievement with their band, orchestra or choir. Still, when judges decide to pass groups from area to region and state, they rank groups in order only, never revealing an actual number (rating) for those groups. Essentially, each judge makes their decision using their own ranking system.

Compare that to what occurs in high school athletics. One difference is that more judges (referees and umpires) are needed more often in a year than for music contests. Each sport has a season and in sports, winning and losing is the yardstick of success. Therefore, ranking is the goal, not rating. Even in states like Texas, that have qualifying events at area, regional and state levels for high school music and do rank, having fewer events, requiring as many judges, than do the 8th-grade basketball teams in their state. Sporting events in high schools are officiated by referees from referee associations. They are approved by state athletic associations and officiate as a full-time hobby. They have formal and informal apprentice programs where younger referees work a mentor and are brought through the ranks. Referees who officiate at the high-end collegiate or pro ranks hold camps and workshops for up and coming new officials. These are commercial ventures. In short, there is an entire cottage industry and professional association structure associated with high school, collegiate and professional sports officiating.

In Illinois and other states, there are referee associations scattered throughout the state. Athletic directors book refs by contacting the association in their area. Most referee associations are local and service multiple conferences or multiple counties. Some conferences, like the Chicago Public League, use more than one refereeing association. In the Chicago Public Schools, all basketball referee assignments are handled by three people.

The Illinois High School Association (IHSA), like most state athletic associations, certifies the referees used for their official state tournament events. Referees are required to test annually, and three levels of testing escalate a ref to a certified level qualified to referee upper-level events. In contrast, the IHSA has a simple online registration with a handful of basic questions for music judges. Most local music contest managers hire people they know, that are good musicians, respected music teachers, at ease with students and consistent with ratings. Because of the low frequency of contests or season-long tournaments in music that exist in sports, there has been little development of adjudicator associations for school music contests. Therefore, the science and art of music assessment has come from outside the educational community.

Since the teaching of assessment, let alone judging methods, has yet to be fully addressed at the undergrad level, it should be no surprise to anyone the graduates know little about assessment or judging, upon graduation. Directors are, essentially, left to create their own systems to determine what standards apply from one contest to the next, how score sheets should be interpreted how scores relate to other groups in a given contest (spread). They are also left alone to determine how to rate, rank and grade students in their ensembles.

The most tested and sound method has been developed in the competitive area of music. The focus on competition, which gets some underserved and deserved criticism, forces judges to make highly distinctive decisions about quality. The system did not occur overnight. It took decades of trial and error. The heretics were many but thank goodness, there were some very smart people in the judging community of early drum corps to keep the process on track and demand it has integrity. We can learn from their techniques. Realizing how little music directors are using valid systems to measure student music performance. And, looking to the long-tested judging system developed in the drum and bugle corps arena, we can begin to construct a process unique to our subject matter but more importantly capable of measuring our desired outcomes. Before examining the system, however, we must first understand the importance of doing a self-assessment of one's background and experience, knowledge of each instrument or voice and our level of mastery of pedagogy.

The Evaluator's Background, Experience & Bias

Music – all music – has context. It is always heard in a personal context. As concert-goers sit and listen to a performance, they are each having a different experience. Surely, only one sound is coming from the stage, and everyone is hearing the same thing, but not everyone is experiencing the same thing. Even among learned and experienced music directors the experience will be something different for each one of them. It is because we all bring to a music performance. It's also a beautiful thing.

When I was a young director attending the Mid-West Band and Orchestra Clinic in Chicago, I would regularly attend some of the finest professional and youth performances I've heard in my career. Evenings, my friends and I would go to the clubs downtown and take in the jazz scene (which was always so rich during "Midwest-week"). Conversations about what we heard during the day would go on well into the evening. I was struck by how many of the observations and opinions spoken by my colleagues, never crossed my mind.

First of all, I was fortunate to have many friends with greater experience than me. I always followed my father's sage advice to "always play with guys better than you or you won't learn anything." I applied that to my teaching career. Fortunately, I met some wonderful mentors along the way who, like so many in our business, were more than willing to "pass down," their pearls of wisdom. Our group was often quite diverse in musical background. I think we enjoyed each other because we all had a different point of view. It enriched us. In those late night discussions about the music performances we had heard through the day, some comments were identical to my reactions. Some comments seemed quite insignificant to me. Some were profound. Some comments would actually stimulate a playback in my mind of the concert we'd heard, and I'd realize I'd missed something on first listen.

One director would comment about how clean the articulation of the brass was at the breakup strain of a march. Another might comment about the appropriateness of the tempo a conductor chose. Finally, one among us would make a statement about the importance of the piece itself – important musically, important for our idiom and important for kids to experience. These sessions motivated me to study more, listen from a different perspective and be sensitive to all the elements in a given composition. This is the pursuit of all passionate music directors in our business. Some never stop thinking about it.

I learned from these conversations. I realized, somewhere in undergrad school, that it took studying, reflection, and an open mind to understand certain music that had more to "say" than most music of my youth. And yet, do I not hear James Brown, Ella Fitzgerald, Frank Sinatra, or Crosby, Stills and Nash differently now than I did then? Of course, I do. And, was I not incapable of experiencing Mozart, Beethoven, Vivaldi or Mahler in my youth as I do now? Yes.

All musical understanding is realized in the context of one's own personal life experiences. For music directors, musical understanding is realized in the context of one's own professional experiences, as well. We must know a wide range of music. We must understand the challenges of each instrument and voice, as well. Most importantly, we must constantly nurture our background by continuing to be listeners, musicians, and technicians

 When assessing students in performance, it is important to start by allowing yourself to listen first. While it will be a natural tendency to begin analyzing, avoid "going there." It is important to acquire an impression during performance. This allows your background and experience to influence your reactions to the performance. There is no need to, nor will you, be aware of your background and experience. Its function is to serve as your "musical DNA." And it will. Allow that to happen as if you were listening with no expectation of the need to assess. You will find that analysis will come to mind as you listen. This is natural and fine. Treat analysis in your mind as "notes written lightly in pencil." It will assist you during the analysis phase which comes later but don't focus there during performance. Receive and retain the performance and your general impression "written in bold ink."

 Not all assessment is a "musical experience" though scale testing or pitch matching can be with advanced students. If you are issuing a scale assessment, you can use a simple "tic" system (described later). Here you are concerned with accuracy. Artistry defines the special effect that occurs when listeners sense the power of mastery as exhibited by a performer. This is part of execution but is secondary here. When marking errors, your background and experience will intuitively take over. Again, there will be no need to think of it. As a student ascends and descends their scale, you will mark errors in accuracy, intonation, tone and perhaps other considerations. Your background and experience will guide you as to your tolerance for error. Tolerance is the point that your standard is not met regarding execution. Tolerance rests on your sense of "what is correct." When assessing execution, it is not required that you "sit back and listen" as when you assess a performance. Here you must be keenly aware of each exposure (accuracy, intonation, etc.) and assess if your tolerance (acceptance) level has been met

While background and experience will and should be "subconscious" during assessment, it should not be subconscious when assessing one's bias. The term bias, in this case, differs from the common interpretation by the general public. In American society, bias commonly refers to someone being overly partial to someone, something or an idea. It's opposite (prejudice) is generally referred to as having an unjustifiably negative opinion or feeling toward a person, groups of people or idea.

Bias in our assessment system refers to something different than the definition referred to in common nomenclature. The term *bias*, in our case, refers to some conscious or unconscious musical or non-musical notion of the importance or insignificance of an element of music or music performance.

Indeed, in some extreme cases, directors *can* experience something similar to the common definition of prejudice. A choral director could express disdain for a required all-state piece, simply as a result of her bad experience performing it in college under a tyrant of a conductor. A band director may cringe at the very sound of his wonderful auditioning oboe students solely based on the excruciating experience in group woodwind class where oboe was an absolute impossibility.

Conversely, directors can experience a bias for music in ways normally defined by social norms. A young orchestra director, still learning the musical capabilities of her group, may program a piece for their first concert she played at her university orchestra brought down the house. A choir director, who is a tenor, may allocate an inordinate amount of rehearsal time working his tenor section while neglecting the equally important sopranos, altos, and basses. An experienced band director may regularly program his favorite composers. While we all have (and should have) our favorites, over programming of any one composer or style shows a bias on the part of the director and may not always provide his band with the varied literature or the accompanying techniques and expressions that come with them. You will notice that the prejudices and bias given in the examples above have to do with like and dislikes of the directors. Here's how their preferences affected the classroom.

The choral teacher that did not like the All-State number did not give her full effort in preparing her students for All-State. The band director failed to give his oboe students an unfiltered assessment due to his dislike for their instrument. The young orchestra teacher failed to select music that was achievable by *her* students. She essentially created a major error in selecting her "text," no different than if the 6th grade English teacher chose an 8th-grade level text. Finally, the band director in love with one composer or genre is not providing students with a broad range of wind ensemble music. He is also locking his students into a narrow perception of what band music is. He has failed to select music based on desired outcomes. The methods used by a single composer or genre never explore a broad enough spectrum of skills for the student musician. This is tantamount to taking a literature class and studying Shakespeare the entire year.

But the bias we speak of relative to assessment is not quite the same as the examples above. Liking or disliking is not the catalyst for bias in this case. Bias, as it affects assessment, is a "blind spot" in an otherwise willing and able director's perception of performance. They center more on one's abilities, performance history, training and repeated practice. Here are some examples:

- A choral director who was trained intently by old voice teacher regarding diction leans heavily on that element and "turns her ear away" from a consistent vowel shaping issue in alto section during an assessment.
- A band director, who is a percussionist, listens to attacks and rhythmic accuracy as his "first point of entry" when assessing his brass players. By this method, he nearly blows right by the wide range of tonal differences in his trumpet section due to improper breathing and embrasure method.
- An orchestra director with a wonderful sense of tone and pitch on the violin may spend all her time sampling that exposure and let tempo or rhythmic accuracy slip.

What usually happens when a director judges with blind spots is, he or she scores with bias toward one element of performance over another. This is not a "like-dislike" issue. It is a background, experience and awareness issue. The director that does this has not taken the time to assess his or her strengths, weakness, tendencies, habits, preferences. This self-analysis should be done all the time. Whether one is in education, business, ministry, sports or plumbing one should always be thinking about what you do and do know about your job. It is not a once a year thing. It should be part of "every drive home," as my old boss in business used to stress with me. In all fields, this is what separates the good from the great.

Having been in business and music education, I found that this principle is the same in both fields. People who don't feel comfortable asking questions assume 1) they're supposed to know everything 2) there is no such thing as a lifetime learning curve 3) people will think they are idiots if they don't know something about music. Ah, but I can tell you that the adage the "older I get the less I know is true."

I learned this lesson about asking dumb questions when I left teaching for the first time, for a business career. I was a total "lifer" when it came to music. But I did music for so long, having played dance jobs since I was thirteen years old, that I was literally bored by thirty-eight. When I got my first job with the Chicagoland Chamber of Commerce, I knew nothing. It was a large group of people totaling, just under, sixty employees. Being a music teacher with two degrees in music education, I knew very little about business. But I had made a decision, and I had to succeed. I asked every stupid question I could think of. To make a long story short, I became a CEO twelve years later. In our business, it is vital that we know our weaknesses, tendencies, and biases - and work on them. It makes us better when we go to assess students, and it assures our growth as musicians.

Beyond analyzing and denoting your tendencies, weaknesses, and biases, it is vital to make use of them when assessing students. While it does sound counter-intuitive, it points to the purpose of the criteria reference system. In the next section I will discuss the big difference between the criteria reference system and the use of rubrics –so dominate in education today. But the use of criteria reference in the act of judging is valid and necessary.

As we have already demonstrated, music performance is a very complex experience. It cannot be experienced in compartments. It is the ultimate synergistic experience known to man. Consider music as simple as "Row, Row, Row Your Boat." A simple ditty like this sung by a young child is light years from Gustav Mahler or the great fugues of Bach. But, consider this. Tone, pitch, note length, intonation, pulse, tempo, dynamics, range, expression, diction, style, communication, mood, resonance, technique – are not all these elements present? Yet, would you like to list these and more words on a score sheet so you can check to make sure they are all present or all achieved? How about if you were judging "Row, Row, Row Your Boat" being sung in its round form by three 5th graders at contest? Would you like to add more words to your list? There are many we could list here. But I will not drive the point any further.

Not only would you not want to assess music by means of a checklist you couldn't do it if you tried. For one thing, you'd miss the performance! Secondly, music performance does not present qualities like commodities. It simply communicates – either well or not well – using the elements of music. Can we diagnose using the words? Why certainly. But we must first experience the performance "as a listener would," then use the words for their intended purpose.

- Performance criteria are used _after_ we have received an impression of the performer's performance. This impression is acquired _exclusively_ as a result of our background and experience.

- Performance criteria are used _once_ an impression range is realized. The impression range is confirmed, narrowed or abandoned based on our _analysis of our impression_ which is done by checking our predesigned criteria.

- In analysis, we _identify_ those _prominent factors_ that were instrumental in our impression formation and provided us with the experience of the performance. It is not true that a higher number of factors present indicate a better performance and more than a lower number of prominent factors dictate a weaker performance. There may be no prominent factors, in which case they may have all been of equal prominence.

- An equally important purpose of criteria reference is to _check against a director's bias._ This assures that his assessment took all factors into consideration – that were, indeed, actually present in the performance.

PART V.

Methodology

Take-away and Build-up

Whether one is talking about student assessment, personnel evaluation, a job interview, or even Olympic skating, there are two ways to measure achievement or assess qualifications. In the competitive music arena, the methods are referred to as either "take-away" or "build-up" technique. I have used both systems when assessing music performance students.

In the take-away method, the judge or evaluator dispenses 100% of the total potential points to the performer prior to the performance. As the performance ensues, points are removed as "errors are perceived." This method is frequently used for such things as scale tests, rhythm tests and other assessments like those intended to measure knowledge of fingering patterns for wind players, scale patterns for strings, and the ability to sing notes in various ranges with a quality, in-tune performance. But when I use "take-away" as my method, my primary interest is to see if my instrumental students know their scales.

The "build-up" method is different. The performer begins with no points. He or she then performs, the evaluator "listens first," and then begins to form an impression. This method does a better job of capturing achievement in the performance of an etude than does the "take-away" system. Conversely, using the "build-up" approach, when giving a scale test, does a less effective job. It lowers our ability to perceive distinction between one performer and the next and also increases the likelihood that we would, in fact, miss errors.

Let me say at the outset that there is a common misunderstanding about "take-away" or what is called "the tic system," by some. At one time in Drum & Bugle Corp, contests judges actually *did* "tic" a corps whenever they perceived an error. There was a term back then that we used called, "zeroing out: when judge ticked so much that the corps ran out of points! I recall this happening to some weaker units early on in my judging career. It usually occurred when an overly zealous and inexperienced judge decided that if the error was missed, he wasn't doing his job. Back then, marching judges who preferred to judge execution on the field were affectionately called "plumbers." I'm afraid the "zero out boys" were somewhat like an unlicensed plumber. They judged as a trained pup might, with no consideration for the *degree* of error. It diluted the value of *any* tics if more than one corps "zeroed out." Fortunately, there were enough smart people around to clarify. Early on, limits were put on how many "tics" a judge could give for certain errors. At some point, the system borrowed from the concept of what was called a "unit penalty."

> *"A unit penalty is an evaluation based on the severity of error and the number of elements and exposures involved in the situation. We use the unit penalty to indicate the severity of error in an exposed situation when there is a great deal of interdependence, and/or to indicate the severity of error when there is a high velocity of error.*

Thus, we did not mark "tic for error" when errors occurred with great velocity - meaning lots, very quickly. Similarly, we did not mark certain situations "tic-for error" when we could not discern precisely how many errors there were and/or how many elements there were involved in an error. Eventually, the marching caption placed a 1 to 6 tic-limit on all errors with the exception of linear cover (straight, front to back) at 1 to 3. This meant that judges were always using *subjective* evaluation even when marking *objective* tics. When recorders were eventually used to record an execution judge's comment, just as they are used at many concert band state festivals, the "tic" was gone. I do recall a transition period in drum corps when we still walked around with our clipboard, marking "tics" while we justified it on our tape recorders. Ugh!

Ah, but if you listen to many judges tapes at your state festival or spring contest performance, you will often receive a tape from a judge that has little to say until an error occurs. This is adequate proof that the judge is not thinking "build-up" during your performance at all. Consequently, when they go to score and have to place a "build-up" number in an empty box, they're lost or have had a running commentary in their mind different from what you heard them say on tape. My point is that "tic judging" still goes on today. Instead of each error being counted and marked on a sheet it is recorded on the judge's mp3 recorder. Tape commentary can point out issues, but judges must primarily recognize achievement (in degrees).

 It is never our job to find every single error. We must keep in mind that our job is to assess achievement, not count errors.

God forbid a 5th-grade band teacher uses *this* objective "tic" method in her assessment model. I have no doubt that most of us could go to an end-of-year beginner orchestra recital and count enough errors to "zero out" the star pupil.

What this demonstrates to us is that, once again, even when seemingly objective assessments are used (i.e., counting wrong notes, bad tone quality, or hesitation in a scale test), the final decision can only be made *"through the prism of a music performance teacher's background and experience as a musician."*

We have made a point here that common-practice testing cannot be used to assess the desired outcomes of our music-performance classes. Consider the nature of the written test in math, science or history. Unless the teacher has constructed a poorly designed question and makes a subjective decision not to count the errors on such, the answers are either right or wrong. They are, as they say, "black or white." These types of tests are "tic for error" systems. Since a music performance is never a right or wrong, black or white outcome, it cannot be measured that way. I might point out that when teachers issue essay questions, term papers, oral presentations, or creative writing assignments they too use the "build-up" system of assessment to grade.

Below is a score sheet for Mary Jones who has just completed the scale portion of her violin audition. She is a freshman student auditioning in the spring for placement in the proper orchestra, next year. She will receive a "raw score" for achievement in 1) scales (30%), sight-reading (25%), prepared music (35%) and a written exam (10%) on musical knowledge understanding. As you examine this score sheet, you can see that a number of assessment methods are being used in one audition. Her *scale* assessment will be done using **"tic for error"** (in the context we discussed above.) Her *prepared music* and *sight-reading* assessment will be assessed using a **build-up method**. And her knowledge of musical terms, string instrument principles, music history, and her understanding of how "counting syllables" are attached to note values, will be assessed using **common-practice testing**. The use of common-practice testing is valid since, in this case, we are assessing understanding of principles, history, and counting - not the performance of such.

BBCHS Department of Music
ORCHESTRA AUDITION FORM
____ Fall   ____ Spring

NAME: Mary Smith

X Violin   ____ Viola   ____ Cello   ____ Bass

SIGHT READING (25%)

Level	Key/Acc	Rhythm/Pulse	Expression

TOTALS

PREPARED (35%)	
SCALES (30%)	1.5
SIGHT READING (25%)	
WRITTEN TEST (10%)	
Notes:	

SCALES (30%)

Scale				Notes
GM (v-1)		I	I	
CM (v-1/a-1/c-1)	II	I	II	Restart
FM (a-1/c-1/b-1)				
EM (b-10)				
AM (v-2)	III	II	I	Slower Tempo
DM (a-2/c-2)				
BbM (b-2)				
AbM (v-3/b-3)				
DbM (a-3/c-3/b-4)				
Gm (v-2/b-2)	|||| II	II	||||	Not Ready
Cm (a-2/c-2/v-4)				
Fm (a-4/c-4)				
G Arp (v-3)			C Arp (v-4/a-3/c-3)	
E Arp (b-3)			F Arp (a-4/c-4/b-4)	

Side notes:

- "Tics" are placed opposite scales Mary played.
- Mary struggles with Level Two scales and her scale assessment is stopped (scales are ranked in four levels – I thru IV)
- Director makes subjective comments to help with final scoring range.
- Director makes a subjective rating based on his objective assessment of Mary's scale performance achievement

Criteria Reference Versus Rubrics

The terms criteria reference and rubrics have merged in recent times. They are not the same thing, nor do they do the same things. The use of the rubric, as we know them now, in education only goes back to the 90's. The use of criteria reference in music performance goes back decades. In modern education circles, rubrics have recently (and misleadingly) come to refer to an assessment tool. Their original use, ironically, was quite like the "unit penalty" we discussed in the previous section under "the tic system." It aided the process of holistic scoring which gave students a single, overall assessment score for a paper (remember our discussion regarding subjective assessments of essays or creative writing).

Let me say up front that education loves paper. They love to write words down and rewrite them. One of the cultural shocks I experienced upon returning to education after being in business for twenty-five years was how obsessed education is with process. Things take a long time because "process" is revered more than action. That's a very unscientific observation, but the inertia I felt attending meetings in educations was real. Writing rubrics is a lot of busy work. Establishing a criteria reference is not.

 The difference between the **rubric** and a **criteria list** is that rubrics try to describe what is to be learned *and* how teachers are to rate students using. Criteria lists tell teachers what to consider when making an assessment but do not tell teachers how to make that assessment.

In this section, I intend to demonstrate why criteria reference is the appropriate and valid system to be paired with music-performance assessment that requires the judgment of an experienced musician for the reason stated previously in this work. To start, take a look at this template for a Holistic Rubric. In brief, holistic scoring gives students a single, overall assessment score for the paper as a whole.

SCORE	DESCRIPTION
4	Demonstrates **exceptional** understanding of the material. All requirements are met, and some are exceeded.
3	Demonstrates **consistent** understanding of the material. All requirements are met.
2	Demonstrates partial understanding of the material. **Some** requirements are met.
1	Demonstrates **minimal** understanding of the material. Few requirements are met.
0	No response; **Task not attempted.**

The immediate question is, "Where do the terms, "exceptional," "consistent," "partial" and "minimal" get defined?" On this piece of paper? Of course, not. They are defined by the teacher, based on standards established as a result of his or her background and experience.

So what do we have here? It is basically a chart that shows five levels of anything. This is not rocket science, yet an entire cottage industry exists around the explanation, formatting, purposes, philosophies, and importance of rubrics and their use in schools. I support the notion that a qualified teacher, in our case a music-performance teacher, can easily assign student performance to one of these categories. It's logical, basic and doesn't take a lot of research and study. My wife is not a musician but, of course, she has been around it our whole life together. It was my initial career, then, our kids all participated, now we follow my son's career as band director, and we talk about my college music students, today. But following band contests years ago, my wife could easily classify bands at a contest in one of five ways:

"They're terrible."
"They weren't too bad."
"They're ok."
"They're pretty good."
"They're really good."

I trusted her instincts so thoroughly that I hesitated to ask her how *my* band did. But, of course, I'd build up the courage and always ask, "How were they?" She'd usually come back with a response something like, "The opener is boring." I'd live with that comment all the way home until I figured out how to fix it. Think about it. Not only did she place bands in the right order, but she could also justify her position.

How many of us have seen the "Man on the Street" interview where a reporter might ask patrons exiting a theater about the new controversial film they'd just experienced. An editor back at the TV station would review the responses and air a cross-section of responses:

"It was terrible."
"It wasn't too bad."
"It was ok."
"It was pretty good."
"It was really good."

If one turned both of these responses on their side, you'd get something that looks like this:

"terrible"	"not too bad"	"ok"	"pretty good"	"really good"

No doubt, teachers need ongoing discussion, practice, and training to assure that they are measuring what they teach. Judges need the same thing to assure that they are measuring what the performance idiom displays. We have already endorsed the notion that the process of evaluation must include a check of the components that make up what we are evaluating. But the job to appraise is ours.

But the educational and judging communities have affixed, what they contend is, a natural extension of this normal distributive range. Education, with its propensity for empirical evidence, and the competitive arena, with the diminished number of formally trained judges around the country, have chosen to add detailed definitions to what they believe qualifies a student or a competitor to appear under one of these five categories. When you over-manage the process you get this:

LEVEL I — An attempt was made to play the excerpt or piece but may not have been completed. Many of the **NOTES** and **RHYTHMS** are wrong. **TONE** quality is uncharacteristic. Choral register is regularly misplaced. **INTONATION** issues are regular and impact key center. Student fails to demonstrate fundamental **TECHNIQUE**. There is little demonstration of a consistent **PULSE** attached to performance. **NOTE VALUES** are treated arbitrarily and do not equate. The student struggles with **ARTICULATION** method often applying a single method the production of each note. **DICTION** for choir is clouded and ill-defined. Music **PHRASING** is not evident and music is performed in a vertical manner. Student struggles to understand the **PRINT MUSIC** system of note, rhythm or expressive notation. Student struggles with **SIGHT READING** demonstrating little resemblance to composer's intent. **MUSICAL EXPRESSION** is limited or non-existent. There is a superficial level of **PREPARATION**. Rhythms are a constant distraction. There is little or no attention paid to **ARTICULATION** and **DYNAMICS**.

Notice: Depending on the system, there could be four, five or six more levels to consider. This box does more than remind the evaluator of the important things to consider. I assure you and all your administrators, that music-performance teachers know when the student "struggles with understanding print music," "demonstrates a superficial level of preparation," or "pays little or no attention to articulation and dynamics…"

Now, instead of asking an evaluator to make **One Choice**, this system is asking the evaluator to make **Many Choices**. This, of course, is impossible and does not serve the teacher or judge. The hours spent writing, rewriting and testing rubrics of this nature are little more than busy work.

- **Overdeveloped Rubrics** are detailed, cumbersome and ineffective expansions of the basic holistic-based rubric which cripples rather than aids the professional evaluator in their assessment responsibilities.

- **Criteria Reference Systems** use a list of components to be referenced by evaluators so as to be complete, distinctive and unbiased in their evaluation process.

The Linear Scale & Impression-Analysis-Comparison

The natural ability of all people to *rate* the actions, creations of man, or the beauty of nature or beast, provides evaluators with a gateway to *ranking*. People observe things, and they express opinions. While their opinion may differ from another person, the fact remains that people can rate things, even when their decision is based solely on a personal bias. As educators or evaluators, it is our duty to rate things divorced from our likes or dislikes. We must evaluate based on defined criteria. But our decision must first reside that part of us where background and experience resides.

Let's start with an examination of the "movie patron" in the previous section. We will call him, John.

Suppose John is interviewed about his opinion of the film immediately upon exiting the theatre and his response is "It was pretty good." Most producers would cringe at the response because even without access to the tone of John's response, one can tell that he would not consider it an Oscar winner. What his response *does* imply however is that he has likely seen other movies.

If this was the very first talkie ever shown in America and it was 1927. I would think that John would have responded with something like "Wow, that was amazing," If John saw his second talkie one month later and his response was, "It was pretty good," what would we assume? We would immediately perceive that John has rated the second film lower than his first. Let's put the two films John has rated on a scale.

If the reporter was astute and had interviewed John following his first movie experience and, now, his second, he would next ask John, "Why was this movie just pretty good but the first one you saw was amazing?" The reporter's question is perfectly reasonable. He wants to know what factors played into John's decision. Let's say, John's response was this:

> "Well, the first movie made more sense. I could follow it from beginning to end. The second one was hard to follow. One thing would happen, and then they'd jump to another idea. I liked the lead actor in the second one, but the rest of the actors around him were not very good. In the first movie, it seemed like all the actors were good. The second movie got long, too. In the first movie, it would create all this confusion, and you'd wonder what was going to happen next and then 'boom' the hero would come in and save the day? It was nifty."

John had a limited background and no experience with talkie films until these two movies. But still, the human instinct to react to a performance, and compare one performance to one previously viewed, came naturally to John as it does to all humans. What can we say about this?

 Evaluators, judges, and teachers who assess, will always have an initial impression and should start all evaluations with that. They should allow the next natural thing to occur which is a conscious inquisition as to why they had the impression.

Let's now compare John's evaluations to my wife's. Let's assume that the first five bands she had ever seen in her life did, in fact, go from very weak to very strong. Her scale might look like this:

Terrible	Not Bad	Ok	Pretty Good	Really Good

In this scenario, there would be one band in each box. This is unusual and unlikely, but for our purposes here, it serves us well. Let's identify each group by number. The band on the far left ("terrible) is band #5, and the band on the far right ("amazing") is #1. By the end of the day, my wife sees twenty-five bands in total. Over that time bands worse than #5 appear and bands better than #1 appear. She is now forced to re-think her original assessment of bands number 1,2,3,4 and 5. She has discovered a "new low" along the way and a "new high." Note: standards are most readily set at the edge of the scale – both at the bottom and at the top. This places all others somewhere in between. This is where the work of a professional, experienced evaluator comes into play. But before we go on, let's look at my wife's placement of bands on the scale now:

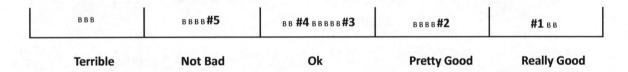

As you can see, things have changed. Let's examine what the twenty-five bands look like now:
- A good portion of these bands settled in the middle of the range. There were fewer in the box to the left and right and fewer, still, in the outside boxes of "terrible" and "really good." Though this looks like the bell-shaped curve, in reality, the curve does not occur in most contests. It takes more the shape of a "fat tail."
- Band #5 has done well. It has moved up a whole range from the "terrible" range.
- Band #4 has moved up also, joining #3 who has remained in the same location.

- Band #2 has not moved into the "really good" range but held its own, maintaining the top position in the "Pretty good" range against four other contenders.
- Band #1 is interesting. They were "leapfrogged" by two other bands. After five bands, my wife had decided that Band #1 was the best band she had ever seen. Then that changed. What occurred when this happened was her *standard* for what's best in the band world increased. From now on, any band she sees in the future will have to exceed what she saw in that last "B" on the far right to be placed at that location on her scale.
- On this scale, there is little information regarding how far one band is from the next other than the distinction by being in one box other than the next. Since the first (and most intuitive) decision was in which box a band belonged, the "evaluation pressure points" were, and are always felt first, at the point where the boxes change.
- The secondary pressure points occur on both extremes where judges have to decide if their standard has been exceeded at any given point during the contest. Clearly, my wife had to make that decision 7 times on the low end (7 bands fell below her previous standard) and 2 times on the high end (2 bands exceeded her previous standard).

Experiencing one performance in a lifetime provides no basis for comparison, and therefore any value (rating) placed on that single performance is meaningless and absent any grounds.

Experiencing two or more performances of like genre or identical composition will immediately dictate a sense of hierarchy (ranking) and begins to establish grounds for a decision (criteria).

 Ranking always involves grounds (criteria). If no grounds are established or considered than the *ranking and rating* is meaningless. This is no different than tossing darts on a dart board. But grounds will always be present when any two performances are compared.

But what do criteria actually measure? Just as judging requires grounds (criteria) to make a judgment, criteria must be affiliated and drawn from something that defines what's being judged. That something is "Qualities."

One cannot compare "apples to oranges." The best apple contest has criteria to measure the qualities of a good apple. The best orange contest has criteria to measure the qualities of a good orange. One quality of an apple might be its stem, but such a quality would not even be part of an orange contest. Conversely, one quality of an orange might be its ability to be pealed easy. Though an apple skin could be peeled, it's not a quality that apple eaters care about. They either cut the apple or simply take a bite.

Therefore, evaluators must be armed with the knowledge of the intrinsic qualities that they are about to judge and what criteria define "excellent" or "poor" demonstrations of those qualities. In other words, "what makes a good apple and what makes a good orange?"

This helps explain the *proper* understating of qualities. *Qualities* are those elements that define the nature, character or cast of something. Their presence is what separates a donkey from a horse. But their presence does not determine the best donkey or the best horse. That can only be done using criteria which provides an evaluator with the means to rank and rate the qualities of ten horses in a contest (or ten donkeys in a donkey contest). For the most part, intelligent men and women can agree on what qualities donkeys and horses possess. Determining the best donkey in a donkey contest, however, requires *criteria* to rate the qualities of a donkey. The same is true for all horse shows.

To further articulate this relationship between qualities and criteria, imagine a horse show where the proper grooming of a horse's tail is a consideration of each judge. The tail is a quality of a horse (part of what makes a horse a horse), and its grooming is one of the criteria used to rate and rank the horses. Were horses not to have tails, then tails would not be a factor in the contest. I'm quite certain that if there was a zebra contest, stripes would be a quality to be measured. Those horses and zebras share many qualities, stripes is not one of them.

But "apples and oranges" <u>can</u> be compared in a contest of fruits, can they not? Does this present a dilemma? It does not. Once a fruit contest is declared then the qualities of a variety of fruits can be measured using qualities such as taste, color, freshness, etc. It does not mean that the criteria of "redness" as applied to the quality of the color of an apple must be applied to all other fruits. In the apple contest, this can be done. But now, in a fruit contest, the quality of color for the apple is measured against the criteria of "redness" while the quality of color for the orange is measured against it "orangeness." This is how the Westminster Dog Show picks a "Best of Show" and selection each "Best of Class." In competitive drum corps and band judging there has been an increase in the number of words added to a score sheet to "help" judges with this matter. Unfortunately, adding words to a score sheet cannot replace training, background, and experience.

- A teacher's training is critical to understanding the important qualities of music, proper production of sound and technique as it applies to each voice and instrument.

- A *teacher's* background points to his or her knowledge and understanding of what they are to teach. Music directors must understand the qualities that define one instrument versus another, what defines a woman's treble choir versus a mixed choir or what defines a good drum-set drummer versus a marching snare drum performance.

An *evaluator's* background points to his or her knowledge and understanding of what they are to judge. An evaluator's experience points to his or her hands-on application of how to evaluate.

 Training in the process of ranking, rating and grading performance has not become critical to successful teaching. Universities and colleges need to add this critical component to their instrumental music education curriculum to better prepare directors for this new teaching requirement.

Were we charged simply with evaluating one student, all we'd be responsible for would be an accurate rating. Like our moviegoer John, we could offer our opinion to a reporter and be done with it. But if determining a valid rating requires the process of ranking (which we have established earlier) then how should we go about organizing our thoughts as one clarinet after another enters the office for their audition.

The professionals in this area were the judges who grappled with this heavy responsibility in drum and bugle contests following World War II. Corps and judges associations were at their peak, and "real money" was on the line. A win at a local contest earned a corps top prize money. A second or third could earn you less. Anyone lower might be "out any money" over the standard appearance fee. The need to understand how to organize the scores in a given contest became paramount as drum corps began to travel in the 60's. While judging irregularities have always existed and still exist today, the use of a scale to organize numbers given to corps was being used by good judges well before it was dubbed "The National Linear Scale."

The use of a scale in drum corps came to a head in 1970 at the first national meeting of drum corps judges associations held in Chicago. A notable early figure named Don Pesceone, who was part of the organizing committee for this event, asked Paul Litteau to present what was beginning to be known as the National Linear Scale. For the competitive band directors, this is the same scale you see on the back of many score sheets. Though some contests have distorted or modified the scale (wide range of scores in the "average" category, for example), the principles of the scale, used by some of the first and second generation judges, was recognized, defined and documented by Paul.

What follows is a general discussion on how it should be used. It is taken from Paul's presentation. As Paul would want me to say, other judges were part of the discovery process that became the National Linear Scale. But it was Paul who was capable of articulating the concept and presenting it in the precise way that only he can do. Others in the field added method to its use, but it first had to be identified, and Paul did that.

To begin with, I should point out the National Linear Scale was used exclusively for General Effect judging at the time of this presentation. All execution judging was assessed using the "tic system," exclusively. General Effect was a measure of excitement, entertainment, communication, artistry and generally inspired programming that engaged the audience (and the judge) in a transparent performance of the aesthetic.

At the far right of the scale (100%) is where a judge would place his ideal. It is here where he would put "the best corps he had ever seen." Few ever reached that standard for some time as the attainment of "perfect" was shunned by most judges. There are reasons for that, but that is a discussion for another time. Yet, there *were* perfect scores given in the modern age. There emerged an anecdotal phrase to describe what judges do once "a ten" is given. It described the reality that a "ten" is never stagnant and art has no defined limit and is fleeting. But the phrase, "last year's ten is this year's 9.5" became part of the lore of judging in the activity.

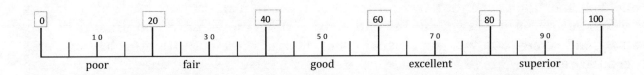

But the National Linear Scale was simply a guide to help judges "see" where groups were "landing" on the scale, how far apart they were, and where the judge was placing the preponderance of his assessments. The real mental gymnastics used by judges to determine the number in the first place was called:

Impression – Analysis – Comparison.

Quotes in the following section are taken from the actual presentation for Paul Litteau's presentation, "The Blackbook," the training guide for judges of Central States Judges Association,(CSJA) © 1970

Impression was discussed previously and required a judge to, first, view or listen to the program and get an impression as to which range a performance belonged (see chart above). Natural intuition was the best way to start. The system had to be **"broad enough to recognize the effect regardless of stylistic approach and still show some consistency."** It was acknowledged that definitions (qualities) and the linear scale approach to numerical evaluation were involved. **"Obviously, the judge's primary function at the any given contest is to properly place and numerically evaluate the corps at that contest."**

"The general effect judge has three direct functions:

1) To help decide the outcome of a particular contest by his proper placing and meaningful numerical score.
2) To give the corps information about their program.
3) To influence the development of the overall program by recognizing achievements, encouraging improvement and suggesting modifications."

Translate these three to the music-performance class the three indicate:

1. To help decide the outcome of spring and fall auditions for ensemble and seating.
2. To give students information about their abilities and ranking among others.
3. To give the director data for measuring student growth (fall to spring) and data on the overall growth of the program (year-to-year).

I used this system with my ensembles since 1977, after being exposed to it as a member of CSJA. When I auditioned for two orchestras, the same material was used for all string students (by voice). This meant the entire string program was assessed using the same material, same standard, same scale, and identical method (impression, analysis, comparison).

Spring Audition
The spring audition determined seating prior to state contest and final concerts. It also determined which ensemble students were assigned to the following fall.

Fall Audition
The fall audition reordered seating, but no changes in ensemble assignment were allowed unless a very unusual amount of growth or decline occurred over the summer.

I have comments on this. With auditions in spring, it also added an additional incentive to the student to finish the year strong. The fall audition assured a little practice over summer in the orchestra program and encouraged preparation for the onset of concert season in band program.

Challenges
I never used challenges with either my bands or orchestras. I found that aggressive students would always want to challenge and usually for reasons of notoriety or the opportunity to play a harder part. I don't besmirch such enthusiasm, but I found that often times, friends would not challenge friends, others feared retribution if they did challenge. I tested frequently enough that I often had enough evidence from rehearsal to switch kids around. The assessment was a way to validate my impression and provide information to the students regarding the reason for the switch.

Let's face it, kids improve and decline during the school year, and we all know when it is happening. We hear them every day. There is another reality. A student, who may struggle to learn a piece at the onset (for a variety of reasons), can sometimes shine as the ensemble gets to the 2nd, 3rd, 4th, and even 5th stages learning a piece. (Only music and sports do this in such a short time). How often have we witnessed the varsity basketball player who rides the bench the first half of the season, become a major factor the second half as a starter?

These are things the coaches and music directors understand. By the way, most kids get it too. They know when the kid next to them is "not cutting it." The student in question knows it too. Talk about peer to peer evaluation and self-evaluations! The kids do it all day. Don't ever let an observer tell you that there is no student lead assessment going on in your rehearsal. Next time you get evaluated; have your evaluator sit with you in front of the band, not in the back. The evaluator will see an entirely different classroom. I did that once on a 2nd evaluation, and my administrator said, "It gave me a very different perspective."

But the three functions of a judge, as stated by Paul, are the same as the three functions of the director when they assess students.

"In order to properly place and numerically evaluate (rank and rate) the corps in a given contest (assessment), it *requires a uniform numerical treatment within the corps in the contest.*" This is my basis for proposing that the same system be used for all like instruments when establishing who is in what ensemble. In my auditions, each violin played the exact same audition, in the same order (scales, prepared, sight-reading).

Litteau further states that "It should be recognized, however, that corps deserve that same uniform linear treatment from contest to contest" In our case, this means the directors must be very careful to maintain their standards regardless of their mental or emotional state or external conditions.

Being consistent requires discipline and concentration. I have always found the use of the National Linear Scale to be my refuge when I lose my focus. Stay the course, use the system.

Another comment from Litteau...

"Corps desire information not only as to how they stand relative to other corps in the contest but also relative to potential competitors through the country. Thus, when a [judge] assigns a number to a [corps], he is telling that corps how it stands on a national level. This obviously requires uniformity of numerical treatment, and the linear chart."

Here are some examples of how your standards (or in the case of execution, your tolerance) is affected:

- It's Monday.
- It's Friday.
- You've just finished freshman and sophomores and will now begin your first junior group with the thought, "Ok, now I'm really going to turn the screws tight."
- A student arrives late.
- A student talks nervously ahead of the audition and has to be prompted to start.
- A student tells you, "This is going to be bad." (I have had this happen, and they were). I've also had that happen, and the total opposite occurred. Their assessment of themselves is often harsher than yours.
- You assess a student that has been having behavior problems in school and are, therefore, tougher on him or her. The issue of attitude should be dealt with in other ways. It is very important to "get the right number" based on his performance, only.
- Within an audition (i.e., all violins or all trumpets), one should never adjust their tolerance for what is acceptable from one audition to the next. Conversely, if new standards are set for performing, ("a new best ever," or "a new worse ever,") adjustments in your standard can and do occur.
- Your tolerance will change gradually as your background and experience grow. If it takes you all week to do auditions, you must maintain your tolerance throughout the week, as you are conducting one audition for the entire ensemble. Tolerance changes over time. New standards can be set at any moment.

You can imagine how professional judges have to concentrate to adjudicate a forty-band marching show. With inexperienced judges, it takes the first hour or two to get their bearings, they get in a groove about ten o'clock, they're hungry by eleven, and during lunch, they look at their scores to see how they're doing. Over lunch, they ponder. With a full stomach at one o'clock, they dig in. Around three o'clock they count "how many are left" And by four p.m. it's a push to the finish.

Kids need to understand what your number means. I should mention at this time that I do not use the scale in my audition to represent a nationwide standard. I have always considered my "10" to be the best audition I have heard in my program. Your standard for your kids should *never* be acquired from:

- What you perceive is "out there."
- The hundreds of kids you've heard play during your entire career.
- The standard from a previous school.
- A standard you would *like* to achieve.
- The ultimate music standard (whatever that is in your mind).

Do not confuse this with "program standards" which are how directors will often describe their program "goals." Growth targets are set year-to-year by establishing "stretch goals" for your ensemble. That, by the way, is what judges were referring to with the phrase, "last year's 10 is this year's 9.5." Only the corps could establish the higher standards. The statement was actually to remind judges not to react to last year's ten in this year's contest when a new standard could obviously replace it immediately after in the same contest and a judge would be "out of numbers" at the top.

Like the directors, and designers in drum corps, we strive to attain a new standard each year. We determine the next level for our kids. But once that goal is set, which usually means, choice of literature for the year or increased demand in the fundamentals (etude, exercises, range, scales, etc.), then the top performance in your fall audition should be the standard set by the best performer you've heard in auditions during your time at your school. Essentially, we wear two hats. We select the program (standard) and then we judge it (assessment). We're the "chief cook and the bottle washer," at different times.

"Basically, the philosophy of the chart is that it is easier for judges to agree on subjective impression than on numerical worth. This is no more than to say that it is easier for two people to agree that a performance is "poor, fair good, excellent, [or] superior, than it would be to assign a comparable number to the performance without some reference (criteria). The chart allows us to begin with impression and converts for us this impression into a numerical range, from which a score is derived. This assures us a measure of uniformity to similar impressions."

"The question of uniformity of impression is not easily disposed of. Obviously, no one can say with precision just what is excellent or good, but by assigning these impressions number values, we have achieved a means of potential statistical quality control (i.e., if a judge's standard is very far removed from the norm it can be easily discovered.)

In the case of music directors, we do not have to concern ourselves with the assessment of another evaluator. We must simply stay consistent with our own standard (as set from previous assessments in our school) the standards are inherent in our ever-changing "textbook" (the literature and training materials we choose).

If you want to make a first step in convincing your administration of the validity of assessing as professional assessment is done in music, show them the chart and start with Paul's statement,

"By assigning these impressions number values, we have achieved a means of potential <u>statistical quality control</u>."

In the utilization of "build-up" evaluation, there are three steps:

1. Impression
2. Analysis
3. Comparison

"In the linear chart method, these steps are applied in that order. Basically, impression is the judge's (professional) subjective reaction to the presence of positive performance (build-up)."

- *Impression* comes first to allow for recognition of musical expression by any possible quality or group of qualities. (Recall our discussion of qualities versus criteria).

- *Analysis* is the objective aspect of the evaluation which seeks out reasons for a director's impression and looks for qualities over and above the performance per se.

- *Comparison* is the mechanical technique to cross-check the validity of the score and/or spread between a student's score and others in the audition.

Impression

"The image of the general effect judge as the uninvolved observer, weighing qualities of effect and arriving at scores through the mechanical processes has long been part of our mythology."

You may recall our discussion about approaching each student's performance "as a listener would." This is only intended to mean that we should receive the performance in that manner. It does not indicate that we should evaluate it in that matter. If we did so, we could ask the art teacher to assess for us, or the dance instructor. I'm sure they have opinions. But they have not grounds (criteria).

"The judge cannot remove himself from the system."

Paul points out that *"the designer of a drum corps show does not (or should not try) to achieve qualities as such, and certainly the audience does not react to "qualities," but to achievement of effect. To properly weigh this, the judge must allow himself to remain part of the system – to subjectively be entertained."*

Analysis

Paul established several reasons why a judge should not skip the analysis stage. No director should listen to a student and "go with their impression." It is not enough to lie in the bosom of one's background and experience and expect a number to drip from your pen. The process of Impression-Analysis-Comparison *trusts* your background and experience to generate an educated impression of performance, but in moving from the subjective to an objective number, analysis must be called upon. It opens the gateway to the final raw number that ranks and rates numerically.

If you want good musicianship in your ensemble, you must call for it at all times. Since we spend a lot of time with the how, in our music performance classrooms, we forget the end goal. Good teachers understand this and demand expression at all levels within their teaching of even the most fundamental technique. Here are some analytical potholes to avoid:

1. Recognize expressive playing even in the face of technical issues or moments of distress.
2. Performance is the aesthetic effect supported by the mastery of technical skills. Some directors conflate artistry with performance. Artistry is the mastery of technical skills. When assessing an etude, directors should guard against rewarding expression on the basis of technical proficiency. They are not the same thing and should be rewarded separately.
3. Some directors reward (or let slide) expression in difficult or intricate passages. Full achievement requires the student to be musical during less technical as well as highly technical passages.
4. Conversely, some students will work the tough passages in detail, gloss over a slow rubato section and fail to express the intensities of the rubato "because it's easier."

A look inside the mind of a director about to consider his impression and work toward a number might sound something like this:

> *"Well, let's see. That wasn't too bad. She's probably about here (placing his pencil tip) to the left side of the "fourth box (excellent). -"Then again, that middle section had some serious intonation issues. I wonder if that really keeps her out of box 4?" No, overall, my impression was a solid box 4." -"Is she in the right place? Let see." The director checks his criteria list, making certain he has not overlooked something. (*He reads it down) - *"Tone, intonation, accuracy, articulation, rhythm, tempo, phrasing, musical expression." He ponders further -Might there be some elements that go beyond his initial impression? "Her phrasing was impeccable. That's worth something."*(he ponders) - *"If her phrasing was done so well, why wasn't I more impressed by her musical expression overall?"- He recognizes that "phrasing" as a quality, does not automatically imply musical expression. -"But why is it that I experienced so little reaction to any expression from her performance?"*

This time the confusion he experienced between his analysis and his impression gets resolved. She played it safe -too slow. It lost a significant portion of its "value" at the slower tempo. The expressive potential of this piece was not realized.

This is a good example of what analysis is. Note that the focus is to resolve any differences between his impressions and qualities present during analysis. Paul describes it in another way...

"The judge looks for qualities over and above those in the impression and assigns "plus" or a "minus" value to them. Again, the judge should not necessarily consider the absence of a quality as a flaw, but he should recognize any quality that exists and be sure it gets proper credit."

All qualities in music are dependent and proportional to an extent on other qualities. To isolate one and say, "oh, there's a problem," is verbal "tic" judging. Musical expression has a fluidity that the visual arts do not. Analysis must occur, but it must be secondary and used primarily as a check against bias or an ill-perceived impression.

 Music-performance teachers must utilize their impression first when reacting to a performance and place the performance in the proper range of achievement, based on their standard (best to worst) but only after they have analyzed their impression against a set of criteria to make certain an error, oversite or bias was not a factor in their initial impression of the performance.

Comparison

The technique of comparison can be controversial. Some feel that if the judge faithfully evaluates performance by the same standards, there would be no need to compare scores. Most professional judges do compare scores and defend the practice this way. We are still human and can make errors during both the impression *and* analysis phases. The primary job of a judge is to properly place and numerically evaluate each performance. Placement can help validate a director's rating number.

Both of these reasons are important to our next section of the book which covers grading.

 When we evaluate for seating within a section or ensemble placement, we must resolve all ties within each section and at ensemble breakpoints.

 Like in the case of analysis, judges and teacher-evaluators must not rush to *comparison* before without first resolving their *impression* with *analysis*.

Part VI

Scoring

Using the Scale

The basic scale

This type of scale mirrors a percentage scale. A score of 50 equals 50%. Were a score placed on this scale at 65, one could interpret that a student played better than 65% of others taking the same assessment. This type of scale is familiar to most people and pretty much understood. Our schooling provided us with a clear understanding of percentage.

The scale below is a bit more manageable and shows clearly the demarcation lines of the 5 ranges. It also shows 100 total points, but each small line is in 2-point increments.

A scale of fewer than 100-points can also be used. The scales below have five ranges within a smaller range of numbers than the 100-point scale. The maximum value doesn't matter. It's the ranges that matter.

50-point scale

25-point scale

15-point scale

10 Point scale

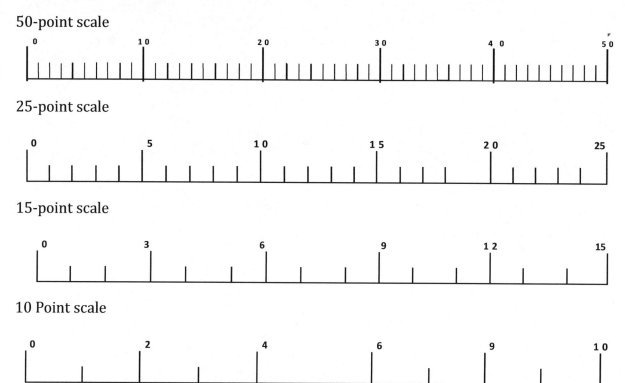

How Judges Judge

In this section, we will use a general description of how a judge uses the linear scale, and the methods associated with it, to assess execution. This section is presented in a narrative form so the reader can follow the mental process in a step-by-step manner. It includes passages in quotes. These are used to designate the private conversation that the judge is having with himself. The contest we are using to demonstrate the process is a marching band show. This is the most common use of the scale and system today.

The judge in question is judging Music Ensemble. Music Ensemble assesses the successful execution of brass, woodwind, percussion sections and also the overall ensemble. The two subcaptions direct the judge to consider his impressions from two very different, but related, points of view. One reacts to the program's inherent ***Demand*** of the musical book and the second reacts to the ***Response*** to those demands. This is very common in "build-up execution" judging. It is, to a degree, a contrived notion to actually *list* "content" on any execution performance sheet for the following reasons:

All execution assessment is always done within the concept of ***Demand***. It is often assumed that judges simply "saw an error and ticked an error." Fortunately, some of the pros around at that time, like Earl Joyce, pointed out that the old system never was intended to be a "tic per error" system and, in fact, that notion was erroneous. A number of judges thought that they were ticking that way. What they were unaware of was the concept of ***Tolerance.*** Tolerance is that point where your tolerance for error has been met, and you thus assess the severity of such, and issue a penalty (tic) to rate the severity. Once a judge's tolerance was crossed, he would assess a penalty from 1 to 6 tenths (1 to 3 for some exposures). Subconsciously, that assessment was based on what was then called "difficulty." Essentially, a judge would come upon a platoon of baritones and sample their highly difficult passage and assess them with difficulty in mind. But giving the judge the leeway to assess using his perception of difficulty was subjective and not valid. This changed once the "build-up" system was deployed. The term "demand" replaced difficulty. Difficulty assumes a judge knows what is difficult for one corps to the next or, for our purposes, one student to the next. This is not always valid.

Now, in our case, as music educators, "we know our kids." But if you are judging a solo and ensemble contest, you do not know all the contestants as their teacher would. You should view achievement as a student's "response to the demands of his or her piece of music," not what you might consider "hard to do." As trained musicians, we understand the inherent musical demands of music. As music educators, we must also understand the inherent demands of each instrument or particularities of each voice, relative to the age of our vocalists and their physical development. The proper way to assess achievement is by knowing the musical demands of a score (***Content***) and the physical demands placed on the instrument or voice in responding to those demands ***(Technique)***.

In short, using the process of "reading all execution through demand," places all contestants on a level playing field regardless of their choice of literature or level of skill. This points strongly to the importance of programming for your own ensemble and the material you select for various formative and summative assessments. We will discuss this in the next section of this book. Returning to our Music Ensemble judge, let's examine the score sheet he has been issued:

> Content (100 pts) and Performance (100 pts.). Content recognizes the demands inherent in the music being played. Performance is the response to those demands (again a "build-up" concept rather than a "tear down" method).

100	Content	
100	Performance	
200	Total	

This sheet will require the use of two scales which appear on the back of the sheet – one 100-point scale and a 200-point scale.

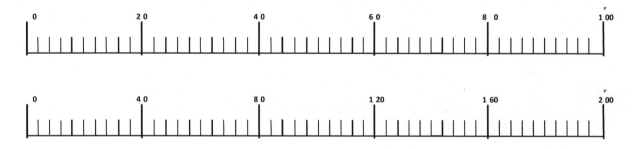

In order to facilitate our discussion, we will assume that the three bands the judge is about to judge all fall above the 50% achievement level. Secondly, in order to demonstrate the "hair-splitting" that goes on in when contestants (or your students seeking a strong chair placement), we will assume that these three bands all give a performance on this day in the low to mid-range of "box 5" which is the superior range. Comparing a student at the very top of the scale, one in the middle and one at the bottom is a much simpler process. All that is required in a contest of three oboes (let's say a freshman, sophomore, and senior) might be which "box" to put them in. Place twenty-four violins in front of the orchestra director to select seating order and 1st part versus 2nd part, and the requirement to be discriminant increases manyfold. So, for our example, we will assume all three of the bands in this example are close in ability. This requires a high degree of discrimination.

Three bands will be discussed.
Place: John Barley Corn High School
Date: Saturday, September 24, 1994

Wallace High School Band

The first band on the field is Wallace High School. They have approximately thirty-woodwinds and forty brass. The battery (drums) includes all voices (6 snares, 2 tenors, 4 basses). The pit includes four keyboards, auxiliary and timpani. The band's repertoire includes arrangements of the following:

"Chester," William Billings
"When Johnny Goes Marching Home," Louis Lambert
"Eternal Father Strong to Save," William Whiting
"The Halls of Montezuma," Jacques Offenbach

Billings Marching Pencil Sharpeners

The second band is from Billings High School. They have twenty-five woodwinds and fifty brass. The battery (drums) includes all voices (8 snares, 4 tenors, 5 basses). The pit includes six keyboards, one amplified synth, auxiliary, drum set and timpani. The band's repertoire includes the following:

"Attack on the Rue Plumet," from "Les Miserables," by Claude-Michel Schönberg
"The Bioluminescence of the Night," from "Avatar" by James Horner
"Snap" An original drum solo by local percussion instructor
"Cadillac of the Skies/The Land Race" from "Empire of the Sun," by John Williams

The Craft School for the Arts

The third band is from The Craft School for the Arts. They have 20 woodwinds and 30 brass. The pit and battery are staged on the field. The percussion does not move during the show but includes all percussions voices. 6 keyboards, synths, snare, toms, bass drums, auxiliary and timpani. The band's repertoire includes the following:

"Spaces," an original composition by William Travis, a local composer.

Wallace High School: Commentary following performance during the scoring process

> "**Well, let's see. Plenty of content here. They're definitely in the 4th box**" (this drawn by his background and experience). "**They're consistent in that area for the most part. But, I have to consider the length of time they presented the drum solo. Then again, I got the chance to sample the winds plenty well, and the percussion solo had a good amount of demand. Except for the initial start, things were played tightly. Few dynamics though…I remember the feeling being the same throughout. The brass definitely has a stronger presence than the woodwinds.**

The arrangements do tend to cause some of that, but the brass *are* solid. I think I'm just to the right of middle in the excellent range at this point. Ok, what did I hear from the woodwinds? They did seem to score the woodwinds to mimic the brass parts, and, frankly, there was a good amount of time when I could not hear them. I have the drum solo which is played well but does not express. Yet, the drums were always tasty in full ensemble work. The woodwinds are the weak link though. If I was just sampling brass, I'd probably feel stronger about placing the band to the far right of middlebox 5. Overall, my impression is that each section seems to play within itself well, but the total ensemble does not feel cohesive to me. I mean, I never feel like they are playing as one ensemble. Their tutti "hits" are fine on the front end, but note lengths tend to vary between sections. The brass and percussion tend to dominate the show. I don't get the sense that each section plays together. Let's see, my first impression was that they go here on content."

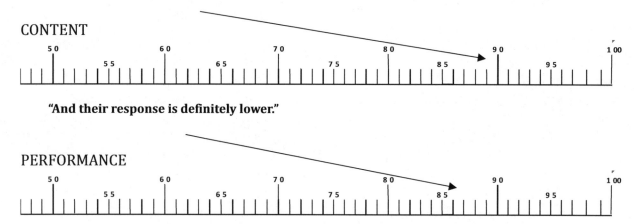

"The only thing is, I can't seem to sample the woodwinds because I don't hear them enough. I may be assuming content here but if I can't hear the woodwinds. That's a "big hole" in my ability to perceive the playing ability of the whole band. I must say, however, that the brass and percussion had very good moments and I think that's why I reacted as I did. Thinking about the brass one more time, they are bright, and upper voices really seem to dominate. I think what we have here is:"

(Now the judge begins to narrow in on his number)

- "A good "book" (the music) but only perceived by brass and percussion."
- "Fairly solid execution overall with the exception of the back of the note."
- "Overall their sound is solid."
- "They "come off" as if they have no issues playing the book (response to demand)"
- "Strong tutti presentations at the major hits."
- "Solid method and execution from the brass, percussion and, what I could hear of the woodwinds was solid."

(This gives you the "spoken thought" of the judge. But also realize that this is probably about 1/3 of the reflection going through his mind. Here's a snapshot of other things he heard that are still in his "impression inventory" as he prepares to select his final number.

> "Trombones had a beautiful statement in the opener...percussion had at least three times where the battery phased with the pit....that second piece was expressed very well....the saxes never seemed to be quite in tune...it still bothers me how bright the band is ...those French horns in the closer were clearly confident, in tune and in control of their upper range, that was pretty amazing...did I hear the flutes? I don't recall...can they play the legato as they do the more aggressive stuff...I think the "brightness" issue for them is placement on the field (drill related) and not really instrumentation because when they were all forward, things were balanced."

And, now to the number.

> "I think I'll pull down that initial impression on content. Without an ability to sample the woodwinds, that leaves a big hole for me. In fact, the more I think about it, there's no way they belong that high... the closer is the only production in the superior range. Besides, I have a slug of bands left here. I need to leave myself room."

The judge lowers the content score from **89** to **87** and, feels comfortable where he has placed his performance number at **86**. He leaves the performance number the same despite his problem sampling the woodwinds. He notes that.

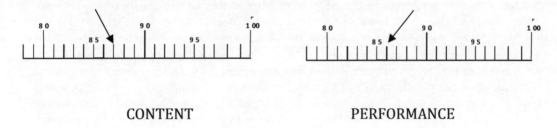

CONTENT   PERFORMANCE

The resulting score is **173** which is converted to **17.3**.

Wallace High School has scored a 17.3 out of 20. This is left of the middle of the Superior Range

100	Content	87
100	Performance	86
200	Total	173

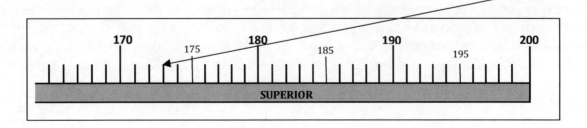

Billings High School: Commentary following performance during the scoring process

> **"First of all, I just don't hear as much linear complexity in this band's book as with the previous"** (Though this is, technically, "comparison" it is proper since it is comparing impressions and not comparing scores, as the system calls for).

The Judge begins his thought process with a dominant impression that began following the opening number. It was clear to him early on that the Billings book (music) did not have the level of demand that the Wallace book had. Isn't this judge comparing too early? Does not the system call for Comparison to occur after Impression and Analysis have been resolved? The answer is, "No." Comparison in our judging model means comparing the *numbers* of one group being considered and other groups who performed before them. This is not what the judge is doing in this case. He is comparing impressions. That is perfectly acceptable. The caution here, again, is not to "rush to the number" or even "rush to the range." This dominant impression is very valuable and does point to a different range or lower position within the range of Wallace High School regarding Content. The judge is still thinking...

> "Ok, yes, the content is lower. There is no doubt. Let me store that in my mind now but focus on what else occurred. This is a very tight band. The full ensemble has perfect balance regardless of volume level or position on the field. The show wonderfully crafted. The structure of this music is different. The Harmonies are more parallel, and the structures have less lyricism than one might hear in more lyrical writing. But the development in the John Williams piece had some wonderful lyrical exposure. Yes, I think the final number gave me a clear indication of this bands ability to express the lyrical line. And the drum feature was "tight as a tic." Man, the middle of that solo when the battery was doing an interplay with the pit was stellar. They had a slight rip."But that problem was really caused by the middle voice solo that dragged and that brought the wind in at his tempo while the drumline maintained. I just don't recall a whole lot of moments when I actually heard intonation, quality or balance errors out there. There's a high level of technique here on all instruments. The "thinness" harmonically and along the lyrical side of the music was striking to me as I got through the opening. This is going to be a situation where I'm going to have to balance the depth of the book (from the content side) to the superior performance. They are different than Wallace. In fact, Wallace has a strong book, but not everyone responded. Ok, let's take that to the chart once..."

The judge glances at the scale to "feel his way" to a range that he feels comfortable with. The question is, "Does he place his **content** number on the sheet totally divorced from his strong **performance** impression. For now, yes. He will get the opportunity to amalgamate those two impressions once he has set a temporary number for **content** and then a number for **performance**. To do otherwise would artificially draw the number closer than they might be when being considered separately. Plus, one must realize that the **performance** number is "read" via **content,** not the other way around. If the proper way to view performance is through content, any conflation of the two allows the performance impression to influence the content number. That creates a backward process.

The judge makes a decision on his first impression of the **content** number for Billings. He places his content impression number at **85**

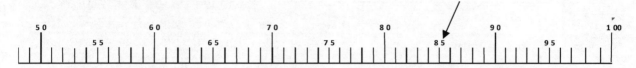

> "I don't know. Is that number right? Some of that pop stuff is so repetitive. How was this thing structured? So much of the pop material is unison chordal movement. Wind instruments need to express lyrically, too."

Ah ha! I believe, our judge has revealed his bias for lyrical music. Perhaps he even has a bias that music written in the popular idiom does not challenge wind players from an expressive point of view. He may feel that too much is written rhythmically and the range of the instrument is not challenged with such music. We don't know what the judge is thinking. Should he score this well-playing band low, he may get pushback from the director in the critique. He could be accused of having a bias against their music and that despite the stellar performance of the brass, woodwind, and percussion, he has placed them under a band that doesn't play as well as they do. The judge continues...

> "Let me think. I do like more lyrical material. I know that. But these kids can play. I guess the question is, did they play well enough to overcome a thinner book? But I have to remember that John Williams closer. They had an opportunity to play lyrically in that tune, and it was beautiful. Was that enough – enough to convince me that they can play in a lyrical fashion? The tune was at least 2 minutes long. No, I'm going to give it to them. I don't care how long they showed me they could play lyrically with expression, the point is they did. And they played the intense rhythmic stuff tremendously."

He goes to his scale. He slaps down an **89**. He feels strongly about his impression of the entire band's ability to perform at a high level. When the playing is that good, it overcomes the book.

He does the math to see how things come out...

> "Let's see, 174...174. What did I give Wallace?"
> (The judge checks his score for Wallace)
> Yep, that's it 174-173. That was my feeling.
> Billings by a hair"

100	Content	85
100	Performance	89
200	Total	174

The judge places the two scores on his tally sheet...

Barley Corn Invitatonal September 24, 2017		Wallace	Billings	Craft
100	Content	87	89	
100	Performance	86	85	
200	Total	173	174	

Though the book of Wallace is stronger than Billings, in the mind of this judge, the stellar performance of Billings convinces him that, despite his bias for lyrical music, the nod must go to Billing. This judge has used the system appropriately.

Craft: Commentary following performance during the scoring process

In the preliminary performance during the day, our judge was judging Music General Effect. As it turns out, Craft was his top band of the day on General Effect. He fully anticipated that Craft, the last band to perform in this finals event, could be a contender to win. In prelims, judging General Effect, he had Craft 1st, Wallace 2nd, and Billings 3rd. Our judge went to dinner between prelims and finals. After thirty bands in prelims, judges have pretty much exhausted their thoughts on bands. So conversations are social in nature and not about the long day. This clears their minds for the night's event. Our judge returned to the stadium with a clear head and was ready to judge finals as a brand new contest.

Still, judges are human, and they do remember performances. By moving from Music General Effect to Music Ensemble, however, our judge is able to judge the finalists bands from a different point of view. Experienced judges can do this with little effort. They use the system.

Craft completes their program, and our judge begins to "talk to himself" about the show.

> "That's weird...I didn't hear that show the same way tonight as I did this afternoon...They seemed tentative tonight...There is no doubt that the complexity of their music is the most advanced I have heard all day. Tonight, however, the students didn't seem to project the subtleties that were present this afternoon...I have to be careful that I'm not reading them with a "general effect" mindset...How *did* they play...There were some issues...most seemed to be with balance...and the intricate lines I heard this afternoon were not always evident tonight...I'm quite certain the general effect judge may be reacting to a flat show tonight... but have they slipped in the execution of the show...Notes heard were in tune and of good quality...The drums, who did such a great job supporting the wind book this afternoon were, if anything, too subtle...at times...too soft...it's hard to say, but I think they sounded tired tonight...the issues were more of an ensemble nature...tempos weren't as crisp...Let me go down this list of criteria..."

Our judge turns to the criteria to make certain that no bias has crept into his reaction and that he is not over-reacting to the musical expression element and failing to consider some other qualities listed on the back of these score sheet.

> **Let's see...tone quality, intonation, attacks, and releases...ok, now here's one area...I did not get the same sense of readiness on the front half of the note as I did this afternoon. On the general effect sheet this would show up in communication, but here, it's definitely a hesitation...Ok look, there's no doubt that I came away from their show feeling uncertain... The cohesiveness I felt this afternoon which allowed me to simply enjoy the effects of the show were not there tonight...The other thing is, I'm quite certain I did not get a clear presentation of the musical book tonight. That impacts the content number. I know the notes are there on paper...I heard them this afternoon... but I didn't hear those second the third lines in the show that made it so interesting this afternoon. It was a flat performance. For whatever the reason, the overall performance in a number of areas was not clear tonight.**

Again, our judge is using the system during Analysis. When an evaluator goes from their impression to the analysis phase, it is a very important moment in the evaluation process. Our judge has done a good job checking his bias. Some may say that he is judging the finals show against the prelim show. Many times a taped commentary like, "you're a little flat tonight compared to this afternoon," will cause directors to be concerned that a judge, is judging her band against their previous performance. The director would be correct in questioning this comment, in my opinion. An important credo I constantly heard during my training years was, "Judge tonight's show." As much as we know about student's capabilities, we must guard against assessing them with a mind on their previous assessment. In other classes, a written test gives every student a fresh start. In our testing model, we must use our system, so each assessment stands on its own merit. Judges do not teach the bands and then judge them. Music directors do both. Being fair and accurate requires discipline. View each assessment as a separate event. Use a consistent system.

Our judge moves to his tally sheet and carefully avoids looking at the scores he has issued to the previous two bands. Even though this is the last band in the contest, he must guard against jumping to comparison and bypassing the same process he used all day – Impression, Analysis, Comparison. When judging execution, he begins with content. He purposely works a side sheet so that he cannot see the other two scores which belong to bands in contention to win the contest (I've done this for years, and it works).

> **"Ok, where are they...? What did I actually hear tonight?"**

He decides to think through the show in his mind. He thinks through the opener and recalls that, during the first production, he did not have the impression the band was under par. Upon review, he remembers his thoughts.

> "I wouldn't say they were noticeably down in the opener. The transitions were very good, and the major impacts were tastefully done and in control. No, I don't think it was the opener."

He thinks quickly about the second production. He recalls two moments when the band struggled visually, and it was noticeable in the music performance. There were at least thirty seconds of insecurity in that production. That was a major consideration. But still...

> "Yeah, that second tune was a factor, but I wouldn't say it was a major impact on content. It was a performance issue, but I wouldn't say it was a content impactor."

The third number was solid, he recalls. It was followed by a drum transition that had issues which came and went. There would be two bars of solid playing, and then the tenors would rush for two bars. Then the bass drums struggled for two measures, and the snares had a rough entrance at the beginning of the final phrase.

> "It's obvious. It was performance tonight. They never quite recovered after the drum solo."

Anytime performance has significant problems, content can be impacted. In simple terms, if a performer or an ensemble is not performing well, the subtle elements of content do not present themselves and achievement cannot be measured against them.

Our judge decides to place Craft's content at an 88. Still, with the issues, it is a significant program.

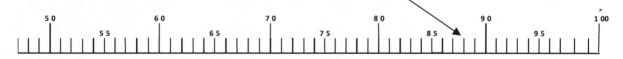

Still working on a side sheet, away from the other scores, he enters his preliminary performance number at 82.

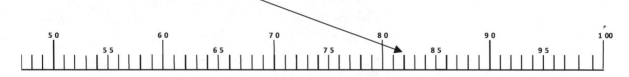

He then tallies the score and places it on his tote sheet, providing him the first opportunity to compare scores with Wallace and Billings.

Barely Corn Invitatonal September 19, 2017		Wallace	Billings	Craft
100	Content	87	89	88
100	Performance	86	85	82
200	Total	173	174	170

He looks…

"Yep, I can live with that. That order feels right. The best performance won tonight. The system worked and I did my job."

If you use the system correctly, you're assured that you will **never lose contact with your initial impression.** If we pull ourselves away from the performance (or our memory of the performance) in those first few crucial moments, we "get mechanical" about our decisions and make errors. The system does not reject criteria reference or a check list of qualities. It believes criteria play an important role in helping evaluators find their way toward an objective rating. But use of criteria must be secondary and used at the correct time. We hope this virtual judging experience at the fictitious Barley Corn Invitational provides a better understanding of how the system works.

The principles hold true for assessment, auditions and placement in our music-performance classroom.

Background and Experience

Evaluator ← Criteria

Performance ← Content

Impression

⇕

Analysis

⇕

Comparison → **Score**

Scoring Assessments and Analyzing Results

You may recall our discussion regarding qualities. We made the point that a performance is never judged by the presence of qualities, alone. It should always be judged based on the actual performance. The reason is that all performances have these qualities or the potential for these qualities. Most performances have them in degrees, and their presence is not static. Their detectability comes and goes during a performance and most certainly in all assessments.

The score sheet on the right is a list of potential qualities that will be present in a brass solo. The judging criteria for these qualities are met when your "conditions" are met or come close meeting your standard. This will occur in various degrees and at different times in the solo.

10	Tone	
10	Intonation	
10	Tempo	
10	Rhythm	
10	Phrasing	
10	Technique	
15	Dynamics	
25	Musical Expression	
100	Total	

This is not a "checklist" however. It should be used to document the listening experience you've just heard. No judge should begin their listening experience in an assessment by staring at this sheet. This sheet will explain to the judge *why* he or she had the reaction they just experienced. It qualifies their reaction and begins the quantification process. It is also not a rubric. We have already stated how rubrics are not effective tools for music-performance evaluation. Like checklists, they force the judge to study the rubric rather than react to the performance.

As a performance ends, I hold on firmly to my impressions as I "go to the numbers." It is that time when we *ease* into the cognitive and keep the performance fresh in our mind during the analyzation process. We will go back and forth between the performance and the presence of the qualities listed on the sheet during performance. This process supports the "build-up" mindset and avoids deploying a "tear down" mentality into the process. It takes effort to avoid the "traffic cop" mentality when judging in a "build-up" system. The traffic cop blows his whistle as traffic moves by. Judges who use this method while listening to the performance will tend to memorialize errors in their mind and miss the good achievements in between. If one judges that way, he or she is using a de facto "mental "tic" system," and his assessment is in error or is misguided and, possibly, invalid. To the extent that a performance disappoints, less credit is given to the performer.

Analyzing Results

On the solo contest sheet, you see a number of qualities listed with point totals attached to them. The sheet has a total of 100 points. Six captions are worth 10 points, one is worth 25 points, and one is worth 15 points. Therefore you need three scales – a "10," "25" and a "15."

Here are a few different profiles that could occur in a solo presentation. Both students are trumpet players and are playing the same etude for seating in the wind ensemble. The director moves from his impression to the scoresheet and after comparing the two scores finds that the numbers line up with his impression.

STUDENT "A"

10	Tone	8
10	Intonation	8
10	Tempo	5
10	Rhythm	4
10	Phrasing	7
10	Technique	8
15	Dynamics	12
25	Musical Expression	20
100	Total	72

STUDENT "B"

10	Tone	6
10	Intonation	5
10	Tempo	9
10	Rhythm	8
10	Phrasing	7
10	Technique	9
15	Dynamics	8
25	Musical Expression	15
100	Total	67

Student "A" has a challenge with tempo and expressing rhythms. "Tempo" and "Rhythm" are in the middle of the middle range. His "tone," "intonation," and "Dynamic" scores are on the border of "Excellent" and "Superior." His "Dynamics" and "Musical Expression" number also approaches the "Superior" Range.

Student "B" is almost the direct opposite to Student "A." She is strong rhythmically but has some fundamental problems with tone production and, likely as result, intonation. In addition to her good sense of time and ability to read rhythms, her technique is in the superior range.

In the case of student "A," the director has placed the weight of the student's success in the expressive areas and has not rewarded as much in the area of tempo and rhythm. Student "B" is given credit in the rhythmic areas but has not generated the same level of significant weight in expression.

Performance Profiles

The weight (points) given various qualities experienced in performance creates a profile of a student's strengths and weakness as in the timpani assessment described as follows:

Tune your timpani to an "F" on the second timpani, and a "C" on the third tympani then perform the following rhythm at quarter note = 120:

1. The student will first be given 1 minute to find his pitches using proper tuning procedure using a pitch pipe or tuning fork. Once the student indicates he is ready, he will signal the teacher who will ask him to play both drums so as to check pitches. If there are issues with the tuning, the student will be given a second chance to tune.

2. Once the student is ready, a metronome is set at 120, and the student performs the etude.

Three different scales are used:

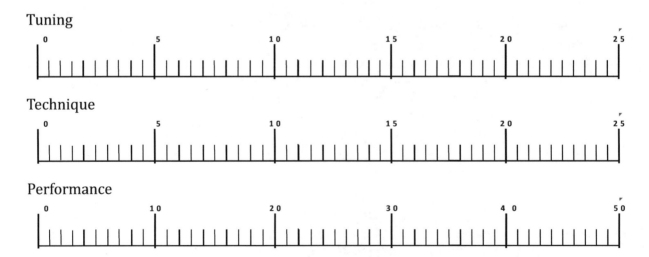

The first question you might ask as you approach the scale is, "What does my top number mean? What does it represent? What standards do I apply? What qualities apply?

Is my top number based on tympani **method and technique**?
Is my top number based on **the appropriate interpretation** of this etude?
Is my top number based on **good music**?

The answer to all three questions is "yes." All three are important, but technique and interpretation lead to a lofty musical standard. Great technique does not assure interpretation, and proper interpretation does not assure great music. Great music relies on the performer's involvement. Great directors never lose sight of that.

But appropriate technique leads to proper interpretation. Proper interpretation provides the opportunity to make great music. And great music should be the standard of highest priority. Most score sheets used in schools and school contests include points for the display of fundamentals. Many contest judges and directors view Musicality or Musical Expression as separate items from things like Tone, Intonation, Tempo, Rhythm, Dynamics, etc. But Musical Expression is reliant on the fundamentals. The reason they are present on contest sheets and in assessment is that we are both teacher and evaluator. Their purpose is to provide feedback to the student on things they are doing correctly and areas where they need to improve. They also provide teacher-evaluators with information that will adjust their lesson planning and teaching methods. But the method of finding the number is the same, whether assessing proper technique or reacting to an amazing performance of expressive ecstasy.

For each performance, situation directors must possess a standard for those performances. Should a director hear a performance for the first time, his or her musical standards provide a solid basis for evaluation. But as teacher-evaluators, we also need to be able to recognize proper technique and performance fundamentals. We must also understand the style requirements of all music used in assessment and in all music we conduct. The conductor of the Chicago Symphony has one standard, and that is a musical one. Technical abilities and fundamentals of performance are a given in professional ensembles. As music educators, our standards encompass three primary areas.

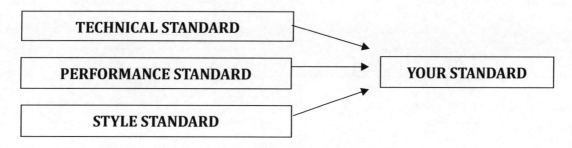

Tuning is certainly important here. So is technique. What is the technique method you teach your students? If you're a bassoonist and cannot describe the technique you require for timpani, then it's time to study.

Tuning, of course, is universal and any trained musician knows if pitches match. But there is a particular way to tune the timpani which is from the bottom, so the drum holds pitch. Does your student adjust tuning simply by backing down on the pedal? This would be incorrect, and directors can assess tune, using tuning technique and pitch, if the director knows the technique.

As we stated before, directors and judges must have enough background and experience to know how voice or instruments produce sound. If you do not have experience on an instrument, then you need to go get some to teach and evaluate properly. If you have a staff percussion instructor than this person would have the background and they should do the assessment on timpani. But if you are like many, the task falls on you.

A perfect score in technique on this timpani assessment would be a fulfillment of your standard (or your percussion instructors' standard) for the technique used for timpani. But you have to have a standard first. If you don't then you will have a difficult time assigning criteria such as 1) finger placement 2) fulcrum placement 3) thumb angle 4) placement of the remaining fingers, and 5) hand location on the mallet... to name a few. With his standards fully in place, the director does the assessment and rates the student's performance. Note the profile of his achievement.

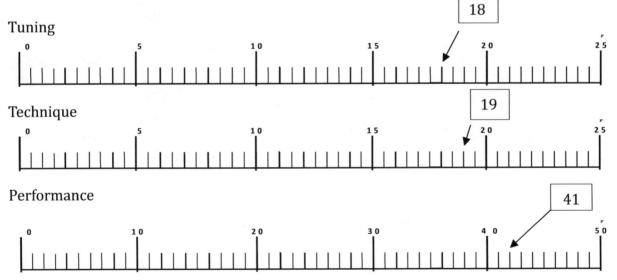

The separate sub-captions added together give Student #1 a score of **78**.

Student #1

Tuning	25	18
Technique	25	19
Performance	50	41
Total	100	78

If you examine the scale, you will notice that the student's ability to tune assessed lower than his technique and technique lower than the performance itself.

Student #2

Tuning	25	23
Technique	25	22
Performance	50	20
Total	100	65

In this case, the student did a great job tuning and displayed proper technique. He obviously did not prepare properly for the assessment or perhaps had issues such as tempo control. He tuned properly and understood technique.

Student #3

Tuning	25	24
Technique	25	24
Performance	50	45
Total	100	93

Student #3 demonstrated proficiency in all three areas. She will likely be chosen as timpanist for the orchestra. If her numbers had fallen in between Student #1 and Student #2, her director would have to make a difficult judgment call.

Assessment Disciplines

Most directors of school ensembles utilized some form of audition in their program. I have always believed strongly in doing a thorough assessment of all students at the beginning and end of the school year. I also had kids play their parts for me on a regular basis. I began assessing in 1972. I wanted to know how my kids played.

In the beginning, I used a haphazard approach that was a blend of my opinion, marking a "tic" every time I heard an error, unannounced playing tests in front of the whole band, scheduled playing tests for a grade, and some written exams on counting, key signatures, expression marks, etc. I always held auditions and seat placement assessments. It simply made sense and it was what I had seen other directors do. It didn't take long to experience some of the challenges one faces when attempting to rank students. When I began my judge training in 1975, I learned that drum corps judges had the same challenges. It was at Central States Judges Association meetings where I first learned the term for these challenges. They called it "numbers management."

Numbers management essentially has to do with the following:

1) Understanding where any given performance fits within your standard.
2) Understanding in what range a specific performance belongs and where.
3) Understanding how many numbers are allocated to each range.
4) Understanding the importance of working within the system.
5) Understanding how to express the proper distance between one performance and another numerically.
6) Understanding the need to check "Subcaption" ranges against the "Total" range
7) Understanding how to properly modify (or maintain) the profile of a performance when resolving ties, breakpoints or spread issues.
8) Understanding how to correct ties, resolve breakpoints and anticipate pressure points in a contest audition.
9) Understanding how to maintain your standard or tolerance over a full-day or full-week assessment or contest.
10) Understanding how to avoid pre-judging.

When it comes to "Numbers Management," these are the "Big 10" issues that face judges and evaluators and they all impact ranking. Every judge and director, regardless of their experience, faces these challenges. Avoiding them requires "staying within the system" and being in-tune at all times when assessing performances. Contests that simply rate each student and do not require ranking are not plagued by these issues. Giving too many or too few of one rating or another or selecting the "Best of Day," are their main challenges.

Let's examine the ten challenges of "Numbers Management."

1) Understanding where any given performance fits within your standard.

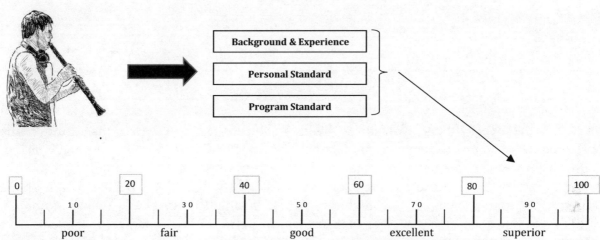

When a student performs an audition, you should have a broad sense of your global standard but also a stronger sense of your standard for middle school alto saxes and the piece of music being performed. Prior to an audition or contest, evaluators should think about their standard and reflect on it. They should be in the frame of mind to experience the performance "as an audience would." It should be noted that impressions can fluctuate. Evaluators should sense the impression range as the performer begins, continues and ends the audition.

2) Understanding in what range a specific performance belongs and where

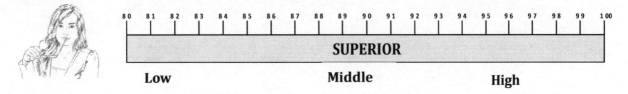

As the end of a performance nears, the evaluator begins to think more concretely about the specific range that a performance belongs. Thinking of number should be avoided at this point. I begin to think about where, within the range, a performance belongs. Essentially does the performance belong on the lower side of the range, in the middle or on the upper side of the range? If my number is far right or left, I consider what criteria keeps those performances from entering the range above or the one below. In these cases, you need to be very confident with your impression and with your placement of the performance in the "Excellent Range." Anytime I place a group or an individual performance at the extremes of any range, I always consider whether or not my process was correct and make certain that no bias impacted by range choice when I began.

3) Understanding how many numbers are allocated to each range

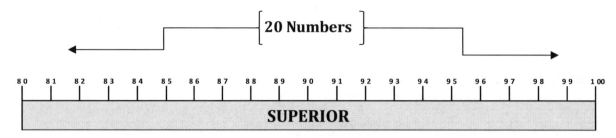

Knowing the score sheet, you have been issued or have created and how many performances you are to judge sounds rather fundamental. But in a field of forty clarinet auditions, it's wise to consider how many might perform in the superior range, for example. If you want to space those excellent achievers properly, you must be conscious of the "number of numbers" you have available to you. In a range comprised of twenty numbers, you should have enough to place varying performers in the correct order with the appropriate amount of space (spread) between performers. Some may perform at a distance from their competitors or may be quite similar to performances within the range.

4) Understanding the importance of working within the system

Staying within the system is key to successful and consistent scoring in the Impression-Analysis-Comparison Linear Scale system. Skipping steps or changing their order of the process can lead to errors. A "70" does not always represent 70% in captions with different point allocations.

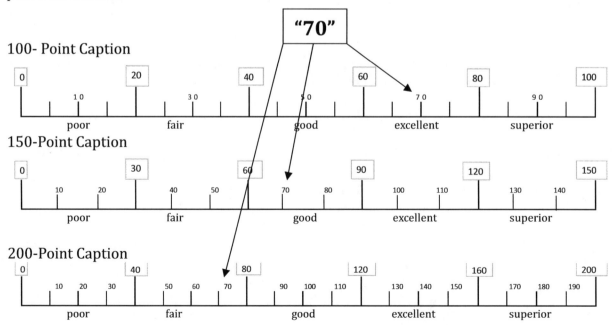

Even the most disciplined adjudicator will fall into the habit of "going to the number" too quickly. Here are a few types of "system abandonment":

Judging by the **system**: (Correct)

Judging by **your "gut"** (Incorrect – no concern for rating or ranking)

> In this case, the judge puts **all faith in his instincts.** He also ignores "Comparison" all together which leads to ties and incorrect "Ranking." In a long contest, this "system" will cause wild swings in scores due to fatigue, bias, conditions and other factors that affect the judge's thinking process.

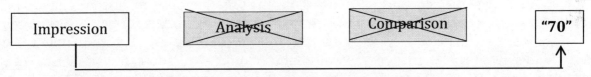

Judging **out of sequence** (Incorrect – ignoring standards)

> In this case, judges are "judging" to rank exclusively with **little consideration for their standards** (the foundation of "Impression"). Their analysis is not the same analysis used in the system. Analysis in this case in analyzing "Comparison" rather than analyzing their "Impression." "Analysis" is designed to analyze impressions not analyze why one performance should be ranked above or below a previous performance. Judges who use this method gather impressions during the performance but always within the context of comparing. During a performance, they will actually compare to the previous performances within the same contest. As a result, the contest is "benchmarked" by the first performance of the day or the first performance in a class such as school size, size of ensemble, grade level or classification such as "Class AA," "A," "B" etc.).

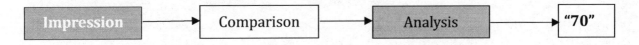

When using the method above, judges use a method (valid or not) to establish a number from the first performance and then base all other performances on that first number issued.

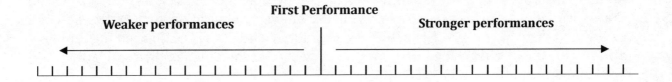

With one performance completed and scored, a second performance follows. Your first question should **not** be "Are they better or worse than the first group?" Your first question should be the same question used following the first performance.

"Where do they belong on my scale?"

You must go through the Impression-Analysis-Comparison process the same way, for each performance. "Comparison" **only** happens after you complete the first two steps. Judges get into trouble if they use "Comparison" as the primary (and many times, only) process used to score based on the first performance they assessed in the contest.

Judging by Percentage (Incorrect – ignoring point allocation)

When judges change the sequence of Impression-Analysis-Comparison, or they abandon it all together, rankings and ratings are always impacted. Wanting to "get it right," experienced and inexperienced judges too often gravitate to "the number" first and abandon the process. Judges will transfer their "raw impression number" to sub-captions. Those "raw impression numbers" are almost always "percentages" as demonstrated here:

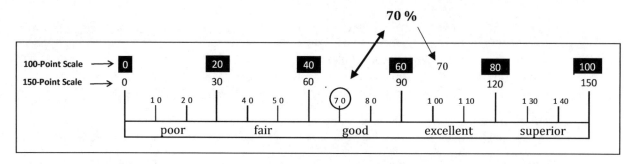

Nearly everyone has a gut feel for the 100 point scale. This, of course, is due to the preponderance of the 100% model in grading, business, and general conversation. People have a strong cognitive and visual image of 100%, 50%, and so on. Very few of us relate to a 350-point scale, a 150-point scale or a 75-point scale. Yet, many sub-captions on score sheets use these totals. When assigning numerical values to individual captions such as "Tone Quality" or "Dynamics," you must be cautious.

This familiarity with the 100 point (percentage) scale can lead to problems if you are not careful to use your visual scale to locate the proper number. Remember, the first step in the process is to identify which range a performance belongs in based on your Impression and Analysis process. Judges and evaluators get in trouble when they "go right to the number" rather than consider the range first and then use the Linear Scale as their guide to locate the actual number.

Above, a judge assigns a number to "Tone Quality" that he believes to be in the middle "Excellent" range at 70%. However, the "Tone Quality" caption totals 150 points. By jumping to his 70% impression and not referencing the chart, he has actually placed the performance in the lower "Good" Range on the 150-scale.

The more we evaluate or judge, the more intuitive we become about our number. This can cause us to fail at the cognitive and mechanical elements of the judging process. Since we are in the business of assessing emotional expression and since we are (and should be) actively engaged "as audience," the cognitive process of determining the numerical value of a performance can be highly affected by our subjective reactions to the performance itself. This is why "Analysis" is used in the system. If we judge with our "gut" excessively, we can forget to use the objective processes along with our subjective "Impression." Analysis helps us bridge the gap between the subjective and the objective. Comparison provides us with an additional means to check our impression.

5) Understanding how to numerically express the proper distance between one performance and another

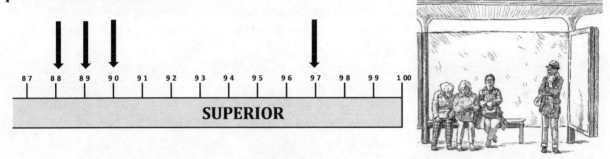

"Comparison" is simply checking to make certain performances in a contest or an audition are in the correct order. But once you have properly determined that one performance is better than another (using "Comparison") the very next question is, **"How much better."**

In the ideal world, if every impression was pure, raw numbers obtained correctly would line up in perfect order. But assessment is a human endeavor. Our system is the best system available, but it is not perfect. Were it perfect, there would be no need for "Analysis" (which double-checks your "Impression") or "Comparison" (which makes certain your numbers equate to a correct "Ranking" of performances). "Comparison," however has other purposes beyond checking for proper "Ranking." It must be used to determine if proper distance has been established between ranked performances. This is called, **"Spread."**

Here is where you must have a keen sense of the **number of points** you have to work with within each range. If the range contains 10 points, a 3-point distance between the two groups is significant. If the range contains twenty-five points, a distance of 3 points is much less significant. Understanding how many points you have in each range is critical to understanding the impact of the distance (spread) between one performance and the next.

Naturally, as more performances "arrive" in a "Range," the choices become more sophisticated and require precise "Numbers Management." If you make an error early-on, you will have significant challenges ranking properly as the audition or contest ensues. The best protection against being "boxed-in" on the Linear Scale is to use the process properly. In most cases, fatigue, distraction, breaks and lack of awareness cause problems with numbers management.

Conditions and Considerations involving "Spread"

1. Design scoresheets with enough numbers in each range to accommodate the audition.
2. If judging a contest, request use of decimals if the sheet is poorly designed, not allowing reasonable room to create a range within a range (create spread).
3. Use the system for every performance to avoid placing performers in the wrong range.
4. Determine the proper location within the range for each performance before considering the rating number.
5. Take note of the number of points allocated to each location within a range.
6. Consider the number of performers in an audition or contest and the likely number that may perform in a particular range.
7. Consider standards when "avoiding" or "approaching" high or low end of the range.
8. Identify distinctions when placing performances near others. Some performances may be very close in "Impression" but distinguishable in "Analysis." Review your "Impression" and "Analysis" first, to resolve a tight spread.
9. Do not artificially create "Spread" between units just to manage your numbers.
10. How to avoid pre-judging.

Every judge or director has tied performances at one time or another. Some are resolvable, some are not. The director, giving an audition, has a distinct advantage over the contest judge who must go on to the next performer. Once a score is submitted at a contest, judges cannot go back and change a score previously issued to accommodate his numbers management issue or resolve ties. A disciplined approach is critical in contest situations so as not to "Rank" incorrectly, suppress or inflate a "Rating," or create ties.

The director holding auditions should take the same approach as the judge. If, however, his or her best efforts create ties, she can go back and review all performances that result in ties and make decisions either using points or "tiebreakers." A director may choose to use certain elements of the audition as a tiebreaker - Sight-Reading, Prepared Music or Scales as other elements. Naturally, the tiebreaker chosen must be a valued quality that the director prefers. Some may prefer Sight-Reading over "Prepared Music." Other may view it exactly opposite or may consider Scales as more significant. Regardless, directors should feel free to use their ability to review after auditions to make the correct choice.

6) Understanding the importance of checking "Subcaption" ranges against the "Total" range.

Once you have entered all your sub-caption scores on the scoresheet and have totaled your score, it is important to double check your math and then check to see if the total score falls within the correct range for "Total Score" Scale. With all the challenges of Number Management, one must avoid mechanical errors such as addition.

7) Understanding how to properly modify or maintain the profile of a performance when resolving ties, breakpoints or spread issues.

We have stressed the importance of ranking overrating in auditions and contests where the order of performances is a "Desired Outcome." Assessment, however, should always have strong educational components. Assessments are not strictly contests to rank. Do not be misled by our insistence on ranking. While there are times when "Ranking," and declaring winners and losers are called for, the primary purpose of assessment is to mark student progress, give feedback to students and parents, improved teaching and provide data for program development. The purpose of stressing "Ranking" as a core component of our system is that it is key to 1) Establishing standards, 2) Sharpening tolerance and 3) Providing data for student growth measurement, ensemble placement, seating, and program growth.

Assessments provide students with information regarding their strengths and weaknesses. In addition to providing scores, evaluators must provide written notes to students about how to improve and where students are achieving. They should also use notes to validate their numerical ranking and raw score. Commentary should align itself with the score issued to students, as well. If a student scores high in intonation, directors should not confuse the student by writing a note on the back of the score sheet such as - "work on your intonation."

But the caption scoring can also tell the student about strengths and weakness. If intonation is mentioned as a problem on the back of the sheet, then the "Profile" of performance qualities should reflect that as well.

The three scoresheets below all have identical "Total" scores. Their "Scoring Profiles," however, are quite different from each another. Each student has scored a **"76"**.

Student A		
25	Tone & Intonation	22
25	Tempo & Rhythm	18
25	Articulation & Technique	16
25	Musical Expression	20
100	Total	76

Student B		
25	Tone & Intonation	17
25	Tempo & Rhythm	21
25	Articulation & Technique	22
25	Musical Expression	16
100	Total	76

Student C		
25	Tone & Intonation	21
25	Tempo & Rhythm	21
25	Articulation & Technique	17
25	Expression	17
100	Total	76

8) Understanding how to correct ties, resolve breakpoints and anticipate pressure points in a contest audition

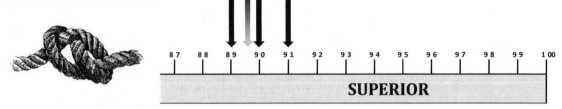

Despite strong adherence to the process, ties between contestants will occur. In large auditions or contests, evaluators will work through the process and inevitably arrive at a number previously issued. There are different types of "Tie Situations." Tie Situations occur when you consider placing a score in an area of the scale that is occupied by other scores in close proximity. "Tie Situations" can occur:

a. When there are <u>plenty of numbers available on both sides</u> of the previous performer's score.
b. When there are <u>plenty of numbers to the left</u> but <u>few (or none) to the right</u> of the previous performer's score.
c. When there are <u>plenty of numbers to the right</u> but <u>few (or none) to the left</u> of the previous performer's score.
d. When there are <u>few (or no) numbers available on either side</u> of the previous performer's score.

9) How to maintain your standard or tolerance over full-day or full-week assessments or contests.

Judging a full day of solos or auditioning an entire week is, in many ways, an athletic event. Like athletes, we do well to come into such events rested. Having a judging routine and using the system religiously allows directors and judges to stay consistent in their assessment of each student. It does little good to assess one way in the morning and then change in the afternoon due to your fatigue, concentration or conditions.

A director's tolerance and receptivity to performance can swing hour-by-hour and day-by-day. Breaks are opportunities to refresh both mind and body and should be utilized. Professional judges learn how to pace themselves and "live inside" the process. Distractions can impact your consistency one day but be a way to relax your mind the next.

Finally, being organized is critical. Proper preparation and a consistent routine are key to delivering professional assessments or contest results. Take assessment as seriously as you do all other aspects of your job. Stay focused and approach each audition or contest performance in the same manner. All student performers deserve a valid assessment.

10) How to avoid pre-judging

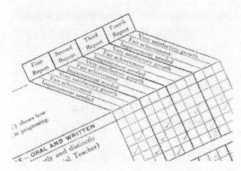

Every student, regardless of past assessments, deserves to be judged based on their performance of the moment. That, in itself, would be enough to motivate any director to assess each performance as if it was the first heard.

But an additional reason is to achieve a valid assessment of progress being made by each student, your ensemble, and your entire program.

Music directors know their students. The time we spend with our music students in the classroom, at performances, and on trips provide us the opportunity to know more about their personalities, motivations, and instincts than many classroom teachers. All good teachers know their students, but music directors, coaches, and other activity teachers spend more time with their students than regular classroom teachers. Music performance classes are unique in that they reveal a student's ability every time music is produced in the classroom. As has been stated, we use assessment not just in formative and summative testing but as our teaching methodology. We assess more often than any discipline in the school curriculum.

This can be a great advantage, but it can also contribute to pre-conceived impressions of how a student may perform in an assessment or audition. Like professional judges, directors must enter each assessment with a clear mind as to the potential of the performance. In professional judging, one learns to do this even though a judge may see a performing group many times in one month.

Directors understand that placing students in the correct ensemble and on the correct part assures students can be productive and provide them the opportunity to succeed and experience music in its fullest. Effective auditions also assure directors that music programmed for each group matches their ability range. Using valid criteria for auditions and assessments that measure our desired outcomes is important. As educators, we have a responsibility to understand the requirements of musical ensembles, to select music written just beyond the reach of our students and to explain the reasons for auditions. In short, we need to know how our student's play. We also need to understand how we'd *like* them to play. Assessment is the only way to assess each student against our musical standards, program standards and Desired Outcomes of each ensemble.

While it is natural to preconceive the achievement range of a student's upcoming assessment, directors should approach each student "as an audience would" and allow the system to assess the performance void of anything they may have heard from the student before. Something new always occurs and you don't want to miss it.

Section Three

Applying Linear Scales to Auditions, Testing, and Grading

PART VII - Assessment Design Considerations

Whether designing assessments and their related scoresheets, evaluators must understand the core principles of the Linear Scale system, when to use the "Take-Away" versus "Build-Up" methods, and how to align the system with grading systems.

PART VIII - Programing & Curriculum Considerations

Along with common criteria used to select large ensemble we have, directors must consider whether all parts contain ample opportunity to assess Desired Outcomes of each voice or instrument. Should any part be lacking, solo and ensemble literature, training materials and private teacher instructional should be used to supplement concert literature.

PART IX - Program, Ensemble & Student Growth

Data collected through the school year can reveal opportunities for improvement, help shape programming, adjust course objectives and provide administrators with empirical evidence of valid assessment and plans for student growth.

PART X Single District, Unit District & Custom Applications

Actual applications of the Linear Scale system in use are explained to serve as models.

PART VII
Assessment Design Considerations

System Review

The Impression-Analysis-Comparison process, synchronous with the Linear Scale, is a well-established and principled method of assessing a live performance. Its authenticity is validated as a result of the following:

1) It draws directly from the nature of music's symbolic expressions of emotion, meaning, narrative and artistry present in live performance.

2) It relies on a receptive and qualified evaluator who "listens as an audience would" and reacts in an unencumbered way before analyzing the cause of his or her reaction.

3) It relies heavily on the background and experience of the teacher-assessor, evaluator or judge to acquire a general sense of achievement before acknowledging an emergent set of oscillating qualities present in the performance.

4) It utilizes the set of criteria, acquired and defined by a knowledgeable teacher-assessor, evaluator or judge, to determine the significance of the expressiveness, artistic, and spontaneous value of a music performance.

5) It provides a numerical scale that delineates the range of an evaluator's standard of excellence on which he or she can place a performer's performance.

6) It requires a final step of comparison to other performances, to validate the proper use of the system and confirm the absence of bias. This can be done within the same instrument, voice, ensemble, program, grade-level, assessment or contest.

7) It requires that ranking take precedence overrating when the purpose of an assessment is determining order or ensemble placement.

8) It allows for numerical ties when executing assessments exclusively for the purpose of grading or informing students as to their placement against the norm of their section, ensemble, or program. If assessments are used to reseat, then ranking must be deployed.

With the appropriate use of the system as described, it can be used for the following:

- Establishing ensemble placement
- Establishing seating order within an ensemble
- Ranking students of like instrument or voice
- Ranking sections and ensembles against each other
- Rating the overall quality of a section, ensemble or program
- Determining grades for specific formative or summative assessments
- Tracking individual, ensemble and program growth using statistical validation

Designing Linear Scales & Score Sheets

Given a 100-point Linear Scale, wouldn't it be hard to audition 120 students and rank them in order, with no ties? Wouldn't at least twenty students have to receive the same score? Furthermore, doesn't the principle of distribution tell us that random distribution never lines up conveniently from "1" to "100?"

The reality is that few students will perform in the "poor" range and a small number in the "superior" range. Since each of those ranges totals 20 points on a 100-point scale, even fewer numbers are "available" to the evaluator. A conservative estimate of "numbers not used" could leave him with a mere 60 points to place 120 students. I can vouch for the fact that in most band contests (with more than 20 units), "numbers management" is always a challenge in the middle of the range.

Some band contests make the process even more challenging by asking judges not to rate anyone below the 50% mark, thus eliminating half the range of numbers available to the judge. Contests that request all bands score above 50%, while not providing additional numbers to work with on the sheets, force judges to compare bands immediately rather than use the Impression, Analysis, Comparison system. Worrying about "fitting everyone in" takes precedence over using the system. This stunts the Impression and Analysis part of the system, which is the natural process to arrive at a number.

One sees a similar phenomenon at state solo & ensemble contests and large organization contests. A judge, who is scheduled to hear thirty-five trumpet soloists at a solo contest, may decide to avoid giving out too many "Superior" ratings in the morning. He does this because he is unsure of the range of performance he will hear through the day. His problem, however, is that students are not scheduled throughout the day in order of ability. His morning may actually contain a number of top performers. But in his caution to avoid "Superior" ratings in the morning, he gets "squeezed" in the afternoon when a high percentage of students perform lower than the top students of the morning who he had artificially placed below the "Superior" range.

Keep in mind, however, that the purpose of the Linear Scale is to provide a scale that reflects five *ranges* of achievement not a fixed set of points. The five ranges reflect the impressions that people naturally get when listening to a range of performances. The total number of points ("0 to 100," "0 to 200" or "0 to 1,000") do not matter. What is important are the five ranges. Therefore, all score sheets and their accompanying Linear Charts must be designed to 1) accommodate the number students being assessed and 2) profile the range of ability of all students being assessed and 3) provide the evaluator enough numerical spacing to use the system properly. That includes ranking and rating with the proper amount of spacing (called "spread") between individual performers.

Anytime judges, evaluators contest managers or contest rules, mechanically alter the Impression, Analysis, Comparison process or manipulate the Linear Scale, as in our examples above, ranking *can* be impacted. Rating is nearly *always* impacted. Unless you are a first-year teacher (or in your first year at a new school), you do not have to guess - as the solo & ensemble judge above did. Fortunately, directors have a good idea of how their kids play. It only takes one audition year to get a sense of the range of your program.

If you want to select the top 24 violins for your advanced orchestra and have a total of 50 to choose from, do you have enough room on your 100-point scale? This depends on the abilities of those fifty students of course. If the range of ability runs from incoming 8th graders to advanced seniors in high school, including three who have the already been offered scholarships for violin in college, then you probably have enough room to rank this entire group. Similarly, if you have a limit of ten to twelve cellos with twenty-two to choose from, you have even more room. But if you are auditioning fifty seniors for twenty-four spots, then you may want to design a scale and a scoresheet with a wider range.

 When designing a Linear Scale, one must base the total number of points assigned on 1) the number of students being assessed 2) the range of ability within the students being assessed

This is important because it assures that scores will align with the standards of the evaluator and of the program. Remember, the standards of the evaluator and those established within the program both apply. In these cases, a pure 100-point scale works fine. But what if you'd like to rank your entire ensemble from the best musician to lowest regardless of instrument or voice? This can be accomplished by using decimal places on your 100-point scale as seen below (close-up shows detail).

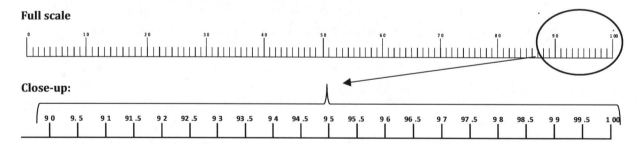

This adds plenty of numbers to your scale. Remember, as we discussed before, the numbers inside the scale do not matter, just the 5 Rangers. When creating your scales always make them devisable by "5." Regardless of how many raw numbers you need, simply add more numbers to your overall range (easily divisible by 5) and then make use of decimal points to distinguish between student performers. The following page shows a 1,000-point score sheet broken down in the total box with a decimal. The student in this assessment scored a total of 858 points or 85.8%. This score can easily be equated to the grading system used in your department or district.

Scoresheet using whole numbers - Then adding decimal in Total Box

	Pts.	Scr	
Tone	100	89	
Intonation	100	78	
Tempo	100	95	
Rhythm	100	93	
Phrasing	100	79	
Technique	100	92	
Articulation	100	89	
Dynamics	100	83	
Musical Expression	200	160	
Total	1000	858	85.8

This is a commonly-used method of scoring. For this particular sheet, you would need a 100-point scale and a 200-point scale for the sub-captions. If the "Total" box is a value different than any of the subcaption boxes, then a different scale for the total needs to be used, as well. This is so you can check each range of achievement in the "Total" box as compared to the sub-caption boxes. An error in math could result in your number "Total" being located in a different range or different location within a range.

Remember, the number of points available within a 5-range scale must provide for the total number of students being auditioned or assessed. This allows ranking with no ties.

Though it is not often necessary, this score sheet would allow a large number of winds to be ranked by "Tone Quality," or "Musical Expression." I don't particularly endorse ranking sub-captions because of the inherent dependence one quality has on another. Problems with "Tone Quality" will certainly bleed into problems with "Pitch." Problems with "Pitch" do not always cause by poor "Tone Quality." It could be "Technique." Challenges with certain "Rhythms" can impact "Tempo." Yet, "Tempo" problems can occur divorced from any rhythmic challenges. Thus, you can see the idiocy of conducting a "Qualities Contest" within the audition or performance contest. In addition, if one perpetuates such a thing, one crosses over to "the dark side" of a quality performance being the sum (or, indeed, the presence) of musical qualities. We'll leave that heresy here and move on.

Can all auditions, evaluations, and judging be done using the "Build-up" system exclusively? In the ideal situation, they can. The "Build-up" system links to the Impression-Analysis-Comparison system better than any other. That is because the "Build-up" system starts with Impression. The "Impression-Analysis-Comparison system was designed *for* the "Build-up System." Contest sheets, like the one on this page, force you to use Impression-Analysis-Comparison and its companion piece – "The Build-up" system. If you have a very specific desired outcome for a formative assessment like "Play the Concert Bb scale, two octaves, up and down," and all you are assessing are accurate fingers and acceptable pitch and articulation, use "The Tic System" rather than contrive a "Build-up" Score Sheet. It will be quicker, more practical and give you a valid assessment of your desired outcome for a major scale.

Applying "Take-Away" & "Build-up" Properly to Desired Outcomes

In conversations with hundreds of directors and contest judges over the years, I have found that many use the "Take-Away" system when listening to students play. In addition, they tend to use it in captions such as "Intonation," "Note Accuracy" or "Rhythm." But when a director or contest judge considers a more subtle quality such as "Musicality," "Musical Expression" or "Tone Quality," they tend to use the "Build-Up" system.

But still, directors tend to lean towards the "Take-Away" system because they use it so often from the podium. Therefore, when we hold auditions or judge a state solo and ensemble contest we "look for errors." It is very difficult to migrate from teacher-director to evaluator-judge. To improve our ability to assess, we need to understand what our tendencies are (as well as our biases as discussed previously). A quick look at a typical score sheet for a contest or audition reveals how we **tend** to use both "Take-Away" and "Build-up" systems for the same assessment.

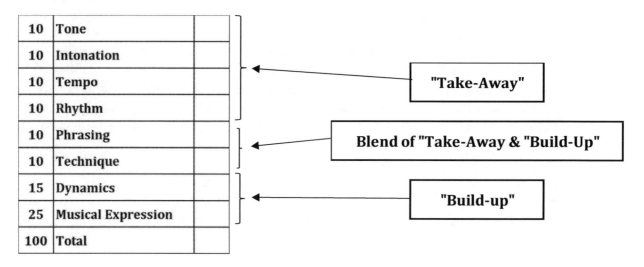

If you have assessed students at all levels of development for a number of years, you, very likely, use the "Take-Away" system more frequently at the lower grade levels and the "Build-Up" system more at the upper-grade levels. This tendency is not as straight-lined as in the graph on the next page, but the graph indicates a general tendency that occurs.

Another tendency that occurs during lower-level performance (with a score sheet like the one above) is that contest judges often spend the entire time sampling "Take-Away" captions *during* performance and then think about "Build-Up" captions such as "Musical Expression" *following the* performance. They must consider both during the performance.

Remember, the graphic above does not infer *how* evaluators should use the "Take-away" and Build-Up" methods. It is an observation as to how evaluators and judges *tend* to use the two methods.

What is important is that directors and judges know *what* method they are using, *when* they are using it and *why* they are using one versus the other. The main reason for using one method versus the other has to do with the instantaneous nature of technical errors (they occur and are gone) versus the developmental nature of expressive achievement during a performance (occurs over time). The other factor is your desired outcomes for any given assessment situation or the requirements of the contest you are judging. If you decide to "count every error" in categories such as "Rhythm" or "Articulation," that choice is valid if it measures your desired outcomes. If you are auditioning 5th graders for next year's 6th-grade band, you would likely get more distinction using "Take-Away" for qualities like "Rhythm," "Articulation" or "Note Accuracy" than if used "Build-up." "Music Expression" is always a consideration and is best evaluated using the "Build-Up" system since it occurs over time. The point is that *both methods* can and should be used when assessing or judging - *and* it is proper to do so within the same scoring sheet.

The graph also shows a correlation between Instructional Method and Judging Method. Clearly, more errors occur at the beginner or lower level. Instructional methods in beginning band or middle school band will tend to be "correctional" in nature. As students advance, there is still a need to correct errors, but technique and method are more developed at that stage. Therefore, we tend to use more of an "explanatory method" of teaching.

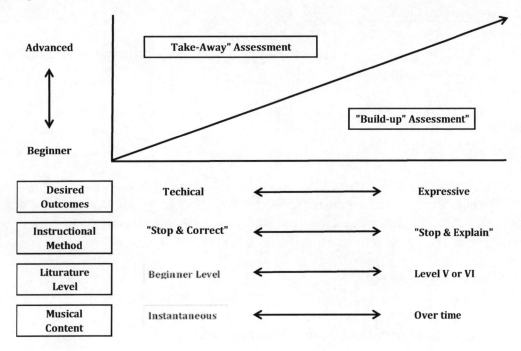

Aligning the Linear Scale with School Grading Scales

We had quite a discussion about the importance of ranking and rating. It was clear that our number one priority in using the linear scale for judging performance was to rank and, secondarily, to rate. In fact, we discussed that the best way to sharpen our standards was to rank *every time* you rate (assess). Schools are somewhat different in that they focus on rating almost exclusively. We live in that world. The two systems are not incompatible. The Impression-Analysis-Comparison system and the Linear Scale still function in the school rating environment because of their ability to place performances in one of five ranges.

When a math or science teacher gives a student an "A," what does that "A" represent? Does it represent a specific and unique grade - exclusive to that one student?

> No. More than one student will receive an "A."

Does it indicate a specific ranking?

> It does not. There are a number of "A's" in every classroom. There are also a number of "B's," "C's," "D's" and a few "F's."

What do these grades represent?

> Very simply they represent ranges of achievement.

What about "number grades?"

> Number grades represent a location within a range of achievement, it does not necessarily infer ranking.

Whether a teacher uses "Number Grades" or "Letter Grades" is immaterial. The more important comparison is to understand when they use a "Build-Up" method or a "Take-Away" method of assessment.

To begin with, most Common-Practice or Standardized testing uses the "Tic-System." Points are removed when an answer is incorrect. An English teacher, grading a creative writing paper, however, can, and usually does, use the "Build-up" system. Similarly, a history teacher who assigns an essay paper will use a "Build-Up" to arrive at a score.

What do *their* numbers mean?

> A number grade does not automatically infer ranking. In a non-ranking system, it represents placement within a range of achievement.

When the English Teacher uses numbers to grade a creative writing paper instead of "Letter Grades" and assigns, say, a **"92"** as the grade, he is still using the number value to locate the student's paper at the lower end of the "Superior" range. He determines that the paper is in the "Superior" range, according to his standards. He then determines that the paper is on the lower end of the "Superior" Range and assigns a **"92"** to represent that area of his "Superior" range. He is **not** ranking and will issue more than one **"92."** He is, however, using "Impression" and "Analysis" to find the proper "Range" of achievement that a creative writer has demonstrated. But what about "Comparison?" He *may* use "Comparison" to check bias or the accuracy of his "Impression" if he is not certain. But he is not using "Comparison" as a means to check rank. He is comparing impressions of one paper versus another so that he is certain that his final grade of **"92"** is proper.

The creative writing teacher may also use "Comparison" to confirm a "tie" between two papers. Two papers receiving a **"92"** in Creative Writing class do not constitute identical papers as does the "Common-Practice" test. When two students achieve a **"92"** on a fifty-point "true-false" exam, they have *identical* papers. When two students receive a **"92"** on a creative writing paper, they do *not* have identical papers. The Creative Writing teacher will have a set of qualities in mind that he uses to confirm his impression range. One paper will have strengths in certain qualities and weakness in others. The second paper will have achieved different qualities and have different weakness than that first. They can both receive a **"92"** for different reasons. He may be considering "spread" when he compares, but he is still checking his Impression and Analysis of 1) achievement level within a range and 2) relieve achievement between others he has scored. In the second example, he is recalling his impression of the first paper, checking his assigned number and confirming its location as compared to others around that first score.

One of the dangers using this system is to shift methods within the same assessment. When the English teacher grades a number of essays in a single class he can use 1) his *personal standard* as determined by his background and experience 2) his *class history standard* achieved in all previous classes of the same subject with the same assignment or 3) the *current class standard,* established by the twenty students in his class.

As he goes through his stack of papers, he may note the "top paper" and "lowest paper" in the pile until a new "highest" and "lowest" appears. This can impact his high and low numbers, of course. And, to a lesser degree, it can impact papers that achieve in between the highest rated paper and the lowest.

He may choose to compare his top paper to the "best paper he's ever seen" or could decide to "grade on a curve," which, in the vernacular, means to place the best paper in the class in the "Superior" range regardless of how it compares to all previous "Superior" assessments he has given over the years.

It is important to understand that teachers use all methods. It is not valid to switch between from one standard to another within the same assessment. Each student should be assessed using the same standard for that particular assessment. Teachers may choose to apply different standards to one assessment versus another. Essentially, each assessment is a "separate contest." If a teacher chooses to apply different standards for certain types of assessments (i.e., a final exam), he should be aware that he is adjusting the "weight" of one particular assessment versus another in that case.

Teachers, who assess creative writing or essay papers, judge more like music-performance teachers than most non-music disciplines. Art teachers assess similarly to us, as well, but they are considered "one of us" by most administrators who have little arts experience. If you are looking for allies in your school regarding our method of assessment, seek out the English or History departments that utilized the Impression-Analysis-Comparison system to assess. Explain our process. It will explain theirs, as well and commonality can be found.

Remember, finding the "Range" is the important part. While ranking is possible in the case of the Creative Writing teacher, it is not necessary. Their "Desired Outcomes" are simply to put student papers in the correct general location of a specific range, based on the English teacher's standards. Most schools use five ranges of achievement just as the Linear Scale does. However, their scale is a bit more skewed to the right.

Here is the standard **Linear Scale** as we have defined it:

Here is a typical **School Grading Scale**:

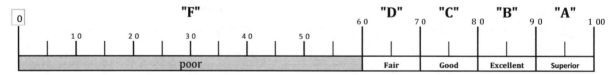

Do math and science students perform in the far left of the scale?

    They do.

Do more students score in the "Fair" category than the "Poor" category?

    Often they do.

Does the distribution of student grades in a large science class, using a school grading scale, look similar to the distribution of orchestra students being assessed using the Linear Scale system?

It does.

One should not view Linear Scales as the distribution of numbers but simply five ranges of achievement with particular numbers or grades assigned to each range. Here is a distribution of grades in a large science class of thirty students using both scales:

Distribution of Grades for Advanced Chemistry (30 students)
School Grading Scale

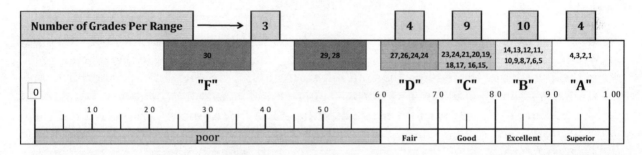

Distribution of Grades for Advanced Chemistry (30 students)
Linear Scale

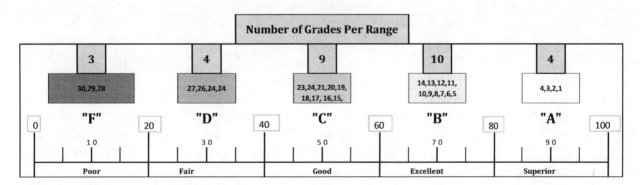

As you can see, "reality" doesn't change. The same number of students achieved. They are distributed the same way across five ranges of achievement. They were assessed the same way. If numerical scores are used, the number grades are the same and placed in the appropriate "Range" of achievement. Even though scales look different, there is no difference. This basic understanding that grading scales are similar is the basis for our contention that the Impression-Analysis-Comparison can be applied to any school grading system. Five ranges hold regardless of the number of points or their allocation.

But it is **how** ratings are achieved in Music Performance Classes that is different from how they are acquired in the science class.

 Since we are a performance discipline and our subject matter is a live (applied) performance of artistic expression, we must use the Impression-Analysis-Comparison system and its accompanying Linear Scale to place performances in the context of our Standards and our Program Standards - which are acquired through our Background and Experience. A science teacher can use common-practice testing, which is a "tic" system, to assess a student's knowledge and understanding of content.

It is also important to understand that **what** Impression-Analysis-Comparison measures is different from what Common-Practice testing measures.

 If we were to use a *written* Common-Practice test to assess 5th-grade trumpet students on the fingering for the Concert Bb scale, we'd be measuring their **knowledge** of those fingerings but not their **understanding.** In music performance, understanding is defined as **doing**. This requires actual **performance** (an applied endeavor). There is no **understanding** in a performance class without live performance. Using Common-Practice testing in a music performance class cannot even be considered formative to a final summative performance. It's helpful, but it's not formative.

With School Grading Scales it is important to realize that there is an additional element to scoring in schools that does not exist in the Linear Scale process. The Linear Scale is simply a range of very likely scores based on what actually occurs in performance. A School Grading Scale has an additional element. That element is called "Passing." Grading in schools is a "qualifying process." The qualifying score on the scale above is a "60." Sixty is passing.

The only number that matters in the School Grading Scale is "60." That qualifies as passing and it gives the student a "credit" for the class and allows the student to move on to the next course and continue on to graduation. That is the desired outcome in this case. But there are other more favorable 'Desired Outcomes."

Grade point average, acceptance to a college and higher levels of understanding are all measured once a student scores above a 60%. This is important too. There are, therefore, additional "Desired Outcomes" beyond the qualifying goal. But the minimum requirement is to pass. A low grade point average could prevent you from graduating, gaining entry into a training school or college, prevent you from getting a job. It can even be an indicator as to your willingness to apply yourself. It is not, however, a guarantee that you will be a failure following school or that you will fail to achieve at a high level.

School records are full of students that failed, dropped out or held a minimal grade point average and yet went on to significant success in life. They include:

- Richard Branson, founder of Virgin Group an international powerhouse currently worth about $4.9 billion. He dropped out at age 15.

- Aretha Franklin who dropped out at age 14 and has since received numerous honorary degrees from universities like Harvard, Princeton, Yale, and the Berkley College of Music.

- Joe Lewis who dropped out of high school at 15 to run his father's catering business, Tavistock Banqueting, and is currently worth about $5.3 billion

- Philip Emeagwali, the supercomputer scientist, dropped out of high-school at age 13 due to war conditions in his native country in Nigeria. Emeagwali came up with the formula for allowing a large number of computers to communicate at once. The discovery earned him the IEEE Gordon Bell Prize in 1989, and he has since been hailed as one of the fathers of the Internet, according to Time Magazine.

Naturally, these are exceptions. Most of the time, our academic performance in school is more of an indicator of our likely *academic* success in the future or the type of career we may select. College degrees have shown to have increased incomes over non-college educated. The Pew Research Center shows the value of a college degree is greater than it has been in nearly half a century, at least when compared to the prospect of not getting a degree. The Pew Research Center has found that the earnings gap between millennials with bachelor's degrees and those with just a high school diploma is wider than it was for prior generations. The school grading systems grade as a final act. The Linear Scale is more functional as a level of achievement at a given point.

Assessing is different than grading. Grading is tied to a point in time. It can be an ending process where a final grade is given, or it can be an "informative grade." An informative grade informs the student what grade they would achieve "if the test was given today." These "informative grades," based on Formative Assessments, essentially give both parents and students progress reports. Formative and Summative Assessments are designed to issue a grade, with no impact on seating or ensemble placement, do not *require* ranking. But once you start using our system regularly, you will find yourself ranking as a natural process even when ties are of no consequence.

Let's suppose you have assigned all clarinet players a formative assessment covering the most difficult passage in a piece programmed for an upcoming concert. Your goal (desired outcome) is to make certain that all clarinets can play the passage at tempo.

Just like in science classes or math classes, more than one student can get a "100." Checking student progress, reporting to both students and parents, and using grades as motivation for students are all valid. Not every assessment requires ranking. In this case, directors can use the grading system as described above where a number represents a <u>location within a range of achievement</u>. When we assess students to check their progress using formative assessment our desired outcomes are different from those when we are auditioning for ensemble placement.

 Ties are **not permissible** in assessments that require ranking for the purposes of ensemble placement or seating order. Ties **are permissible** when numbers are used to locate student performance in a particular location within a range of achievement (i.e., "Superior," Excellent" etc.)

The Linear Scale is simply a snapshot of a specific performance. In some cases it is used to rank performances, in which case, ties are not permissible. In other cases, it is used to provide an achievement range and qualify the performance to be in either the low, middle or high end of an achievement range. In this case, ties are permissible. When the actual grade is assigned and submitted into a student's record, it can easily be correlated to most school grading systems. The Linear Scale can be used in all forms of assessment used in schools today:

Assessment
Assessment refers to the wide variety of methods or tools that educators use to **evaluate, measure, and document** the academic readiness, learning progress, skill acquisition, or educational needs of students.

Reassessment
A second-chance to **repeat an assessment** taken previously.

Formative Assessment
Assessments used to conduct **in-process** evaluations of student comprehension, learning needs, and academic progress during a lesson, unit, or course. Formative Assessments may or may not be registered as grades. They may or may not include a grade but a rating to show student progress leading to a final Summative Assessment which is graded.

Summative Assessment
Assessments used to evaluate student learning, skill acquisition, and academic achievement **at the conclusion** of a defined instructional period—typically at the end of a project, unit, course, semester, program, or school year.

Part VIII

Programing & Curriculum Considerations

Literature

We have already discussed the lineage of bands, orchestras and choirs and how they entered the American School System. The principles that were established by the pioneers in the early days still drive what is considered quality, today. Most band, orchestra and choir directors in America consider their concert groups to be the core of their program. Many have multifaceted programs and consider them all equally important. jazz bands, marching bands, swing & jazz choirs, pop orchestras, drum lines and winter guard programs all make up the vast landscape of music performance in our schools, today.

Through Fredrick Fennel's efforts and many others, wind literature came into its own after World War II. Over the years, composers and arrangers of all types have written for wind ensemble, concert band, solo & ensemble, jazz band, marching band and various "athletic bands," which perform numerous times throughout the school year. Choir music has a significant body of work in secular music along with religious and folk music arranged for female, male and combined voices. Even orchestras, with their penchant for "the classics," have a significant body of contemporary music that is educationally sound and good music. But still, serious music directors must "dig deep" to find composers, publishers and self-publishing composers who write lyrical, expressive, and significant music. While there is more music available, a good percentage of it is uninspired.

In my days as an orchestra director, I would often read a lot of music with both my developmental string ensemble and the advanced group. After sight-reading through a new piece, I would always pose the following questions to them. "Is this piece written by a music educator or a composer? Now, this is a bit of a tongue-in-cheek question, but it was not to infer that music educators couldn't write good music. Nor was it intended to mean that composers never write bad music. In fact, a good portion of quality material written is written by teachers and former teachers. Some of my best "finds" are works by inspired writers who understand the student-musician and write with sensitivity to the developing musician. Nevertheless, it surprised me how accurate my student's responses were to this question. Over 90% of the time they would answer accurately. Even student musicians can sense when music is good.

My observation is that kids tend to develop musical taste along the lines of their director. I think many of us have observed this. In my five years at Bands of America, where I witnessed thousands of kids, passionate for their music, and after forty years of judging, interacting with directors, and witnessing the performance of their kids, I became fully convinced that our students learn to appreciate the music *we* appreciate and are passionate about. This may be the most profound thing about teaching music. It's not just **how we teach** kids about music. It's not just **whether we assess** what they've learned. It's really about **what we teach** our kids. That means good music, expressive music, and music that is about something substantial. Dynamic directors *live* their passion for good music.

I'm fairly opinionated on this topic. As I reflected back recently, it was surprising to me that I began composing over forty-five years ago. Little of it made me much money, for I was always composing for my own students. This was often out of necessity. Even in the beginning, I could never write about "nothing." There had to be a story, a mood, a meaning or a realization behind the work. Like many a would-be composer, I tossed out more manuscript than I ever put in front of an ensemble. But compositions that are simply "playable" and offer little substance are not good choices.

Here, I am not speaking of genre, style or type of music selected though there is certainly "light" material out there. In the band world, there are outlets for the most serious and the most sublime material. I believe there is room for both but in the proper season. The same kids that play "Shut up and Dance," by Walk the Moon, at a fall football game can perform "Armenian Dances," by Alfred Reed in the spring. In addition, innovators in the marching band world have brought serious music to the competitive arena over the years out of a desire to make the fall season more meaningful from an aesthetic point of view. The great programs in our country are those that explore all idioms in an artistic way. Poor writing, bad arranging, and music that does not challenge our students, regardless of the season, should be avoided. Choosing bad literature for your high school orchestra is tantamount to handing a 5th-grade math book to a senior calculus class.

There are many examples of poor literature. Some examples that come to mind include:

- Music that removes most lyricism from woodwind parts only to relegate them to repetitive and extended ostinato rhythmic patterns, short changes our students.
- Scoring for full orchestra that is dominated by wind and percussion parts with an obligatory "string feature" distorts the nature of symphonic orchestra music.
- Pop material for choir that is poorly adapted to student choir and written with no consideration for the range or development of young singers is harmful.
- Chopped up medleys of program music that provide abrupt transitions and little effort to modulate artfully from one selection to the next are probably not the best choice.
- Compositions that ignore the dynamic of full percussion contribution significantly to distill the experience our percussionists receive in large ensemble class.
- "Themes from" pieces chosen simply to be current with kid's tastes and interests in popular music from film, games or the latest pop star, without consideration for their artistic merits, debase our efforts to teach quality music in the classroom.
- Certain novelty pieces that are of little artistic merit, lessen student's sense of taste.
- Music that fails to explore the inherent nature of what wind ensemble, concert choir or symphonic orchestra produce reduces the development of our art form. I struggle to find new music with significant lyricism in primary, secondary, tertiary parts in both band and orchestra literature, today.

There is no doubt that the publishing business drives many of the choices available to directors, today. "What sells" is equally, if not more, important to publishers sometimes than "what teaches" or "what is profound." But with the rise of print-on-demand, small start-up publishers and entrepreneurial composers can produce their own printed music at low cost. Finding music for school ensembles that is educationally sound and is "good music," is a challenge. But recalling that music is our textbook, all directors should take great pains to select quality literature. Beyond your artistic requirements, a few other considerations come to mind:

> Music is graded by difficulty by publishers. But as any experienced director knows, these grading systems are "all over the board." One publisher's "2" is another publisher's "1." Is **difficulty** the only criteria for which we select music?
>
> Directors will often select music based on the strengths or weaknesses of their group. That is certainly valid and a consideration. But should **matching ability level** be the primary criteria for selecting music for our group?
>
> Directors will often select music that is programmable in their school. We are all in the entertainment business to a degree, and it is not a crime to select material for a concert that will entertain and be enjoyable for audiences and students alike. But should **entertainment** be our standard by which we select music?
>
> Directors will select music they hear performed by other programs they respect. But should choose **music that others perform** with no regard for the abilities of our students?
>
> State Music Education Associations maintain standards for literature by creating optimum playing-lists for students at the high school, middle and elementary levels. Committees of directors determine required literature and select prominent conductors to conduct it from the ranks of university, school and professional conductors for festivals. But should we select **state or association required music** if our group is not ready to perform it or simply to pronounce that we have "played" it?

I posed no answers. I posed the questions to prompt a thought process that we should all practice when we select literature. To be certain, all of the considerations above, and many more should go into one's thinking when choosing music. No one consideration should be used exclusively, and it is not a requirement that they all be considered. Each director should use the method that agrees with their philosophy and upholds quality music performance education in the context of your community, school, and program.

Why is this discussion of literature important, here? Music selection creates our body of work. It is our text-book. Most importantly, it is our product. What we play determines what we teach. Literature also plays a very significant role in the development of our standards. It can be easily argued that picking good and appropriate literature is our most important job.

- Programming for your ensemble should be comprised of artistic, expressive and substantial music you deem appropriate for your ensemble, program, and community.

- Programming for your ensemble should explore a wide variety of composers, styles and periods to provide your students with the complete breadth of music written for each idiom.

- Programming for your ensemble should challenge your ensemble technically, musically and cognitively to provide for continued growth as student musicians.

- Programming for your ensemble should be designed to stretch the level of all of your program's ensembles from year to year.

- Programming for your ensemble should provide ample material on each instrument or part to assess defined Desired Outcomes of musicianship, artistry, and skill within the context of each music performance class offered within the curriculum.

- Content in your Music performance classes should include compulsory scales (rudiments for percussion), etudes, exercises and technique builders included to provide for development beyond your ensemble literature and to support it. Solo and small ensemble literature should be utilized. It provides musical experiences not available with the large ensemble experience,

Beyond selecting music that is well written, that explores a range of music styles and is programmable for your various performances, the music you select should provide you with ample excerpts throughout the year to assess student achievement in a range of musical challenges. Compulsory scales (rudiments for percussion), etudes, exercises and technique builders should be included. Finally, solo and small ensemble literature also provides musical experiences not available with the large ensemble experience.

Why is it that the great directors are always talking regularly about works for band, orchestra compositions, and exceptional choral arrangements or spend hours searching for that "ideal piece"? Simply stated, to develop artistic, complete and significant student-performers we must select artistic, complete and significant music. There is no substitute for this, and the great programs in our schools play great music.

Compulsories

You might find my use of the term "Compulsories" in the context of assessment a bit unusual. It's certainly a borrowed term, most famously associated with figure skating. Drawing figures on ice, most notably the "figure eight," was a technical contest in and of itself. The compulsory figure patterns gave way to what the skating community calls "Moves in the field" or "MIFs. Similarly, ballet has a long tradition of highly specified skill-based fundamentals still used in dance training, today.

It goes without saying that music performance has its compulsories. One of the beautiful things about our discipline is that the fundaments have not changed for centuries. Like skating and dancing, we are a physical science and the body has not changed much. The equipment we use has improved over the years but the principles of how to produce a quality tone on a brass instrument, how to develop vibrato as a singer, how to shift to third position on violin, have the same purpose – to master the art of physical performance. As we all know, technique is not an end product, as it was during figure skating compulsory contests of yore. It is a means to an end. Issues of technique are as old as musical expression itself, and they are never static. The masters of the trade practice many more hours than they perform. As the music gets more complex, the physical stakes get higher.

We've discussed the selection of literature as being the core element to quality music performance programs. But we cannot approach any of it unless we have trained musicians. This is, in fact, the essential part of our job. It is how we spend our day. To borrow two terms from my business background…

> Selecting music is **strategic.**   Teaching method is **tactical.**

Unfortunately, contact time with music students to teach fundamentals has eroded. Many of us are teaching "method" from the podium as time in and out of the school day has depleted. In many cases, those fortunate enough for some sectional time during the school day often have sectionals with heterogeneous instrumental groupings or from different ensembles. Many directors teach before and after school hours. Students spend lunch and study hall time practicing and getting assistance from teachers and fellow students.

Academics and the demands for student time outside the school day have changed the landscape of music performance instruction. Some programs are holding rehearsals outside of school time much as it was done in the early part of the 1900's. Still, there are programs that have adequate opportunities to meet with students during and after the school day. There are schools with private lesson teachers incorporated into their program. The profile of student contact across the country varies wildly from state to state and schools within ten miles of each other. Analyzing and providing solutions to this issues goes beyond the spectrum of this book but is worthy of research, proposed solutions, and action.

The topic of scheduling and teaching fundamentals during rehearsal time is a topic unto itself and a research project beyond this book.

Acknowledging the varied restrictions many programs face, the importance of including skill development teaching and materials in your curriculum is critically important. Whether we teach it in full ensemble class, sectionals, private lessons, or outside of school time, the need is always there. In order to reach the Desired Outcomes, method must be taught and assessed.

The following two graphics show a sample of an Assessment Schedule for a freshman percussionist. You will note that the assessments are always comprised of **Compulsories** & **Literature**. The 1st quarter is comprised of Marching Band literature exclusively. Our sample student is a **tenor drum** player. All his literature for 1st quarter is memorized material. His percussion curriculum includes the three primary instruments in percussion – snare drum, marimba, and timpani. Note that these compulsories occur simultaneously to the marching band season. Technique and Etude material supplement his Concert Band assignments. You will note that only certain segments are chosen in his concert literature. These are selected by his director and are the most challenging sections in his part. Finally, you will notice an etude selection for snare, timpani, and marimba during his first year as well as exposure to drum set. Some of the selections are customized to the student's ability level, but most are standard for first-year percussionists.

SAMPLE ASSESSMENT SCHEDULE

1st Quarter Freshman
Percussion

Compulsories	Literature	Due Date
Marching Band Tenor Drum Warm-up	**Tenor Drum** School Song from Memory	Sept 8
Level I - Snare Technique Exercises Number 1,2	**Tenor Drum** Show Opener	22-Sep
Level I - Marimba Technique Exercise 10	**Tenor Drum** Show Drum Solo	Oct 6
Level I - Timpani Etudes Number 1,2,3	**Tenor Drum** Show - 2nd Tune/Closer	Oct 20

SAMPLE ASSESSMENT SCHEDULE
Freshman Year – By Quarter
Percussion

Compulsories

Marching Band -Tenor Drum Warm-up
Due – Sept 9
Level I – Snare Technique Exercises 1, 2
Due - Sept 22
Level I – Marimba Technique Exercise 10
Due - Sept 6
Level I – Timpani Etudes Numbers 1, 2, 3
Due - Oct 20

Literature

Tenor Drum - School Song by Memory
Due – Sept 9
Tenor Drum - Show opener
Due -Sept 22
Tenor Drum - Show – Drum Solo
Due - Sept 6
Tenor Drum -Show – 2nd Tune/Closer
Due - Oct 20

Compulsories

Technique –George Stone Stick Control #4
Due – Nov 3
Snare Study – Ted Reed Syncopation 1-6
Due – Nov 18
Marimba Study- Goldenberg Ex 1
Due - Dec 2
Timpani Study - Goodman Mod Meth #2
Due -Dec 16

Literature

Snare Etude – John Pratt Cadence #4
Due – Nov 3
Perc Ens. – Snare Duet - Letter B to D
Due – Nov 18
Concert Band – Concert Piece #1 – H to end
Due - Dec 2
Concert Band-Concert Piece #4 – 1 to 5
Due - Dec 16

Compulsories

Technique –George Stone Stick Control #14
Due – Jan 12
Snare Study – Ted Reed Syncopation 7-12
Due Jan 26
Marimba Study- Goldenberg Ex 4
Due - Feb 9
Timpani Study - Goodman Mod Meth #5
Due - Feb 23

Literature

Contest Solo –Timpani Salvatore Rabbi
Due – Jan 12
Perc Ens. – Contest Piece - Letter B to D
Due - Jan 26
Concert Band – Concert Piece #2 – Letter G
Due - Feb 9
Concert Band-Concert Piece #3 – A to D
Due - Feb 23

Compulsories

Technique-George Stone – Act &Rebds #4-6
Due – Mar 9
Set Study – Beat Patterns 1 to 10
Due - Mar 23
Marimba Study- Goldenberg Ex 6
Due –Apr 6
Timpani Study - Goodman Mod Meth #7
Due - Apr 30

Literature

Marimba Final – Etude #3 – 2nd Section
Due – Mar 9
Perc Ens. – Recital Piece - Letter A to F
Due - Mar 23
Concert Band – Contest Piece #1 – A to D
Due –Apr 6
Concert Band-Contest Piece #3 – F to end
Due - Apr 30

Steps in Building Compulsory Requirements in Music Performance Classes

1. **Identify components** of your compulsory curriculum (scales, exercises, sight-reading) for every instrument and voice in each ensemble or at each grade level.
2. Draw components from **literature** programmed for the year and add to the compulsory requirements as appropriate.
3. Categorize different **levels of difficulty** to compulsories and assign to either grade levels or ensemble levels.
4. Determine the **number and type** of compulsory assessments each quarter (or semester)
5. Plan appropriate **instructional time** during the school day, outside the school day or in coordination with private teachers to prepare students for assessments.
6. **Schedule** compulsory assessments.

Acquiring Assessment Performances.

In our percussion example, there are 16 separate assessments over the full school year. If your high school program has 20 percussionists the total number of assessments in the percussion section alone would total 320. If you have one band and your winds total 80, you assess 16 times in one year. That would total 1,280 assessments for a grand total of 1600 assessments. **How in the world will you find time to listen to 1600 in one year?**

The first point to make is that you can **only assign a number of assessments that you, your staff and your technology can assess**. Many directors use phone recordings, Dropbox, SmartMusic and other methods to acquire assessments for evaluation. New technology will continue to make these "listen later" methods more efficient and quicker. But here are a few non-technical methods that have been deployed:

1. "Down the row" assessments in full ensemble class (different instruments selected for each day of assessment week).
2. Assess individuals in sectional class.
3. Individual assessments during ensemble performance. An example of this is asking the snare section of your marching band to play through their drum solo assessment as a group while you assess one at a time (5 snares = play 5 times or assess individuals during one play-through as drums are judged.
4. During a "play-through" of the full ensemble ask certain students to perform near your podium. You can easily hear clearly most instruments in this way (flute is an exception). Voices are easily perceived this way. I've assessed two or three of the same part in this manner, and it works well. Also, there is less pressure on the students as the ensemble performs behind them.
5. Quick assessments of individuals at the podium while class is dismissed (good for one or two students). Instrumental classes are often dismissed to pack up prior to the bell. This provides opportunities for short assessments.

Establishing Your Book

All of us spend a good amount of time selecting music for our ensembles. Whether you pour over bins of music, listen to sample recordings or listen to other groups to find literature, it goes without saying that it is an important and ongoing part of our job as directors. Most directors hope to find music that will challenge and yet appeal to students. One should not conflate "appeal" with either "easy" or "popular." It is most educational when appeal comes as students master a piece of music over time, providing them with a lasting memory of their performance in final form. At the same time, well-written arrangements of certain popular or contemporary music can be found and used in our concert repertoire, as well.

There are times when we *do* select music that "plays well" or is easily accessible to student musicians. It can be technically easy to play, and yet substantial and subtle in its expressive demands. This can provide a significant learning experience for students. Music with a lesser degree of technical demands can expose the expressive possibilities to students in a well-written piece of music. Though harmonic and phrasing structures can reveal such works, the end result can often be realized more fully if one listens before buying. The history of music is loaded with compositions and arrangements of a low technical nature and yet very demanding and unveiling from an expressive point of view. Expressive and lyrical music should always be a consideration in your selection process. Directors often look for music that provides ample opportunities to teach either technical or structural concepts to students. Often times, they seek music that will simply meet their programming needs of concerts or contests. They will select music to feature certain sections of their ensemble or even a particularly outstanding soloist.

Finally, the most well-trained directors also understand the importance of certain "required" or "important" literature. Our regional and state organizations point to this material in their required lists and festival choices. Bands, orchestras, and choirs all have a body of work that is considered "important." But it is most important to program music to *your* ensemble. Advanced ensembles will often play works of this significant nature, but directors should never program music beyond the reach of their students because it's "an All-State number."

The above is a partial list of what directors consider when making literature choices for the school year. Good musical and educational considerations should always be the driving force behind your music-choice decisions. Realizing that we do not always spend our summers selecting music for the entire year, or that we often adjust our choices when music is released through the year, it is important to analyze the profile of your "textbook." You should supplement with etudes, exercises and other methods for students that address the curriculum requirements in each ensemble class. Were we simply in schools to perform, this would not be a consideration. Like professional ensembles, we'd leave the training to someone else.

But we are not. We must develop musicians. It is our job to lead student-musicians to good music while, at the same time, select music that can support what they need to develop as musicians over time. In music education, selecting music and educating students are not two different things. The lofty is not possible unless we teach how it is acquired. While some programs have a good percentage of students with the opportunity and financial ability to take private lessons, most do not. But whether your program includes extensive private lessons by certified staff or outside professionals or whether you have no individual contact time with students or very few students taking private lessons, you must make certain that the fundamentals, required techniques are being covered. This often happens from the podium in some schools. But it takes away from the required ensemble development of the group. But ensemble method is moot if the kids can't play anyway so many directors are doing everything required in each class to teach method and ensemble performance. These are true master teachers in my mind. Yes, I am always amazed to hear wonderful groups perform at the end of the year who possess insurmountable challenges with scheduling and routines disruptive to student contact time.

"Your Book," as we have dubbed it, is defined as the body of literature, studies, methods, technical exercise, scales, rudiments and other materials that round out the training of each instrument in the band or orchestra and each voice in choir. Being a tuba, bass-viol major with a third major in percussion. I can give testimony to the "thinness" of many parts for these instruments in music that is otherwise extensive and challenging to the other instruments in band and orchestra. This is particularly true for basses in orchestra, for example. How significant is the percussion experience in your band if you do not supplement it with percussion ensemble, solo work on the three primary percussion instruments (snare, timpani, and keyboard)?

In my years directing band and orchestra, I have always drawn first from the programmed literature for assessments. This requires going through each piece for significant excerpts to be assessed. I have also documented my expectations for each grade level on each instrument. In the case of tuba, bass viol, and percussion, this was a simple process. When it came to the other instruments, I relied on my knowledge from methods classes but more importantly from other directors and private teachers who were trained musicians on instruments other than my own. Each quarter, my students were assessed on method materials germane to their instrument either drawn from the literature we were performing or from our standard "book" of method, etude or technical exercises assigned to their particular instrument. "Your Book" is essentially their textbook for the year. It takes a good amount of work and will change as your ensembles improve. But each year, directors should take student development into consideration when planning for performance and instruction.

Part IX

Student, Ensemble, Program & Professional Growth

Individual, Ensemble and Program Assessment

Student assessment is a major topic of discussion in education today. Though my view is that most of it has had minimal impact on the education of our youth, I find that, in the hands of good teachers, it can add to the quality of our teaching and, hopefully, the degree of learning that occurs as a result. But the task of a music director includes more than simply measuring the progress of individual students as they come and go from our classroom each day. Unlike all other classroom teachers, we must also assess the success of our students in *group performance*. Documented numerical evidence becomes valuable to music directors as they assess specific sections, different ensembles or the entire program.

Individual student progress

Individual progress can be documented by tracking audition scores over time as demonstrated below:

		Frederick Miller - Assessment Record 2011-2014							
		Raw Score	Weighted Score	Raw Score	Weighted Score	Raw Score	Weighted Score	Raw Score	Weighted Score
Prepared	35%	1.2	8.4	1.7	11.9	3.2	20.3	4.1	27.3
Scales	30%	1.3	7.8	2	12	3.4	20.4	4.3	25.8
Sight-Reading	25%	1.2	6	1.6	8	2.9	14.5	3.9	19.5
Written	10%	2	4	2.5	5	3	6	4.5	9
			26.2		36.9	5	61.2		81.6
		Freshman	1.310	Sophomore	1.845	Junior	3.060	Senior	4.080
		Fall 2011		Fall 2012		Fall 2013		Fall 2014	

- Frederick assessed above his grade level at the start of 2011.
- In 2012, he scored lower than the 2.0 required for sophomores.
- At the beginning of his Junior and Senior years, he was on par with his grade level.
- His most significant rate of growth was in the area of Prepared Music.
- His highest level achieved in high school was in Sight Reading 3.0.
- He grew a total of 2.8 in Prepared Music and 2.9 in Scales.
- His musical understanding, assessed on written exams, rose 2.5 in four years.
- Frederick advanced to the Symphonic Strings his junior year.
- Frederick's chair level dropped his Senior year as more students in his section scored above his score of 4.080.

Section Assessment

The chart below demonstrates the growth pattern of each instrument in the string program over an eight-year period. The number is calculated by simply averaging the scores of all instruments by section following the fall assessment. Spring assessments can be added, as well.

		2009	2010	2011	2012	2013	2014	2015	2016
Violins	35%	1.2	1.5	1.7	2.1	2.2	2.3	2.8	2.9
Violas	30%	1.1	1.3	1.6	1.7	2.1	2.4	2.6	2.6
Cellos	25%	1.3	1.8	1.8	2.1	2.4	2.3	2.8	3.0
Basses	10%	1.4	1.7	2.5	2.3	2.7	2.5	2.7	3.2

- The best year for all instruments was in **2016.**
- Basses assessed higher than any section over an eight-year period at 3.2.
- The **viola** section showed slow growth for the first four years until the arrival of strong freshmen over a four-year period raised their average to 2.6 in 2016.
- Being the largest section in the orchestra, the **violins** grew less rapidly and, overall, at a slower rate than other sections. This was due to a large influx of freshmen violinists each year that were at or below high school level of 1.0.
- After four years, the **cellos** had a consistent average in the 2.1 to 2.8 range culminating in the only other 3.0 average in addition to the basses.

By averaging all string players, directors can track the overall progress of each ensemble in their program as follows:

Program Assessment

Most directors have an intuitive sense of the quality of their ensemble. As the saying goes, "we know how our kids play." But measuring actual performance levels adds *Analysis* to your *Impression* and allows you to use *Comparison* over time. It also presents strong evidence that administrators can relate to – providing additional support for

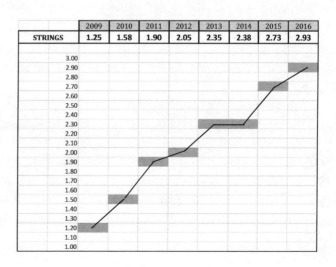

Resetting year-to-year Standards

No one becomes a director in a new school simply to maintain the status quo. We all go into new endeavors with the desire to make things better - which means making better music. We understand that "getting better" is all about the literature our ensembles perform year-to-year. Ironic, is it not, that the most important outcome to us is invisible to most administrators, audiences, community, and most parents.

Can you picture the morning bunch at the local café in town having breakfast and someone pipes up and says, "Wow, did you hear that the wind ensemble at the high school played Hindemith Saturday night?" Humorous, I admit. But most of those around us would not know "Symphonic Metamorphosis" from "Emperata Overture" - nor should they. Yet, the music we choose to play is our most significant decision each year. Few teachers or curriculum committees in other subject areas select a new textbook each year. If we're doing our job correctly, we must do so. Choosing the material for our classroom has been left up to us for as long as we have existed in the public school.

All other subjects teach and assess individual students. They "teach the class" so the "individual learns." In music performance, we "teach the individual" so the "class learns." We have "Desired Outcomes" for <u>each student</u> but also have "Desired Outcomes" for the <u>entire class</u> (ensemble). There are, in fact, lessons we teach the class that are separate and distinct from those we teach the individual student. If we know we have a responsibility to teach and assess each student, then we must also understand that it is our responsibility to teach and assess those things unique to the ensemble. The proposed assessment system provides a means to student, ensemble *and* program assessment.

<u>Student Growth</u> is an important component of individual learning. It follows, then, that <u>Ensemble Growth</u> is also an important component of group learning. We are the only discipline in schools that "teaches individuals" so the "class learns." In other classes, the method is to "teacher the class" so the "individuals learn." We must, in fact, do both. It follows, then, that it is not enough for students to simply increase their ranking each year on music that is of the same content, depth, and demand. It is important that directors select music that is always "a step ahead" of the ability of their groups so that <u>Ensemble Growth</u> is realized.

Music directors must set growth targets for *Ensemble Growth* with the music they select. These targets are best realized when planned two, three or four years out, but they should also be revised based on annualized assessments of your students. We all know there is no end to the musical journey. Your ensembles, as well as your students, should take significant steps each year if growth is to be realized each year. This means that literature, training materials, and audition materials should change to reflect the growth of your program each year

Personal Assessment

How good of a musician are you?

I know of no music director that has not asked that question at some point in their musical life. A good number ask it many times over in their career. In the beginning, music is just fun. But once we acquire even a fundamental level of proficiency, we listen and observe the music and musicians around us – *and* - we take inventory of what we can do and what we cannot do, what we understand and what we do not, and what we might do about it. These moments of self-reflection are different for everyone. I have met young students obsessed with the question and others than never consider it. Some just enjoy what they do and are not driven to do more than what comes to them. They don't ask the question much. I've met other students that seldom ask it because they played better than those around them. I believe most music directors do ask the question.

I used to believe that I knew a lot more than I did. I also recall my days as a young musician, and later a director, when I felt music could be achieved, much like fixing a clock, mowing the lawn or winning at chess. I was also independent (friends of mine might use another word) enough to think I could "achieve" by figuring it out on my own. Upon reflection, the one thing I would do differently were I a young twenty-five-year-old director again would be to ask more questions. Fortunately, I had enough friends to turn me around when I ran into a brick wall.

But once we realize that musical achievement is fleeting, that the depth of expression is endless, that meaning in music takes a lifetime to grasp, that a composer knows much more than we perceive, that demand is not the same for everyone, and that "there is always someone better," we understand the endless pursuit that is music. As we have stated previously, we believe that all assessments must be done "through the prism of a director's background and experience." It is for this reason that a director's personal growth is so vital to the process of teaching and assessing student musicians. Though I did not ask as many questions of others as I could have in my youth, I asked an endless amount of myself. Reflection has *always* been part of my performance and teaching life. I first learned how little I knew when I began my training with the Central States Judges Association, in 1977. In undergraduate school and even graduate school, I was one to question and debate more than listen and learn. But such is youth.

Part of the reason we don't reflect upon our work enough is that it is nonstop! The build-up and ultimate performance occur so regularly at times that there is little time to reflect before the next performance is at hand. During my teaching years, my summers were the time when I could analyze the previous year and plan for the next. It was in business that I learned to ask questions. Fortunately, for me, I had tremendous mentors that were more than willing to guide me and answer my questions.

- If your program grows, it is because of your diligence. If your program is growing, you must maintain your diligence.
- If your program is growing it is because of your passion. If your program is growing, you must maintain your passion.
- If your program is growing it is because of the musical experience you are providing students. If your program is growing, you must continue to provide a good musical experience.

Though the statements sound like double-talk, they are not. Determination, passion and the musical experience are contagious and inspiring. As educators, we are fortunate to be working with young people who can be convinced, inspired and impacted by you and the music they play. This places a large responsibility on all directors and requires that they continue to grow as musicians and revitalize themselves each year.

This is not always easy. The conditions of your teaching environment, your school system and other requirements that come with the education profession can all have an effect on what you do. Some districts provide more than adequate support for the needs of music performance classes, and others create dismal situations for directors attempting to set and maintain a standard of performance for their student ensembles. How you deal with the negative elements of your job, assess the trajectory of your career and measure your satisfaction with is something only you can assess. But, in the end, you must be happy, motivated and inspired to teach, or students will recognize your either lack of zeal and or your overwhelming determination to make them better musicians and better people.

Just as performance comes easier to some than to others, so does teaching, directing and managing. I've observed many different music directors in my time. Some bemoan their situation while others love what they do every day. I can honestly say that of all the wonderful people I have met in the music education business in my lifetime, many more are inspired than despondent. Furthermore, there is little connection between a person's view of their job and the conditions that surround them, be they glorious or abhorrent. Regardless of any of the factors discussed above, it goes without saying that to be a superior teacher and evaluator of students you must seek to learn and assess yourself. Essentially, you must "walk the walk" and "talk the talk."

As most of us know, even the most proficient evaluation performed by your administrator merely skims over the hundreds of things you must consider when assessing your own performance. Self-assessment should occur after performances, lessons, semesters, contests, and any time you engage your job. In business, I learned the importance the CEOs place on balance in their professional and personal lives. This too must be part of your considerations. You will not always remember or have time to reflect. But make it a part of your profession. The good ones I've met always do. And, they ask questions...their entire career.

Part X

Single District, Unit District & Custom Applications

Prelude to Part X

Part X begins with a detailed discussion of how Standards and Linear Scales are put to use in school music-performance programs. This section also explains how standards are set when a director enters a new school for the first time and contains valuable information for first-year teachers. Sections two and three present two case studies where Impression-Analysis-Comparison and their relative Linear Scale are used in different situations. Case Study #1 involves orchestra. Case Study #2 involves band. The studies demonstrate how the system can be used for auditions, ensemble placement, ensemble seating, formative assessments, summative assessments and grading, in different ensembles, different school systems and using different standards.

Ranking and grading using the Grade Level Method

Case Study # 1 *Ranking and grading using the **Grade Level Method***
This model examines the use of the Linear Scale in Orchestra at a single high school district in Illinois. In this case, **4** high school grade levels are superimposed over the standard Linear Scale.

The director's musical standards and program standards, established over the history of the program, are used to evaluate. All five (5) ranges of the linear scale are used for both auditions and assessments. For auditions, seventy-five string players are ranked as one group. There is a single breakpoint that separates an upper-level string ensemble from the developing string ensemble. The same scale is used for formative and summative assessments with no impact on ensemble placement during the year. Seating changing within ensembles is at the prerogative of the director. There is no challenge system.

Ranking and grading using the Ensemble Level Method

Case Study # 2 *Ranking and grading using the **Ensemble Level Method***
This model examines the use of the Linear Scale in Band at a unified school district in Texas. In this case, **8** ensembles (four in the high school and four in the middle school) are superimposed over the scale.

Directors' musical standards and program standards required for entry into one of four wind ensembles at the high school and four at the middle school are used to evaluate. The five ranges of the linear scale are subdivided to create ten levels of performance from beginner to collegiate and profession levels of achievement. There are eight (8) breakpoints in the scale that correlate to entry one of eight ensembles across the school district. Though middle school and high school ensembles are separated, the same 10-level scale is used to unify the system.

Establishing Standards and Linear Scales

Establishing a System

Upon my arrival at Bradley-Bourbonnais Community High School in 2011, I had no knowledge of the performance ability of the orchestra, nor did I have any first-hand knowledge of the performance level of a single student. As I had done in my previous positions, I sought the answer to the most important question all first year or experienced directors ask when entering a new school. **"How do these kids play?**

As young directors, we all recognized the success of the more experienced directors in our field, but we were much less adept at determining how success had been achieved by the pros around us. If we were smart, we asked a lot of questions of our mentors and learned. Nonetheless, all directors, coaches, and quality teachers ask the same question when starting a new job, "How good *are* these kids?"

Sports, music, business and all "doing" activities must ask this question. Regardless of their objective, they also must know where to start. More to the point, they must know with whom they are staring. In business, every supervisor, manager, senior manager and CEO asks the very same question. I asked the question each time I took on additional management responsibilities, and I always asked it during my teaching career. Good leaders must have high standards and goals. But they must start with understanding what their players, students, or employees know how to do.

What distinguishes successful leaders from the mediocre is:

1) They understand ***where they'd like to be.***
2) They do an honest and valid assessment of ***where they are currently.***
3) They ***create a plan*** to get to their goal, and
4) They create a system to ***regularly measure*** how they are progressing.

Therefore, having a vision of where the BBCHS Orchestra program could be someday, I set out to do a complete assessment of each student, when I arrived on Day One.

Three possible standards could be used to rank and rate my new string students.

1) My **Musical Standard** established through my background and experience.

2) My **High School Standard** acquired from all the previous orchestras I had heard, judged or conducted at the high school level.

3) The **Program Standard** for Bradley-Bourbonnais Community High School.

Musical Standard

I certainly possess a musical standard after some fifty years of music making. One's *Musical Standard* is always present. It is our foundation - vested in our background and experience. It's our intuitive sense of quality. And it's the standard against which we make all musical decisions. But it is also somewhat like a view from 30,000 feet. It would give me information about my program in the grand scheme of things, but it would not provide me with much *relevant information* about my 58 string players who were about to audition.

Would it matter if my violinists were placed on a scale with the finest violinist I had ever heard on the far right and the fledgling first-year Suzuki student on the far left? Hardly. The Linear Scale that represents my broad *Musical Standard* would provide little distinction for me. While my *Musical Standard* was available and established, it would not be the best standard to use when auditioning my BBCHS string players for the first time. It might be interesting to see where my top and bottom violinists placed on such a scale but I would learn more about each student's ability if I narrowed my view.

High School Standard

I knew that most of my students would fall somewhere on a Linear Scale of all high school string players I had heard to date. I had a keen sense of that standard and decided it was the only logical standard to use in my *initial* assessment of the BBCHS string program. Where would my new students fall on that high school Linear Scale? Might someone fall below my standard for high school violinists, for example? If they did, they would become my new low standard for high school violinists. Might I find a "diamond in the rough" and be treated to an audition that surpassed any I'd heard in my years teaching? Perhaps. Nonetheless, I would take my *High School Standard* into that first audition.

The Chart below shows how my *High School Standard* for string playing correlated to my *Musical Standard* when I arrived at Bradley-Bourbonnais Community High School.

		Musical Standard			
Poor	Fair	Good	Excellent	Superior	
		High School Standard			
	Poor	Fair	Good	Excellent	Superior

Keep in mind that this is not a comparison of high school orchestras to professional orchestras. It is a scale representing the range of achievement by high school student-musicians I've heard, aligned with the scale of achievement that represents all music and musicians I've heard over a fifty year period.

The Program Standard

We all understand what it means to "set a standard." Setting standards refers to setting minimum requirements. Your decision to include a student in your top orchestra, for example, is based on the minimum standard you set for entry into that ensemble. Directors understand that the playing ability of their students is a major factor in determining the music they select for those students. They also understand that selecting students for certain ensembles is based on the music they *plan* to perform.

A band program will have standards for their primary concert ensembles, another for their jazz band, and a third for their marching band. Choir programs will set different standards for their men's choir, their jazz choir, their freshman girls' choir, and their advanced mixed choir. Within each program, standards are set for specific ensembles at varying levels and playing a variety of styles of music.

But, "setting a standard" is very different from "having a standard." Having a standard means that you have a "sense of quality." You know what your "best" is and what your "worst" is. You understand the distance between the two. You understand the factors that create that distance (criteria based on inherent qualities). When you hear a performance, you quickly have a sense of whether that performance comes close to your "best" or "worst." With experience, you can narrow that location further to a specific location on your Linear Scale. By using Impression-Analysis-Comparison, you can delineate between even the most subtle differences in ability between one performance and the next.

The distinction is this. In order to "set a standard," you must "have a standard." The standard you have for your program is rooted in your <u>Musical Standard</u>. It is framed by your <u>High School Standard</u>. And, it is set in the <u>context of your school program</u> and what your students have been able to achieve under your direction. This is your <u>Program Standard</u>. My use of the term <u>Program Standard</u> is not the same as program evaluation, used in the classic sense by people like Richard Cowell and others. Program evaluation relates to the overall conditions, status, and prospectus of your music program. A <u>Program Standard</u>, in the context of evaluation, is the range of achievement established by your students over time. It is used in conjunction with a Linear Scale, to demark the performance of individual students in auditions and assessments during the school year.

A <u>Program Standard</u> is not static. In fact, it should grow each year if you are doing a good job of teaching. We all have those years when our students raise the standard previously set by students before them. This is a wonderful thing. Even though our goal is always to be better each year, we know that there are good years and bad. We have years where certain sections are stellar and other years when those same sections are less than desired. But no matter what kind of year you face, the <u>Program Standard</u> does not retreat. Your "best" and "worst" is always present whether it was discovered this year or seven years previous.

If you have taught at the same school for eight years, your standards have been established over time. The best cello you ever had. The best horn player you ever had. The weakest bassists ever to grace your concert hall. They all fold into your *Program Standard*.

You set your *Program Standard* the first time you audition your students. Conducting a comprehensive audition of all students is the best and quickest way to establish your *Program Standard.* What you chose to assess is your decision. The materials you select, however, should give you the adequate evidence you need to choose music for the year and the Desired Outcomes you have for each instrument or voice. You should have different materials that explore the unique challenges of each instrument or voice range.

The *High School Standard* has a position on the Linear Scale that represents a portion of my *Musical Standard.* Following an initial audition, my *Program Standard* now has a defined position on the Linear Scale aligned with a portion of my *High School Standard*. The chart below demonstrates a possible correlation between these three standards.

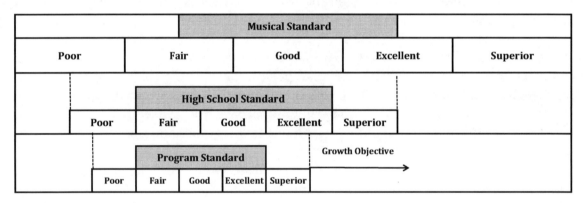

The Gradient Scale

It strikes me that all directors possess a standard that increases as students move from one year in school to another. In other words, we all have a sense, I believe, of our standard for what a freshmen student should be able to do on a particular instrument, what a sophomore should be able to do, and so on. How many times have we heard a director rave about a particular student's performance and conclude by saying, "And, she's only a sophomore!" Coaches do this all the time, as well. Experienced directors, in fact, have an intuitive standard for school musicians – relative to the student's year in school.

When I came to Bradley-Bourbonnais Community High School in 2011 as the new orchestra director, I knew that all my string students at BBCHS came from the same middle school and few had private lessons. I also knew that few of the high school students took private lessons. So, it struck me that lacking any extraordinary "accelerants" like private lessons or other intense individual help in the classroom, the high school students would likely come close to ranking in order relative to their grade level.

The preliminary research I did on conditions prior to my arrival indicated to me that in general, individualized instruction and technique development was lacking for about five years or more. When I examined the literature performed over that same time period, the level of difficulty did not increase significantly. This was an indication to me that whatever increase there was in student ability it had a strong correlation to the number of years students were in orchestra class. I also noticed a higher than normal drop off of upperclassmen students which can indicate attrition caused by musical boredom. Like many high school orchestras, our orchestra was comprised of motivated and academically successful students. Most music students come to us voluntarily so this is expected. I know one thing about most high school students. If they don't get better at what they do, they can lose interest.

With this in mind, I deployed what I called a *Gradient Scale*. The *Gradient Scale* simply aligns four ranges of achievement on a Linear Scale with the four grade levels in either high school or grade school. The *Gradient Scale* is not a standard in its truest form but is, in fact, part of, and dependent on, the standard for student musicians drawn from college, high school or middle school standards. It is simply a relabeling of the four achievement levels as grade levels. In high school, freshman through senior is used. In elementary and middle school 5th grade through 8th grade is used.

High School Gradient Scale

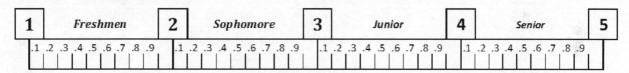

Elementary/Middle School Gradient Scale

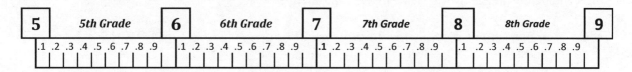

As we've discussed, our *Musical Standard* is fine-tuned and intuitive. But for the average person, a music teacher's grade issued to a student-musician is often considered, in many cases, "opinion." Many administrators without a music background also have the same notion of how grades are issued in music performance classes. Indeed, music directors will sometimes express their opinion of a musical performance with the phrase, "I just like them better than the previous group." As musicians, we understand what's behind that statement, but it has different connotations to the non-musician.

The *Linear Scale* provides directors with a means to delineate their assessment decisions better. But the *Gradient Scale* expresses results in ways that students, parents, and administrators understand better. In this day of accountability stating our opinion is not an effective way to communicate how we assess. We need to communicate with some specificity on grades.

You will note that in addition to demarking the four primary divisions by year, the Gradient Scale also identifies the months within each school year. This was done to reflect not only the year-to-year standard but also a month-to-month standard.

Each grade level is quantified with a numerical value that represents both the year and month of a student's ability. In the high school scale, the number "**1**" indicates freshman level, "**2**" equals sophomore level...and so on. Furthermore, each year is divided into ten months with use of the decimal point, as follows:

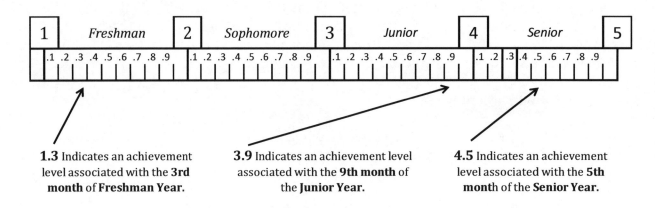

1.3 Indicates an achievement level associated with the **3rd month** of **Freshman Year**.

3.9 Indicates an achievement level associated with the **9th month** of the **Junior Year**.

4.5 Indicates an achievement level associated with the **5th month** of the **Senior Year**.

Some of the elements of this system are as follows:

1. It brings **more distinction** to your grading procedure beyond the five letter grades (A,B,C,D,F).

2. It reveals a student's ranking **relative to other students** at their grade level.

3. It **adds clarity** to student achievement levels beyond number or alpha grading.

4. It helps to **remove the "mystery"** from the grading process for students, parents, and administrators.

5. It creates a **specific numerical ranking** of students for the purposes of ensemble assignment and seating.

Since assessments are drawn from music being played in large ensemble, as well as, exercises, scales and knowledge tests (written) associated with that literature, assessment materials would naturally increase in demand as your literature intensifies. Audition materials should be upgraded as the quality of your ensemble increases, and the high-end demand should exceed the current ability of your top players to stimulate and account for musical growth. Since not all students achieve at the maximum, audition and assessment materials should be graduated to reflect the ability level of students in the same grade level. Therefore, four demand-levels of audition material are used in my audition system.

The rationale in establishing four levels of audition material has to do with the fact that band, orchestra, and choir are really four-year courses and all students at each level are participating in the same class (though they may be in different ensembles year-to-year). Though we know there will be exceptions, freshman students auditioning on senior-level material would provide us with little evidence of their relative ability or distinction from others within their grade level or playing ability. Many would look at the senior-level audition material and state, "I can't play that."

The <u>Gradient Scale</u> does not infer that freshmen are only assessed on Level I material. Nor does it infer that juniors are assessing on Level III materials exclusively. The <u>Gradient Scale</u> rates students anywhere on the scale, **regardless of their year in school.** Furthermore, the audition requires that *all* students begin their audition on Level I (freshman level) and work their way up. The proximity of a student's numerical rating to their actual month and year in school generates a grade for any given assessment. Auditions, if graded, can also be done in this way.

Freshmen in their fourth month of freshman year should be performing at a "fourth month-freshman year" level. Students who assessed at their "Grade-Month Level" or above would be doing "A-level" work. Students that fall behind the grade level would receive corresponding "B," "C," "D" or "F-level" work for their assessments and auditions using this system. A score of 1.8 in an assessment by a freshman student in their 8th month (April) would indicate that he or she was "on track" with the minimum standards set by the program. This would constitute "A" work. From there a deviation of "2" points left of 1.8 would equate to a "B." "4" points a "C" and so on.

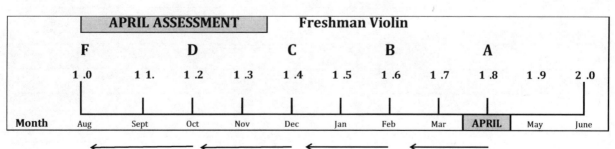

The next logical question becomes:

"How are music achievement levels assigned to these grade levels?"

Key to establishing a grade-level standard for the ensemble is to have data from previous school years. Only the data collected by a director can establish his or her standard going forward. Naturally, when a director has no previous data in their first year in a new position, they must first establish their *Program Standard* by assessing their students. Once completed, the range and profile of the initial audition can be used to assign grade levels to the four ranges of achievement present.

The *Program Standard* will become fully established once the new director has cycled through four years. Remember that the *Program Standard* is a result of assessments by a specific director or staff. Once an ensemble is comprised of students who have played exclusively under the same director or staff using the same system for four years, the *Program Standard* is well established. What is important in the *first year*, however, is to establish the very *concept* of a standard against which all performance achievement will be measured.

As I approached the first audition, I considered how the *Gradient Scale*, (4 ranges), could align with the *Program Standard* (5 ranges). I knew that there would be some students who would not play up to my *High School Standard* on that first audition. I also wanted to account for any advanced students who may score some distance from the pack – the "diamond in the rough." While my *Program Standard* is a range of performances from the weakest to the strongest it is also important to recognize performances that are **significantly distant** from the norm – either on the low end of the high end.

I could provide for those extreme performances by utilizing a ½ range on both ends to place students on the scale and bring an additional perspective (more distinction) to my top and bottom student's abilities. The result was a scale constructed as follows:

FOUR RANGE ASSESSMENT SCALE
(½ range below standard ~ ½ range above standard)

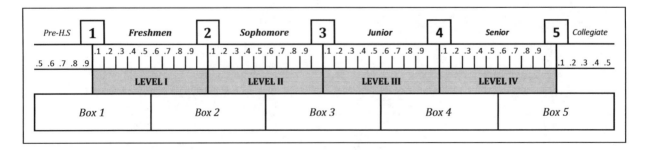

A **half range below** the freshmen year is designed to capture string performance achievement that falls below the minimum standard established for entering freshman string players at BBCHS. A **half range above** the senior year is designated to capture string performance achievement that exceeds and sets a new standard for senior string players at BBCHS.

One question you may ask is how only a ½ range could accommodate the two extremes on this scale. The matter of "the number," again, becomes irrelevant (remember our discussion about the range being more important than the number). In both cases, students falling above or below the *Gradient Scale* would be assessed using a *"Customized Standard."* This standard is used to chart individual student progress both on the low and high end.

The Customized Standard

The *Customized Standard* is used to measure individual growth of a student who is either below the minimum *High School Standard* or beyond it. (note: this applies to Middle School, as well) Again, armed with one's acceptable minimum standard for high school freshman violinists, a director can identify students who are significantly below that level. They then customize a program to get those students to the required grade level within a prescribed period of time. An accelerated instructional plan, with increased one-on-one contact, can bring students up to their grade level.

This chart on the next page shows student **Robert Jones'** plan to improve at a rate double the norm of a freshman violinist. Although the *Program Scale* for high school is expressed as whole numbers of 1-4 for freshman through senior, the number "9" is used for freshman year in this example. This adds clarity to the transition from 8th grade to 9th grade in this case. The same *Customized Standard* could be fashioned for any student who falls significantly behind the standard set for his grade level – i.e., 9th to 10th, 11th to 12th.

	Accelerated instuction →		
	8.2 8.4 8.6 8.8 9.0 9.2 9.4 9.6	9.8	9.9
Normal Freshman	9.0 9.1 9.2 9.3 9.4 9.5 9.6 9.7	9.8	9.9 10 .1 .2 .3 .4 .5 .6 .7 .8 .9
Robert Jones Audtion 8.2			
8.2 .3 .4 .5 .6 .7 .8 .9			
	FRESHMAN		**SOPHOMORE**

On the scale above, you will note that incoming freshman **Robert Jones** was assessed at an **8.2** achievement level (8th grade, 2nd month). He had started violin late in 7th grade and did not have sufficient remedial teaching in 8th grade. Robert would be allowed to enroll in freshman orchestra under the provision that he agree to the extra instruction. His *Customized Scale* was designed to "double" the amount of learning required in one year to get caught up to his peers by the end of freshman year. This individualized instruction model included an agreement between Robert, his parents, and the director.

Roberts Jones had significant issues with his sound due to an incorrect bow grip that caused "sliding" of the bow up and down the strings. He also had an excessive and constant "tilt" of the bow. Consequently, he had significant tonal issues. His bow speed never varied, and he seldom used the entire bow. He played the "G scale" one octave only and had significant pitch issues due to finger placement and improper "grip" on the violin neck. This was caused by his not having a shoulder pad during middle school allowing the chin to maintain a proper hold on the violin. These technical issues, along with an irregular pulse and note reading difficulty, would make it difficult to perform first-year freshman music.

Though he was allowed to enroll in freshman orchestra, he would be given remedial help with private lessons from his director and a student mentor from the upper orchestra. He would be assessed on the remedial materials exclusively but gradually assess on the same excerpts from the orchestra repertoire.

Remedial Migration from *Training* to *Concert Orchestra Literature*

Robert was assessed both on the concert music being performed by the orchestra and his remedial materials. His grade for orchestra class was 100% based on assignments from his remedial plan at the beginning of the school year. As he improved, his assessments comprised of a percentage of concert material used to assess all students in freshman orchestra along with his remedial materials.

Assessment Literature								Robert Jones - Freshman Violin			
Norm	9.0	9.1	9.2	9.3	9.4	9.5	9.6	9.7	9.8	9.9	10
Month	Aug	Sept	Oct	Nov	Dec	Jan	Feb	Mar	April	May	June
				REMEDIAL MATERIALS							
								PERFORMANCE LITERATURE			
	100/0	90/10	80/20	70/30	60/40	50/50	40/60	30/70	20/80	10/90	0/100

When designing a customized lesson plan you need to consider what portion (percentage) of the student's assessment will be based on their customized skill development materials and what percentage based on programmed music the ensemble is playing. This can vary month-to-month, but students should be assigned excerpts from the full ensemble that they can play. This is important because it keeps the student engaged in the orchestra and reminds them that the goal is to play at their grade level.

It has been my practice to schedule assessments following *each* concert. I assign excerpts well in advance. They are comprised of the more challenging part for each instrument. By adding the assessment the week following the concert, I add an additional incentive for the kids to practice prior to the concert on the material that is the most demanding.

But remedial assessments should occur monthly. On months when there are no *concert assessments*, the remedial assessment is 100% of their grade. In months where a concert is scheduled you assess excerpts from the concert material, the student can play. You then determine the weight of the two assessments as you see fit.

The assessment schedule for **Robert Jones** is below. Grading in this school is done quarterly.

	\multicolumn{6}{c}{Customized Assessment Schedule}						
							\multicolumn{5}{c}{Literature and Skill Development}				
1	100/0	90/10	80/20	70/30	60/40	50/50	40/60	30/70	20/80	10/90	0/100
2	Aug	Sept	Oct	Nov	Dec	Jan	Feb	Mar	April	May	June
3	\multicolumn{3}{c}{1st Quarter}			\multicolumn{3}{c}{2nd Quarter}			\multicolumn{3}{c}{3rd Quarter}			\multicolumn{3}{c}{4th Quarter}		
4	Audition		Concert		Concert		Concert	Solo & Ens	Contest	Concert	Audition
5	0%		20&		40%		60%	70%	80%	90%	100%
6		100%	80%	100%	60%	100%	40%	30%	20%	10%	0%
7	Assess	Skills 1	Skills 2	Skills 3	Skills 4	Skills 5	Skills6	Skills 7	Skills 8	Skills 9	Skills 10

Line 1 shows the percentage of the music mix for each monthly assessment.

Line 2 shows the months of the school year.

Line 3 shows the grading periods – in this case quarterly.

Line 4 shows scheduled performances including auditions, concerts and solo & ensemble contest, and full orchestra contest.

Line 5 shows the percentage (%) of each assessment based on Concert music being played by the orchestra. Note how this percentage increases through the year and becomes 100% of the assessment by year's end.

Line 6 shows the percentage (%) of each assessment based on the remedial music assigned to the student. Note how this percentage decreases through the year and becomes 0% by year's end.

Line 7 shows the remedial music being assessed each month. Note that the audition is held in August, so no assessment is issued. The audition at the end of the year, which determines seating for the following year, *is* assessed and a grade is issued.

Grading on the Customized Scale

You will recall the scale presented earlier that showed how grades are calculated using the Linear Chart. In the case of the Customized Scale, the same basic technique is used, but in the case of the Customized Scale, the grade level that determines an "A" will change each month.

	GRADING BY DEVIATION					April Assessment					
	F		D			C		B		A	
	1.0	1.1	1.2	1.3	1.4	1.5	1.6	1.7	1.8	1.9	2.0
Month	Aug	Sept	Oct	Nov	Dec	Jan	Feb	Mar	Apr	May	June

In the case of Robert Jones, his grade used the Deviation Method also. The difference is that his "A" is not determined by his year in school but his month target.

The two charts below show how **Robert Jones'** grading scale adjusts to the progress he is making as the school year ensues. In January, you can see that "Normal Freshman" level for the 5th month of the 9th grade is **9.5**. Since **Robert** is working to catch up to his grade level, his target level to receive an "A" is a **9.2**. Robert has been making progress on his customized accelerated instructional plan and is only 2 points away from being grade using the norm for freshmen students.

Customized Grade Scale in **January**

Customized Grade Scale	Aug	Sep	Oct	Nov	Dec	Jan	Feb	Mar	Apr	May
Normal Freshman	9.0	9.1	9.2	9.3	9.4	9.5	9.6	9.7	9.8	9.9
Robert Jones Assessment	8.2	8.4	8.6	8.8	9.0	9.2	9.4	9.6	9.8	9.9
			"F"	"D"	"C"	"B"	"A"			

As you can see, Robert will be at the norm by April and will need to score a **9.8** to receive an "A"

Customized Grade Scale in **April**

Customized Grade Scale	Aug	Sep	Oct	Nov	Dec	Jan	Feb	Mar	Apr	May
Normal Freshman	9.0	9.1	9.2	9.3	9.4	9.5	9.6	9.7	9.8	9.9
Robert Jones Assessment	8.2	8.4	8.6	8.8	9.0	9.2	9.4	9.6	9.8	9.9
					"F"	"D"	"C"	"B"	"A"	

The complete grading scheme for **Robert Jones** is below. It shows the <u>required levels</u> across the top, <u>achieved levels</u> down the left and the resulting <u>deviated grade scale</u>.

		Customized Grade Scale				*Robert Jones* - Freshman Violin						
	Norm	9.0	9.1	9.2	9.3	9.4	9.5	9.6	9.7	9.8	9.9	10
	Month	Aug	Sept	Oct	Nov	Dec	Jan	Feb	Mar	April	May	June
Required →		8.2	8.3	8.5	8.7	8.9	9.1	9.3	9.5	9.7	9.9	10
Achieved	8.2	A	A-	B	B-	C	C-	D	D-	F	F	F
	8.3		A	A-	B	B-	C	C-	D	D-	F	F
	8.4		A	A-	B	B-	C	C-	D	D-	F	F
	8.5			A	A-	B	B-	C	C-	D	D-	F
	8.6			A	A-	B	B-	C	C-	D	D-	F
	8.7				A	A-	B	B-	C	C-	D	D-
	8.8				A	A-	B	B-	C	C-	D	D-
	8.9					A	A-	B	B-	C	C-	D
	9.0					A	A-	B	B-	C	C-	D
	9.1						A	A-	B	B-	C	C-
	9.2						A	A-	B	B-	C	C-
	9.3							A	A-	B	B-	C
	9.4							A	A-	B	B-	C
	9.5								A	A-	B	B-
	9.6								A	A-	B	B-
	9.7									A	A-	B
	9.8									A	A-	B
	9.9										A	A-
	10.0										A	A-

The <u>Customized Scale</u> is used on the high-end also. As your program grows and improves, individual students will "lead the way," establish higher standards of performance within your program and "raise the bar" for all others in their section. But these students should not be used simply as "pace cars." Too often, the development of advanced and motivated students is ignored. These students must also grow musically. For some advanced students, the <u>Program Standard</u> does not sufficiently challenge a student who is performing at a level well beyond your ensemble literature. Avoiding the needs of these students creates the risk that they will feel unchallenged, will fail short of their capabilities, and become bored.

Educators should always be focused on student growth. If using your <u>Program Standard</u> for these advanced students fails to present opportunities to grow and denies them advanced musical experiences, you should utilize advanced literature, technical studies, and performing opportunities in addition to the music being performed by your large ensemble group. In addition, the material used for assessments should be enhanced. The <u>Gradient Standard</u>, which is applied to the majority of your students, does not apply to the highly advanced student. In this case, a <u>Customized Standard</u> and its accompanied <u>Customized Scale</u> is used. The requirements to receive an "A" under the <u>Customized Standard</u> are higher than that of the <u>Program Standard</u>, in this case.

Assessment is used to measure desired outcomes which mean music performance outcomes. Establishing a Customize Standard for these students and using a Customized Scale to determine their grade, maintains a valid system of measurement for students that perform beyond your ensemble or beyond a student's grade level.

If a student advances easily through the standard audition material, directors should present advanced material to the student to determine how far a student is beyond the _Program Standard_ or Grade Level. The additional assessment can be performed at the same time as the first audition or at a later date which may provide you more time.

When a student is performing significantly beyond their grade level, the standard used to assess them should be set higher. What determines their grade is a mix of the literature, etudes, or technical studies being used to assess other students and advanced material designed to provide for growth in the student's abilities.

The _Customized Scale_ is for high-end performers and is used in a minority of cases. It represents a _Customized Standard_ established for the advanced student who performs well beyond the standard set for either the student's grade level or beyond the high level of the ensemble of which they are a member.

Naturally, if there are two or more major ensembles in your program, students can audition up to a high-level ensemble. But programs with one ensemble or even two can limit an advanced student's ability to grow if limited to the literature being performed by your band, orchestra or choir. The need for a _Customized Standard_ for certain advanced students applies primarily to programs that are still developing. High school programs whose standards align with the _High School Standard_ present in the United States will have less need for the _Customized Standard_

Mary Erickson FRESHMAN Audition

Below	1	2	3	4	5	Above
.5 .6 .7 .8 .9	.1 .2 .3 .4 .5 .6 .7 .8 .9	.1 .2 .3 .4 .5 .6 .7 .8 .9	.1 .2 .3 .4 .5 .6 .7 .8 .9	.1 .2 .3 .4 .5 .6 .7 .8 .9	.1 .2 .3 .4 .5 .6 .7 .8 .9	.1 .2 .3 .4 .5
	FRESHMAN Level	SOPHOMORE Level	JUNIOR Level	SENIOR Level	Above	

Mary's Customized Standard

	.5 .6 .7 .8 .9
Symphonic Orchestra Literature	20%
Advanced Music and Skill Development	80%
Enhanced Instruction & Performing Opporutnities	

Mary Erickson's Customized Orchestra Experience

	MARY - Year One	MARY - Year Two	MARY - Year Three	MARY - Year Four	
	.1 .2 .3 .4 .5 .6 .7 .8 .9	.1 .2 .3 .4 .5 .6 .7 .8 .9	.1 .2 .3 .4 .5 .6 .7 .8 .9	.1 .2 .3 .4 .5 .6 .7 .8 .9	.1 .2 .3 .4 .5
	Orchestra Assessments	Orchestra Assessments	Orchestra Assessements	Orchestra Assessments	
	Customized Assesssments	Customized Assessments	Customized Assessments	Customized Assessments	
	Solos, String Quarter, IMEA District Auditions, State Solo & Ensemble Contest, Honors Recital Private Lessons, All-Area Youth Symphony, Summar Orchestra Camp, University Auditions				

The figure above demonstrates how a Customize Standard and its related scale align with the Program Standard. Mary Erickson is a freshman violin student who recently moved into your district from Boston, Massachusetts. She has studied violin since the fourth grade with a private teacher and plans to continue lessons with a professional violinist locally.

Deciding when to use a Customized Standard for a student is a decision that a director must make based on the student's ability relative to the Program Standard of your program. A variance of one year may not require a Customize Standard in a student's first year but may be necessary in year two as the student advances.

*You will notice that Mary's freshman audition at the beginning of her freshman year placed her at a **3.5**. This score is equivalent to a junior in their 5th month on your Program Scale. This wide of a gap would likely necessitate a Customized Standard for Mary.*

You will note that the mix of Mary's customized instruction, literature and technique development materials are shown as 20% from the music being played by the top orchestra and 80% form customized material. This mix can vary based on a director's assessment. It can also change from year-to-year and, in fact semester-to-

A customized curriculum can include any number of the following:

a) Solo preparation and performance either with piano accompaniment or within the context of a concerto piece with the large ensemble. A good approach is to assign a significant solo piece each semester for an advanced student. The second semester piece can sometimes be used as the entry for solo & ensemble contest, but in some cases, students can play an additional solo for that event.

b) Small ensemble work with other students that presents a higher level of demand not currently present in your large ensemble. If students, ether advanced or highly advanced, are available in any given year, directors can establish quartets, duets or other groups comprised of advanced students.

c) Required participation in solo & ensemble contests auditions for all-state groups, and other performing opportunities in community youth or profession ensembles. If these performing opportunities are utilized, directors can use literature from those experiences in the assessment of advanced students.

d) Private lessons with outside private teachers or the director provide more advanced literature that can be incorporated into the assessment of more advanced students. The private lesson also provides additional opportunities for advanced etudes, exercises, and technical studies that will challenge the advanced student. In this case, assessments are taken from assignments by outside private lesson teachers, directors or "in-house" private teachers who teach during the school day.

e) Highly advanced students often audition multiple times for college scholarships regardless of their planned major. Visits to universities as early as a student's sophomore year can include auditions with applied faculty who are more than willing to listen to advanced students. Preparation for such auditions can be incorporated into a student's assessment program.

f) Any and all other performances that enhance the advanced student's potential become opportunities for directors to assess them at advanced levels. To be fair to the student and allow them to continue to grow musically, this is important.

g) Advanced students are respected by other students for their playing ability and in many cases, their leadership abilities. Music directors often entrust these students with additional responsibilities. We look to these student-leaders to set an example for other students and assist in the management and logistics of our performing groups. These enabling and motivating practices should <u>not</u>, however, be used as substitutes for materials that will contribute to the advanced student's musical growth.

Additional Questions regarding the Customized Standard:

1. Should these advanced students be assessed on the literature, he or she is playing in your ensemble as well as the customized literature assigned?

>Yes. As a member of your ensemble, the advanced student has the responsibility to prepare properly for his or her ensemble performances and this literature should be assessed in the same manner you assess other students. It goes without saying that this literature will also challenge the advanced performer in ways that solo, small ensemble and technique development exercises do not.

2. Is the advanced student's grade determined against your _Program Standard_ or the advanced curriculum you have established for them under your _Customized Standard_?

>Both. Assessments for advanced students are held with the same frequency, at the same time, and on the same experts as other students in his or her ensemble. In addition, they are assessed on their customized material as well. To receive an "A" for an assessment requires "A-level" achievement on the standard literature being assessed as well as their advanced material.

3. Should all highly advanced students have a Customized Standard for assessment?

Yes, but not identical. _Customized Scale_ is scalable. A freshman clarinetist may require only a portion of customized instruction be advance in order to measure growth. If they move to the upper ensemble in their sophomore year, less supplementary material may be needed. By their junior year, it may return as they advance. And by their senior year, the majority of their assessments are drawn from supplementary material using a high percentage of a _Customized Standard_.

4. Is there an issue of "fairness" in grading individual students against a higher standard?

Yes, but only if the student and parent are made aware in advance of the _Customized Standard,_ you will be applying to the advanced student. It is not unusual to assess students in the same ensemble using different materials. First, Second and Third clarinet parts often vary in their level of demand. First violin parts are frequently much more difficult than second parts.

Directors have the prerogative to add appropriate additional performance requirements to an advanced student's curriculum. Keep in mind, however, that parents have the ultimate right to approve outside activities such as community ensembles or private lessons with associated costs. Because of this, directors should always work directly with students and their parents when constructing a customized curriculum for the highly advanced student.

Ranking and grading using the Grade Level Method

Linear Scale / Grade Level Format

Bradley-Bourbonnais Community High School

Bradley-Bourbonnais Community High School is a High School district that serves 2,400 students in Bradley and Bourbonnais, Illinois, located 50 miles south of Chicago, The Orchestra program consists of a developing orchestra of 24 strings, a symphonic string orchestra of 47, and full orchestras at each level. The program is fed by one middle school district in Bourbonnais. Each orchestra is paired with the top wind players and percussionists from the corresponding wind bands.

Bradley-Bourbonnais Community High School
700 West North Street
Bradley, Illinois 60915
Department of Music – **Orchestra**

Kevin McNulty, Sr. Director (2011-2016)
Orchestra Director and Assistant Director of Bands

Ensembles
Symphonic Strings
Symphony Orchestra
Concert Strings
Concert Orchestra

Schedule and Student Contact
- There are 8 teaching periods in the school day (0-7).
- Each period is 54 minutes in length.
- Symphonic Strings and Concert Strings meet daily.
- Symphony Orchestra meets 8:00 AM to 8:54 on Thursdays.
- Concert Orchestra & Concert Band winds rehearse separately, then rehearse twice together prior to concerts.
- Concert Strings have a 30-minute sectional each day.
- Symphonic Strings are divided into two 30-minute sectionals.
- There is no in-school private lesson schedule.

HOW THE LINEAR SCALE IS APPLIED

The scale below shows how the Grade Level System aligns with the standard Linear Scale. All five boxes of the Linear Scale are used, allowing directors to rank students against the standard for all grades on specific instruments. The "4 against 5"structure in this adaption allows for a half range below and above expectations for high school musicians in orchestra at this particular high school. Essentially, the school year is perceived as 10 months long. A score of 2.3 represents a level equitable to "third month of the sophomore year. Students can instantly perceive if they are ahead or behind the standard.

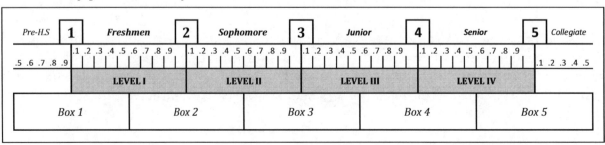

THE AUDITION   BBCHS Orchestra

The first assessment in a new school establishes the position your program has <u>within</u> your <u>*High School Standard*</u>. When conducting your first audition, you would use your <u>*High School Standard*</u> to rank and rate each student - for no <u>*Program Standard*</u> exists until you establish one through audition. If you are a middle school director, you will use your <u>*Middle School Standard*</u> when assessing for the first time.

Once you complete your first audition in a new school, you have established the <u>*Program Standard*</u> for your program. The second audition at the end of the year would be based on the <u>*Program Standard*</u> set in the first audition. The only change that can occur in your <u>*Program Standard*</u> in future auditions is when a student surpasses your highest standard or falls below your lowest. Keep in mind that when you assess your band, orchestra or choir for the first time, you are actually establishing a <u>*Program Standard*</u> for **each** instrument or voice. A <u>*Program Standard*</u> is actually a collection of standards for each instrument or, in choir, voice.

Having a sense of my <u>*High School Standard*</u> for string players in 2011, I proceeded to put in place my first assessment of Bradley-Bourbonnais Community High School string students. In addition to learning who my top and least developed player was in each section (and overall), I would learn how all current BBCHS string students and the string program compared to all other high school string players and programs I had witnessed in the past. Once I held the audition, I would then have a place to start. Not only would this first assessment rank and rate my students, but it would also determine my literature for the year, my developmental materials, and all of the activities for the BBCHS Orchestra for the year.

Just as my <u>*Musical Standard*</u> provided little distinction between the 58 students I was about to audition, I felt my <u>*High School Standard*</u> would not provide enough discrimination to establish a proper order (ranking) of my students, either. My focus was on placing each student in the correct range of my <u>*High School Standard,*</u> and then goes back and makes decisions on spread and ranking. I decided <u>not</u> to rank but simply to rate students in the initial phase of this first audition. I would apply my intuitive standard for good musicianship, proper string technique, and expression and rely heavily on my "Impression" and take significant notes on each student. I could then rate strictly on my "Impression" – basically, not over-think the process the first time. I would rank, resolve ties and set spreads after the entire group was assessed, using the *Comparison* process. I did not use a score sheet with qualities listed such as "tone," "pitch," etc. for the same reason that I chose to simply rate in the first phase. Referencing qualities on a score sheet would have me focused on sub-captions and their relative merit. While I would certainly recognize and think about those qualities as they appeared in performance, I wanted *Impression* to take "front seat" in this first audition.

I utilized my *Impression* of each performance and arrived at a raw number based on my *High School Standard*. I determined that *Analysis* would be utilized in the first phase of the process even though I planned to establish ranking after the entire audition was completed. My use of extensive notes on each student would give me the opportunity to reference them during the *Comparison* phase of the process. *Analysis* is often called upon during the *Impression* and the *Comparison* phases.

Why judge this audition different from the way I've judged competitive events over the years? There is a big difference between a contest and an audition. In a judged contest each judge must complete each contestant's sheet prior to moving on to the next contestant. Score sheets are turned in and, short of a math error, judges cannot make changes once a score sheet is turned in. In the case of a closed audition such as my string audition, you have the luxury of *consideration* though out the audition. You can take your time to consider the order of each section carefully. You can deliberate, check your impression and consider your extensive notes before making a final decision. The important thing to understand is that Impression-Analysis-Comparison is used in both situations. In the audition, it is used in the same way it is used in a contest. The closed audition, however, allows for more time and more consideration to get the ranking and the rating correct.

Essentially, my string audition is four separate assessments using different scoring methods.

The Take-Away ("tic system") used to assess the accuracy of **Scales.**
The Written Text is used to determine non-performance **Musical Understanding.**
The Build-Up system is used to assess the performance of **Prepared Music**.
The Build-Up system is used to assess the overall accuracy of **Sight Reading.**

These methods are used to determine the top and bottom performers in the orchestra and in each section of the orchestra – violins, violas, celli, and bass. This will establish the range of your *Program Standard* and its placement on your known *High School Standard*.

The four assessment categories are weighted. The weight you decide to place in these four categories is your choice. I have always chosen to emphasize the performance of Prepared Music as a priority. My second priority is a student's ability to Sight Read. The ability to sight-read not only demonstrates an understating of notation it also demonstrates an understanding of keys, scale-wise patterns, and other skill sets. It also reveals the level of stability a student has under increased pressure. I have found Scales to be best assessed using "tics," while the understanding of music theory, history and terminology are best assessed using a writing exam.

The audition profile used in my string audition is detailed in the chart below

		Level I	Level II	Level III	Level IV
35%	**Prepared Music**	1st Year Etude	2nd Year Etude	3rd Year Etude	4th Year Etude
30%	**Sight Reading**	1st Year Demand	2nd Year Demand	3rd Year Demand	4th Year Demand
25%	**Scales & Arpeggios**	3 - 1st Level Keys	3- 2nd Level Keys	3 - Third Level Keys	3 - Four level Keys
10%	**Written Exam**	60-69%	70-70%	80-89%	90-100

I determined my objectives for the first assessment:

1. **Rank every player** in each section from best to least developed.
2. Determine who my **top players** were and how they ranked against my *High School Standard.*
3. Determine any students **significantly lacking skills,** place them at the bottom of my scale, and determine if they ranked below my *High School Standard.*
4. Place each audition on my Linear Scale with **appropriate spread** to determine the natural breaks in the ranking.
5. **Determine the profile** of my students within my *Program Standard*.
6. **Establish seating** for each section.

I created Four Levels of material for each performance category.

1. **Prepared Music** was comprised of <u>four separate etudes</u> ranked from Level I to Level IV. All students were required to start at Level I and work their way up as far as they could go. In this first assessment, I did not allow older students to choose a higher level as became my practice in later years because I did not know one student from the next.

2. Four levels of **Sight Reading** were also used. Again, each student would begin with Level I and work their way up until their abilities were overly challenged.

3. I grouped **Scales and Arpeggios** into four levels as well. The demand consideration was based on the particular instrument – violins beginning with "G," and violas with "C," for example. I was aware that the majority of students did not play 3-octave scales, so I began 3-octave requirements at Level III - with the exception of bass, of course. (The 3-octave requirement was in place by the spring audition following training and assessments during the first year.)

4. The written exam, which assessed **Musical Understanding,** was graded in a standard way and the four levels were assigned to the four passing grades (A, B,C,D).

The materials were designed to capture many various musical components. Music with less technical demand in Level I could reveal the expressive capabilities of a student. Increased demands in Level II could reveal their more technical abilities. Level III might begin to reveal those capable of 1st Violin material. And Level IV would offer a group of students I might consider as principles, soloists, and candidates for high-end ensemble groups.

Choral ensembles will use different tests such as pitch matching, note reading, and other skill sets. Middle School directors may choose to emphasize more fundamental skills than the high school level. What you chose is your decision, but it should encompass the broad spectrum of what you believe defines a competent, trained and expressive student musician.

Audition Scale

If you recall, I mentioned how the first audition was actually four auditions in one. Though the scale below compresses only fifty possible points, my largest section was the violins (25 students). This scale would provide me with enough numbers to establish my _Program Standard_. I would use the "Above" category for any students that were particularly advanced and the "Below" category for students that fell below my _High School Standard_ for string players.

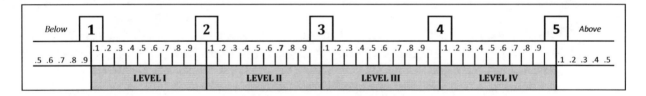

Audition Process

I determined that every student would perform the same audition in the same way. This meant that the top violinist from the previous year, for example, played the same audition as the incoming freshman. Each student would begin at Level I and work their way up. If I felt their abilities called for additional demand they would perform music at the next level higher. Advanced students moved up from Level I to Level IV. Others "washed out" at Level I, II or III. But once complete, I had a very good idea of how each student could perform.

Tabulation

The net rating for each student determined their ranking within their section and ensemble. The raw score in each category (prepared music, sight reading, scales and musical understanding) were weighted to reflect the priority of my Desired Outcomes for the audition.

The chart below shows the tabulation for four studies and the ranking of the violin section Each component of the audition has a different weight as indicated by the **weighted score.**

		Raw Score	Weighted Score	Raw Score	Weighted Score	Raw Score	Weighted Score	Raw Score	Weighted Score
Prepared	35%	2.5	17.5	1.9	13.3	3.2	14	2.2	10.5
Scales	30%	1.3	7.8	1.2	7.2	1.7	10.2	1.5	9
Sight-Reading	25%	1.2	6	1.2	6	2.0	10	1.5	7.5
Written	10%	3.1	6.2	2.5	5	2.6	5.2	3.1	6.2
			37.5		31.5		39.4		33.2
		Student 1	1.875	Student 2	1.575	Student 3	1.970	Student 4	1.660

Ranking		
1	Student 3	1.970
2	Student 1	1.875
3	Student 4	1.660
4	Student 2	1.575

INST	YEAR	NAME	SCORE
Violin	11	Kaitlynne Johnson	2.245
Violin	9	Bryana Reed	2.240
Violin	9	Guadalupe Martinez	2.200
Violin	9	Kendra Reasoning	2.130
Violin	9	Megan Malone	2.125
Violin	9	LaurenLaMontagne	2.100
Violin	10	Alisha Washington	2.075
Violin	9	Patrick Wilson	1.995
Violin	9	Sydney LaGrange	1.755
Violin	10	Benjjamin Shaw	1.715
Violin	9	Erick Newberry	1.510
Violin	9	Jessica Washington	1.465
Violin	9	Arianna Landrow	1.320
Violin	9	Nicole Mason	1.280
Violin	9	Madison Orchard	1.170
Violin	9	Ashley Simpson	1.165
Violin	9	Nora Maloney	1.150
Violin	9	Emily Norton	1.145
Violin	9	Nick Legacy	1.130
Violin	10	Fredrick Jordon	1.050
Violin	10	Dawson Bernardy	0.875
Violin	9	Sheila White	0.850
Violin	9	Alexis Mendoza	0.675
Violin	9	Mike Reniger	0.600

The chart on the left shows twenty-five violinists ranked in order of their assessment total score.

Three of the students at the bottom of this list failed to rank at a high school level and will be assigned a *Customized Standard* to get them up to a 9th grade level.

All scores are fairly tight. The top 8 violinists would be assigned to play 1st violin parts. The next 15 students will play 2nd violin.

As the three bottom violinists improve during the year they will be able to contribute more consistently which could result in adding one additional 1st violin for better balance.

Score Sheet

One scoresheet was used for the entire orchestra. The scale column is coded to indicate which instrument and scale apply to which particular level. All scales are three octaves with the exception of the Bass.

BBCHS Department of Music
ORCHESTRA AUDITION FORM

NAME _____

___ Fall   ___ Spring   ___Violin   ___Viola   ___Cello   ___Bass

SIGHT READING (25%)

Level	Key/Acc	Rhythm/Pulse	Expression

TOTALS

PREPARED (35%)	
SCALES (30%)	
SIGHT READING (25%)	
WRITTEN TEST (10%)	
Notes:	

SCALES (30%)

GM (v-1)				
CM (v-1/a-1/c-1)				
FM (a-1/c-1/b-1)				
EM (b-10)				
AM (v-2)				
DM (a-2/c-2)				
BbM (b-2)				
AbM (v-3/b-3)				
DbM (a-3/c-3/b-4)				
Gm (v-2/b-2)				
Cm (a-2/c-2/v-4)				
Fm (a-4/c-4)				
G Arp (v-3)			C Arp (v-4/a-3/c-3)	
E Arp (b-3)			F Arp (a-4/c-4/b-4)	

The back page of the score provides for extensive notes for Prepared Music. This is the most important section to collect data on each student. It often served as a "tie-breaker." This and the front page of the audition sheet is copied and issued to each student following auditions. It becomes a game plan for the student for the semester.

PREPARED MUSIC (35%)

Level I

Level II

Level III

Level IV

Notes to Student:

How the Written Exam score equates to the scale

All of us know how written tests are graded. There are a few variations but the preponderance of grading deducts a certain number of points for each question, and a percentage is calculated. Schools have varying formulas for grading such as:

1
90 -100 = A
80 - 99 = B
70 - 89 = C
60 - 69 = D
59 or below F

2
92 -100 = A
85 - 91 = B
77 - 84 = C
70 - 76 = D
69 or below F

Regardless of your school's grading policy, grading scale #1 is best equated with the Linear Scale in our system. The following graph shows the relationship between the "raw number" earned in the audition's Written Exam and an equitable ranking on the audition Linear Scale.

Below Standard	Level I	Level II	Level III	Level IV
	1.0 1.1 1.2 1.3 1.4 1.5 1.6 1.7 1.8 1.9	2.0 2.1 2.2 2.3 2.4 2.5 2.6 2.7 1.8 2.9	3.0 3.1 3.2 3.3 3.4 3.5 3.6 3.7 3.8 3.9	4.0 4.1 4.2 4.3 4.4 4.5 4.6 4.7 4.8 4.9 50
		Audition Rating		
		Written Exam Score		
0 ← 59	60 61 62 63 64 65 66 67 68 69	70 71 72 73 74 75 76 77 78 79	80 81 82 83 84 85 86 87 88 89	90 91 92 93 94 95 96 97 98 99 100

Your *Program Standard* Profile

Though we will discuss your Program Profile in a subsequent segment, it seems appropriate to point out the difference between your program **Range,** your program **Profile,** and your Program **Position** on the High School Scale.

    a) The **Range** of your *Program Standard* is the distance between your best student-musician and your least developed. (A wide range can show weakness at the lower grade levels)

    b) The **Profile** of your *Program Standard* is the location of all student-musicians across the spectrum of that range. (Having a high percentage of students on the right side of your range demonstrates solid training at the lower grade levels).

    c) The **Position** of your *Program Standard* relative to your *High School Standard* reveals the level of music and musicianship your program is producing relative to other programs and student-musicians that comprise your *High School Standard.*

The extensive data drawn from the Linear Scale assessment system allows you to consider empirical evidence to support your strategy to improve the abilities of your student-musicians, increase the capacity of your school ensembles and expand the depth of musical expression capable within your program.

Audition Literature

If it has not crossed your mind yet, the question of audition literature is one that you must carefully consider in your first (and subsequent) auditions. The level of demand contained in scales and, to a lesser degree, written tests (which assesses certain musical understandings), is easily recognized and fairly standard. String teachers understand what a three octave scale on violin entails. Tempo, articulations and even expression can vary, but for the most part, the level of complexity for scales, arpeggios or any other exercise designed to develop technique can be scaled to match four levels of demand. In addition, anything short of an elaborate music theory concept like assessing the understanding of fundamentals such as scale construction, or note value, is also fairly fundament in any written exam use as part of an audition.

But the criteria used to select literature for both Prepared Music and Sight Reading in an audition requires a bit more insight. As previously stated, I chose to use my *High School Standard* in my first assessment of BBCHS string students. You will also recall that while I used this standard, I anticipated that it was *likely* that most of my students would not perform at the high-end of that standard. As it turned out, not one of my students approached the upper level of my Excellent Range or the Superior Range of my 4-range *High School Standard*. I did, however, have material ready that would measure achievement in that range, should I find a student unchallenged by Level IV Prepared Music or Sight Reading. audition material.

In sectional classes, students prepared for auditions individually, in small groups as I roamed the room offering guidance and assistance. Many asked questions. And I made a point to check on each student as they prepared. I was able to quickly identify students who were struggling and those who were the strong performers. I spent two weeks preparing students in sectional rehearsals this way. In the final days prior to auditions, I made adjustments in both my Level IV and Level I prepared music and sight reading materials.

All of us have gotten the question "How does this go" from students. That usually means is a student's sight reading abilities are low. I was asked that enough upon my arrival at BBCHS that I was convinced me that I need to adjust to a *lower level of demand.* In most cases, all Sight Reading material will be of lower demand than Prepared Music. All of us perform better each time we play a piece of music than we do in the first "read-through." While the accuracy of an excellent sight reader will be high the first time, their level of expression and nuance will take some time "living with the piece," before full expression is achieved.

The selection of Prepared Music has similar considerations. If I was using my *High School Standard*, would that not demand that I utilized Prepared Music for Level IV that matched the level of demand associated with my High School Standard? The answer to that questions is, "no."

Utilizing a High School Standard does not require you to present each student with literature associated with the best high school string students I had ever heard. While I had such high-level material for both Sight Reading and Prepared Music, students would only be asked to perform it if they successfully "climbed the ladder" of Levels I through IV and performed Level IV with ease. Keep in mind all students were required to begin Prepared Music, Sight Reading and Scales at Level I and move up to Level IV if they passed each level. Had a student sailed through all four levels of Sight Reading, I had a higher level ready. Also, if they performed Level IV Prepared Music at an unencumbered and expressive level, I would issue a highly advanced piece to them to play for me within a week. This student would establish the top level *Program Standard* for Prepared Music performance ability at BBCHS, and I would adjust my Level IV Prepared Music for the next audition. That new Level IV material would, in fact, become my Level IV for my Program Standard going forward.

Therefore, my *High School Standard* was used to measure students in the first audition, but I selected music for Prepared Music and Sight Reading that would *likely* capture the range of ability within the program. The Literature I chose the first time was simply how I constructed my audition. Remember, in addition to assessing each student, the purpose of the first audition is to establish your Program Standard. Should a student or group of students exceed my high-end level of literature, all the better. I would then know what level of literature to assign to my Level IV *Program Standard* for Prepared Music and Sight Reading.

I based my music choice on 1) my informal observations during preparation classes, 2) the level of literature performed by the ensemble prior to my arrival and other 3) anecdotal information such as the number of students who took private lessons prior to my arrival and information from my band and choir colleagues. The scale below represents the approximate range of literature used for my first audition of string students at BBCHS.

Prepared Music and Sight Reading Materials for Audition

High School Standard				
Level I Demand	Level II Demand	Level III Demand	Level IV Demand	
Level I	Level II	Level III	Level IV	Contingency Material ⟶
BBCHS Audition				

The low-end Level I literature is based on my High School Standard. Students who fail to meet that standard are assigned to the <u>*Customized Standard*</u> (and associated literature) until they catch up. Naturally, the goal is to establish a <u>Program Standard</u> that does <u>not</u> begin at the bottom of your High School Standard but is higher. "Bringing up the tail" of your <u>*Program Standard*</u> is an important first step in improving your program. The second step is moving the overall profile of the students in your Program Standard to the right.

<u>The Audition Profile</u>

Once all auditions are completed, the next step is to analyze the profile of your ensemble. This adds to and, in some cases, clarifies the impression you have of the overall ability of your ensemble. While your "stars" may be memorable and while your weak players may gnaw at your optimism, the Audition Profile can reveal the strength of the middle of your ensemble. As we have stated previously, it is that "middle range" that will often determine the level of literature you can successfully perform with your ensemble.

As a result of the initial audition of the 58 string students at BBCHS, I had a fairly even distribution of abilities in Levels I, II & III with a mere seven students playing at Level IV. The distribution after "the first pass" looked something like this:

Distribution of Students - 1st Assessment

1	**13** Students	2	**21** Students	3	**17** Students	4	**7** Students	5
	Level I		**Level II**		**Level III**		**Level IV**	

As you can see, the large percentage of my students rated to the left side of the scale. Naturally, this gave me an immediate view of the level of literature I would be able to choose with an assurance of some level of success. The distribution (profile) of these scores revealed much about the condition of the program. Of the 58 students who auditioned:

- 34 performed below the 50% level / 24 performed above the 50% level
- 7 students performed a Level IV. Of the seven, six took private lessons.
- The bottom 5 scoring students were below my <u>*High School Standard*</u>.
- The orchestra was comprised of 8 Seniors, 9 Juniors, 18 Sophomores, 23 Freshmen

The number of students below the 50% level in this audition was evidence that a developmental orchestra was needed at the high school level. Increased quality of literature in a "top group," could also increase retention of upperclassmen. In year two, the number of string students grew from 58 to 76. Two orchestra classes were offered. literature.

The Ensemble Standard

With two ensembles established in the BBCHS String Program, the fourth and final standard of excellence came into play. This is the standard set for my top orchestra - called the *Ensemble Standard*. What ***is*** the *Ensemble Standard* and how is it determined? How does the *Ensemble Standard* fit into the system of standards we have established thus far?

The *Ensemble Standard* establishes minimum entry requirements for certain ensembles that play music with higher demand. It, therefore, establishes a "firm bottom" or barrier to entry for students if they are to be accepted into an ensemble that plays music of an elevated demand. As was stated previously:

> *"Directors understand that the playing ability of their students is a major factor in determining the music they select for those students. They also understand that selecting students for certain ensembles is based on the music they plan to perform."*

In my description of the first audition held for string students at BBCHS, I explained <u>how</u> I determined what music I would play with my new orchestra by doing the following:

    a) **RANK** all students in the program using my *High School Standard*
    b) **RATE** all students in the program to establish my *Program Standard*

In year two, when the **Symphonic Orchestra** and **Concert Orchestra** were established, I could now determine what music I would play with my two orchestras by doing the following:

    a) **RANK** all students in the program using my *High School Standard*
    b) **RATE** all students in the program to establish my *Program Standard*
    c) **SET A MINIMUM** entry requirement for the top ensemble based on the **prescribed number** of string voices needed for the Symphonic Orchestra.

The notion of a "prescribed number" may take you a bit by surprise. But standard instrumentation for a string orchestra, as well as wind bands is fairly established. Some directors prefer a large concert band. Others prefer the modern wind ensemble instrumentation established at the Eastman School in the 1950's by Frederick Fennell. Choral directors often determine the size and balance of voices off of the number of men's voices. Based on the developing voice at the high school level, choral directors will shape the size and balance of their singers with considerations different from their wind and string cohorts. Certain choral music is better suited for the smaller mixed choir while major Beethoven or even Mozart works work best with large choirs. The choice is up to the director based on the size and quality of the students in a school's program.

In my first year at BBCHS with one orchestra class, I was limited in my choice of the "ideal size" and balance of string voices. All students were in one orchestra, but students who were below standard were assigned supplementary training material and were graded based on the _Customized Standard_. In year two, only students in the developing orchestra (Concert Strings) needed a customized curriculum to catch up. In the top orchestra (Symphonic Strings) students could be assigned a customized curriculum to develop their skills and expand their musical experiences beyond the capabilities of the top orchestra.

This is what occurs when a band, orchestra or choir program has more than one ensemble. For my friends and colleagues in the judging community, this is no different than establishing the fact that you have to score in the "top ten," or "top twelve" (or some other number) in prelims - to "make finals."

The foundation of the proposed system is the directors _Musical Standard_. This ties directly to the principle established in the early section of this book which reads as follows:

> *"The only way to accurately measure the desired outcomes of music performance is through the prism of a music performance teacher's background and experience as a musician, and not simply against a list of criteria or an extraneous written exam."*

Therefore, all standards within a music program have their foundation in the directors Musical Standard and the only way to measure the desired outcomes of a music performance against those standards is through the prism of the director who has brought the standard to the classroom in the first place. The chart below shows the correlation between a director's _Musical Standard_, _High School Standard_, a school's _Program Standard_ and a program's _Ensemble Standard_

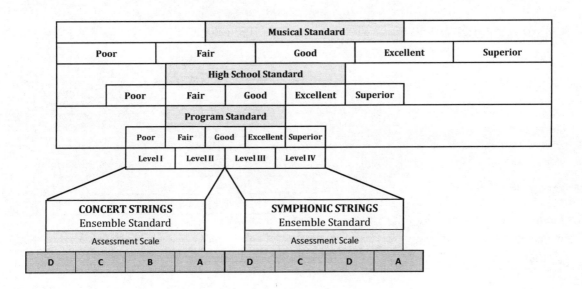

Grading Scales

Three grading scales can be used in the proposed assessment system:

   a) The Grade Level Scale measures a student's grade in relation to the standard established by other students in their same **Grade.**
   b) The Ensemble Scale measures a student's grade in relation to the standard established by other like instruments in a student's **Ensemble**.
   c) The Customized Scale measures a student's grade in relation to the standard established by their director that is **individualized**.

Grade Level Scale

If your program has **ONE** band, orchestra or choir for all grade levels, then the Grade Level Scale and its accompanying grading scale works best when doing assessments.

Grade Level & Ensemble Level Scales

If you have **TWO** or more ensembles for band, orchestra or choir, you can use a combination of the Grade Level Scale and the Ensemble Scale. The Grade Level Scale is applied to compulsories and training materials assessed during the year. The Ensemble Scale is applied to music being performed by the ensemble in which a student performs.

Grade Level Scale

Used for all compulsories and training materials such as Scales, etudes exercises

Ensemble Level Scale

Used for all compulsories and training materials such as Scales, etudes exercises

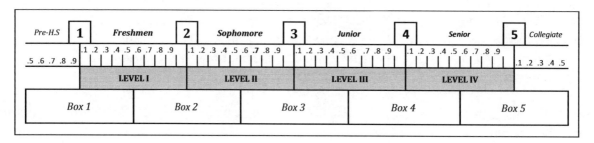

In the next section, we will examine a program with four bands at the high school level. In programs with more than two ensembles of the same kind (band, orchestra or choir), the Ensemble Standard can be used exclusively regardless of grade level. Students from all grades are eligible to audition for any ensemble and are graded according to the Ensemble Standard exclusively.

Formative Assessment
This type of assessment is done during the learning process in order to report progress, to modify teaching and learning activities to improve student attainment. The Formative can be used to assess performance of literature, and ensemble work, or compulsories such as scales, etudes, and exercises. These types of assessments are either graded or not graded depending on the grading policy of your school district.

Summative Assessments
This type of assessment is used to evaluate student learning, skill acquisition, and musical achievement at the conclusion of a defined instructional period—typically at the end of an audition, concert, contest or semester. These types of assessments are almost always graded.

Which assessment should be used?

The choice to use either Formative and Summative Assessments or strictly Summative Assessments is often the choice of the director, though some school districts may require Formative Assessments (graded or not graded) as a matter of policy. At BBCHS, the music department used Summative Assessment exclusively. This is usually the best choice since programming for concerts, contests, and public performances vary in style and content. Longer projects such as a recital etudes or contest pieces may require frequent checking by the director but may not require formal Formative Assessments, particularly ones that are graded. The nature of a piece, varied approaches to learning a piece of music and the synergistic requirements of music performance make Formative Assessment less relevant.

When to perform assessments?

It is best to hold Summative Assessments following performances. I found this to be the time when students were at their peak. In addition, music is not repeated from one concert to the next, so assessments following final performances measure desired outcomes best. Auditions can also be used as graded assessments. Within the structure of my fall or Spring Auditions, I would assess Prepared Music, Scales, and the Written Exam as graded Summative Assessments. I did not apply grades to the Sight Reading assessment since that learning curve developed over a longer period of time. In addition, the preparation for Sight Reading is best achieved by simply sight reading but is not directly tied to the actual music used for Sight Reading in the audition.

BBCHS Orchestra Performance & Audition Schedule

SEPT 12-16	Fall Auditions
OCT 24	Fall Concert
DEC 11	Holiday Concert
FEB 8	Combined Middle School-High School Concert
FEB 23	University of Illinois String Festival
MARCH 8	IHSA Solo & Ensemble Contest
APRIL 14	IHSA Organizational Concert
MAY 15	Spring Orchestra Concert

Below is a Summative Assessment used following the Holiday Concert. It also assesses a compulsory scale to end the semester. Note the particular excerpts.

SYMPHONIC STRINGS
Holiday Concert Summative Playing Tests

1st Violins
    "It's Christmastime   Bar before 19 to "Suddenly Slower"
                                            2 before 47 to 55
    "The Christmas Song   42 to "hold" 8 before the end
        SCALE   Ab Major 3 octaves

2nd Violins
    "It's Christmastime   2 before 19 to "Suddenly Slower"
    "The Christmas Song   42 to "hold" 8 before the end
        SCALE   Ab Major 3 octaves

Viola
    "It's Christmastime   Bar before 19 to "Suddenly Slower"
    "The Christmas Song   Bar 6 to 22
        SCALE   Db Major 3 octaves

Cello
    "It's Christmastime   6 Before 133 to 133, 144 to end
    "The Christmas Song   14 to 22
        SCALE   Db Major 3 octaves

Bass
    "The Christmas Song   Beginning to 14
        SCALE   F Major 2 octaves
        SCALE   E Major 2 octaves

Ranking and grading using the Ensemble Level Method

Linear Scale / Ensemble Level Format

Keller Central High School

Keller Central High School is one of four high schools in the Keller Independent School District located in Keller, TX, a suburb of Fort Worth, Texas. The high school has approximately 2,500 students. Keller Central is fed by one Middle School (7, 8), one Intermediate School (4, 5, and 6) and 3 Elementary Schools (1, 2, 3),

Band students begin in 6th grade. The high school band program consists of 4 Bands of equal size (50-65). Keller High School serves students from Keller, Fort Worth, Watauga and North Richland Hills, Texas.

Keller Central High School
9450 Ray White Road
Fort Worth, TX 76244
Department of Music – **Band**

Kevin McNulty, Jr., Director of Bands
Kye Rudnick, Assistant Director (Brass)
Jessica Maus, Assistant Director (Woodwinds)
Matthew Stephens, Assist. Director (Percussion)

Private teachers for each instrument teach at the school. Approximately 78% of students take private lessons.

Ensembles
Wind Ensemble
Symphonic Band
Concert Band
Concert Ensemble

Schedule and Student Contact

- There are 5 periods in the day (block scheduling)
- Each block period is 90 minutes long
- Wind Ensemble meets for 1 ½ hours each day
- Symphonic Band meets for 1 ½ hours each day
- Concert Band meets for 1 ½ hours each day
- Concert Ensemble meets for 1 ½ hours, 2 or 3 days alternating.

HOW THE LINEAR SCALE IS APPLIED

The scale below shows how the Ensemble Level System aligns with the standard Linear Scale. While the five boxes of the Linear Scale are referenced in this scale, the focus of auditions is the "minimum entry points" required to be accepted in any one of the four ensembles. Ensemble size and instrument is set by the directors, and the size of each band is roughly the same. The scale extends downward to the middle school level where four additional bands have entry requirements. While the scale shows ensemble names under a range of numbers, only the primary numbers (4, 5, 6, 7) matter in terms of ensemble qualification. Students can (and do) score all the way up and down the scale allowing students, parents and administration to see how students achieve across the spectrum.

	KELLER CENTRAL HIGH SCHOOL BANDS				
	4	5	6	7	8
.1 .2 .3 .4 .5 .6 .7 .8 .9	.1 .2 .3 .4 .5 .6 .7 .8 .9	.1 .2 .3 .4 .5 .6 .7 .8 .9	.1 .2 .3 .4 .5 .6 .7 .8 .9	.1 .2 .3 .4 .5 .6 .7 .8 .9	.1 .2 .3 .4 .5 .6 .7 .8 .9
MIDDLE SCHOOL	CONCERT ENSEMBLE	CONCERT BAND	SYMPHONIC BAND	WIND ENSEMBLE	COLLEGIATE
Box 2	Box 3		Box 4		Box 5

Introduction to Keller Central High School Bands and the Texas System

In the Bradley-Bourbonnais Community High School Case Study, we examined a single high school district with two feeder school districts, one of which had a string program. The case study examined the high school program during a development stage when one orchestra grew to two. We examined an audition and assessment system that measures the musical growth of individual students but can also be used to assess sections, grade levels, and entire orchestras. Central to the system is the implementation of a _Program Standard_ within the _High School Standard_ of the director.

In our second case study, we examine a band program in a school district that is structured quite differently than BBCHS. Keller Central High School is in a K-12 Independent School District located in the suburbs of Fort Worth, Texas with multiple elementary schools, middle schools, and high schools. Keller Central High School has four bands at the high school level and four bands at its Middle School feeder school. As a unit district, the program is viewed and structured as one curriculum, one teaching methodology, and an assessment system that covers the 6th grade level to 12th grade.

Keller Central is among those schools that utilize the standard associated with high school bands in the State of Texas. Many programs in Texas set standards for school bands nationwide. This, along with the highly defined standards established over the years by the *Texas Bandmasters Association* (TBA), the *Texas Music Educators Association* (TMEA), places Texas bands at the forefront of some of the best bands in the nation.

Another reason for the highly defined nature of the "Texas Standard" is their all-state system, run by the *University Interscholastic League* (UIL). UIL is designed to support and enrich the teaching of music as an integral component of the public school curriculum in the state of Texas. Each year approximately one half million middle school, junior high and high school students reap the benefits of participation in the ten UIL music events. UIL has an established repertoire guide that has been developed over time. This Prescribed Music List sets a repertoire standard for over 3,800 performing ensembles each year. Not only does UIL hold state qualifying events for large group, solo & ensembles, it also has the same state championship structure for marching band.

Auditions for UIL are extensive, using three territorial qualifying segments namely, "Area," "Region," and "State" level auditions. The audition process is highly competitive, resulting in All-State groups that represent less than 1% of the total student-musician population in Texas. Because of the legacy and national prominence of Texas bands, it behooves school music programs in Texas to strive for high standards, and many of them do. School district and community support are also significant to the standards set by Texas bands. The TMEA, TBA, and UIL, along with the level of support for music in Texas schools, have a major impact on the standards being set by Texas band programs.

The Keller Central Program Standard

The audition and assessment system used by Keller Central Bands does not have a *Program Standard* separate from the *High School Standard* as perceived and accepted by the Texas band community. As mentioned earlier, the Keller Central notion of quality is more closely aligned to a national *High School Standard* because of the overall quality and status of top band programs in the State of Texas who are often included in a list of standard-setting programs nationwide. Each band program, including Keller Central Bands, strives to reach the ultimate standard that prevails in their state. Therefore, the only standard at Keller Central is the *High School Standard.* That standard fully provides adequate <u>distinction</u> to rank, rate and place students in one of four ensembles.

Remember, a *High School Standard* is one that directors in a school or school district possess as a result of the high school performances they have experienced in their lifetime. No committee or group establish this standard. It is acquired by each director. It is analogous to widely accepted standards of quality for high school music ensembles but is always a director's personal standard for high school music performance based on his or her background and experience. Musical judgments (assessments) always draw on the *Musical Standard*. But it, too, is recognized, formed and possessed by, and unique to, each individual musician-teacher.

In practice, musical standards are not established out of context. The works of the great composers and arrangers of band music are the lens through which our standards are realized. It could be argued that the *High School Standard* for band is, in fact, the achievement of high school musicians playing literature that *presents* the opportunity to achieve at the highest level. Thus we see the logic and appropriateness of the Prescribed Music Lists of Texas and other states.

The staff at Keller Central will be the first to tell you that they are on a journey to meet (and further embellish) the standard for band performance. They will also tell you that they feel they have some way to go before their program approaches or exceeds that standard. With that said, the important thing to understand is that their scale is aligned with the *High School Standard* set by the bands in Texas and the country. Furthermore, their audition, assessment and grading system is aligned with the *High School Standard*. The alignment of the *Keller Central Standard* with the *High School Standard* appears as follows:

High School Standard			
Level I	Level II	Level III	Level IV
Keller Central Program Standand			
Concert Ensemble	Concert Band	Symphonic Band	Wind Ensemble

Students at Keller Central are placed in one of four ensembles, according to an *Ensemble Standard*, *regardless* of Grade Level. Essentially, each ensemble has a barrier that students must exceed to gain entry. Therefore, an ensemble's standard expresses the rating of a student's audition or assessment with more clarity, just as the use of the *Grade Level Standard* added more clarity to the numerical rating given string students at BBCHS. At Keller Central, a student's playing ability can be expressed as being at "Concert Band Level" or "Wind Ensemble Level." Students hear other students in the various ensembles at school. The number ranking may be somewhat abstract to them, but being rated at the "Wind Ensemble Level" has some real tangible meaning.

Hillwood Middle School, which feeds Keller Central, uses a similar system when placing their Middle School band students in ensembles. They use a *Middle School Program Standard* that aligns with the *Middle School Standard*. In reality, the *Middle School Standard* grows out of the *High School Standard* at Keller Central.

Middle School Standard			
Level I	Level II	Level III	Level IV
Middle School Program Standand			
Beginner Level	Concert Band	Symphonic Band	Wind Ensemble

A look at the *Keller Central High School Scale* and the *Hillwood Middle School Scale* shows how they correlate.:

Keller Central High School/Hillwood Middle School Scale

			Keller Central Program Standard			
			Concert Ensemble	Concert Band	Symphonic Band	Wind Ensemble
LEVEL 1	LEVEL 2	LEVEL 3	LEVEL 4	LEVEL 5	LEVEL 6	LEVEL 7
Beginner Level	Concert Band	Symphonic Band	Wind Ensemble			
Hillwood Middle School Program Standard						

Looking at the **Entire Scale** in detail on the next page reveals the range of ability in the program and how it plays a role in both **auditions** and **assessments.** It shows the numerical range of the program. In addition, you will note that the scale includes a **Collegiate** level and a **Professional** level. The point of including the ranges beyond high school is to project the endless range of achievement in music – a laudable concept. It reminds students that there is a significant standard well beyond high school.

1				HIGH SCHOOL - 9th Grade - 12th Grade			
2		H.S. Inst. Techniques	Concert Ensemble	Concert Band	Symphonic Band	Wind Ensemble	
3		MIDDLE SCHOOL - 6th Grade - 8th Grade				Collegiate	Professional
4	Beginner Level	Concert Band	Symphonic Band	Wind Ensemble			
5	LEVEL 1	LEVEL 2	LEVEL 3	LEVEL 4	LEVEL 5	LEVEL 6	LEVEL 7	LEVEL 8	LEVEL 9
6	1.0 - 1.9	2.0 - 2.9	3.0 - 3.9	4.0 - 4.9	5.0 - 5.9	6.0 - 6.9	7.0 - 7.9	8.0 - 8.5	8.6 - 10.00
7	Box 1 *	Box 2		Box 3		Box 4		Box 5	

*Standard Scale extends down to "0"

Line 1   Indicates the **High School Range**

Line 2   Shows Range of **High School Bands** – plus remedial range.

Line 3   Indicates **Middle School Range**

Line 4   Shows Range of **Middle School Bands**

Line 5   Shows the **9 Levels of Achievement** on the scale

Line 6   Shows **Numerical Values** of each level on the scale

Line 7   Shows alignment with **Standard Linear Scale**

The Hillwood Middle School Program

Students at Hillwood Middle School begin band in 6th Grade. The average number of beginner students at Hillwood Middle School each year is 250 students. Band in 6th grade is structured so that students spend the entire year studying in classes with other students who play the same instrument. Directors do form bands at certain times for performances but, for the most part, 6th grade band meets as an instrument-specific class. This has a significant effect on the entire Keller Central/Hillwood band program. The intense "first year" of study accelerates the learning process and, as a result, 7th graders are placed in one of three (3) bands following their full year of instrumental class in 6th grade.

The distribution of **7th Graders** following one year of band in 6th Grade are as follows:

Concert Band   (Level II)   Approximately 15%
Symphonic Band   (Level III)   Approximately 75%
Wind Ensemble (Level IV)   Approximately 10%

At times, certain 6th graders will be moved into the Concert Band at the end of one semester of band instrument classes. While this is the exception, it does occur each year. The Distribution of **all band students** at Hillwood Middle School is represented below:

Beginning Band   6th Graders (100%)
    Beginning Band is a class grouped by instrument.
    Bands are formed a few times for concerts second semester.

Concert Band   7th Graders (95%)
    6th Graders   (5%)   2nd semester

Symphonic Band   7th Graders (80%)
    8th Graders (20%)   lower level

Wind Ensemble 8th Graders (75%)
    7th Graders (25%) upper level

The structure of instrumental classes in 6th grade at Hillwood Middle School provides students with the opportunity to acquire musical fundamentals and playing technique at a pace that often takes two years in schools with group brass, woodwind classes and three years in schools where a single band class is scheduled. As a result, a number of students in the top two bands at Hillwood are playing at levels comparable to the lower two bands at Keller Central by the time they get to 7th and 8th grades. The Wind Ensemble at Hillwood, for example, regularly explores Level IV music which is typically seen at the high school level.

The Overlapping Scale

If you examine the Keller Central/Hillwood Scale below you will notice how the Numerical Scale runs through the Middle School Wind Ensemble range and the High School Concert Ensemble and Concert Band range.

MIDDLE SCHOOL - 6th Grade - 8th Grade				
1.0 - 1.9	2.0 - 2.9	3.0 - 3.9	4.0 - 4.9	5.0 - 5.9
Beginner Level	Concert Band	Symphonic Band	Wind Ensemble	
LEVEL 1	LEVEL 2	LEVEL 3	LEVEL 4	LEVEL 5
			High School (Lower Levels)	
			Concert Ensemble	Concert Band

The same **Numerical Scale** (shadowed boxes) extends from **Level 1** at the Beginner Level to **Level 7** at the high school Wind Ensemble level.

			Keller Central Program Standard			
1.0 - 1.9	2.0 - 2.9	3.0 - 3.9	4.0 - 4.9	5.0 - 5.9	6.0 - 6.9	7.0 - 7.9
LEVEL 1	LEVEL 2	LEVEL 3	LEVEL 4	LEVEL 5	LEVEL 6	LEVEL 7
Hillwood Middle School Program Standard						

Therefore, a middle school student that performs a **4.1** in an audition is playing at the same level as a high school student who achieves a **4.1**. Further examination of the **Overlap** reveals how middle school and high school ensembles, comprised of similar-scoring students, are different despite being comprised of students who have an audition score at the same level.

- The scale <u>does not</u> infer that "overlapping bands" all play the same level of literature (though that does occur a few times per semester).
- The scale <u>does</u> infer that members of both the middle school Wind Ensemble and the high school Concert Band achieved the **same** numerical rating on the **same** audition material, to gain entry into their respective bands either at the high school or middle school.
- The scale <u>does</u> infer that middle school and high school students who score the same are at the same playing ability.
- The scale <u>does not</u> infer that the profile of the ensembles in the high school and middle school comprised of students with the similar scores are of equal quality.

The reason "overlapping" bands, comprised of students with similar abilities, are not identical is due to the student composition of middle school versus high school bands as demonstrated in the chart below:

	Keller Central High School	
Band	Concert Ensemble	Concert Band
Profile	95% Freshmen 5% H.S. Beginners	85% Sophomores 15% Freshmen
Numerical Scale	4.0 .1,.2,.3,.4,.5,.6,.7,.8, 4.9	5.0 .1,.2,.3,.4,.5,.6,.7,.8, 5.9
Profile	75% 8th Graders 25% 7th Graders	
Band	Wind Ensemble	
	Hillwood Middle School	

All music directors understand the difference between "musical skill" and "musical maturity." How many times have you heard a nice performance by a very mature middle school or young high school band and commented, "They're still young." This comment is common among music director audiences and judges. It is an acknowledgment that despite even the most distinctive assessment or audition system which measures "one student-musician at a time," no system can measure the true ability or potential of an ensemble until it performs. When musician-directors hear a performance, however, they sense maturity clearly in some of the most subtle ways that only a professional can perceive.

Assessment of individuals that comprise an ensemble cannot predict or measure the dynamic or the quality of the ensemble of which they are comprised. Ensemble performance is a performance by individual musicians in synergy. Things happen (good and bad) in an ensemble performance that are never revealed in the assessment of each individual member of any given ensemble. Knowing this, directors will select music based on the potential of "the group" to perform the music with the maturity and understanding required of an ensemble – not solely their individual ability.

Ensemble playing is certainly much more than a collection of individual performances. The very nature of ensemble performance requires that the individual express exclusively through the ensemble. As soon as one musician becomes two, three or eighty, an entirely new set of requirements take hold. At that point, individual skill becomes a means to a new end. The finest ensemble performances are ones where, in fact, individual skills become secondary and, in many cases, invisible to the audience and the musician. They are assumed and serve the great ensemble need.

THE KELLER CENTRAL AUDITION SYSTEM

Concert Ensembles

Each spring, eighth grade students from Hillwood Middle School and the freshmen, sophomores, and juniors audition for placement one of the four ensembles at Keller Central High School. Students audition for one of four the high school directors. Each instrument type is issued its own customized audition packet. You may recall that the BBCHS Audition system places students in one of four (4) levels of aptitude from Level I to Level IV. Students play prepared music, sight reading and scales beginning with the lowest demand and proceed up to the more demanding levels until they reach their maximum capability. Students are ranked from Level I to Level IV which determined orchestra placements – either Symphonic Orchestra or Concert Orchestra. Their numerical rating also determines seating order. With two orchestras, only one barrier to entry exists for auditioning students. The barrier for the Symphonic Orchestra is determined by the number of strings required for that orchestra. Students who were not accepted into Symphonic Orchestra were placed in Concert Orchestra.

The Keller Central audition system places students in one of four (4) ensembles from Concert Ensemble, Concert Band, and Symphonic Band to Wind Ensemble. Students perform **Scales** and a **Required Etude**. Students who wish to be considered for the top two ensembles, namely the Symphonic Band and the Wind Ensemble, must perform a **Supplemental Etude** which has technical demands not present in the Required Etude. All Required Etudes and Assigned Scales are the same for each student on their particular instrument.

The **Required Etude** is a lyrical etude and is performed by all auditioning students. It is designed to assess the expressive capability of each student and other musical elements (tone, phrasing, etc.) not measurable in the scale element of the audition

The **Supplemental Etude** is a technique etude required of all students interested in Wind Ensemble and Symphonic Band. The Supplemental Etude measure a number of capabilities not present in the Required Etude. Students are not selected for these ensembles without performing the supplemental audition.

Marching Band
Band auditions decide band placement for the fall and spring concert bands. The Keller Central Marching Band is made up of students from all four Concert Bands. Participation in Marching Band is required. Separate auditions for arching positions are held during Summer Band Camp in August for brass and woodwind players and in May for percussion.

Percussion and Color Guard
Marching Percussion and Color Guard have separate auditions prior to the winter season.

Keller Central Band Audition - **Clarinet**

Wind Ensemble
Scale segment
- Play the Concert C, G, D, A, E, B, Gb, Db, Ab, Eb, Bb, F scales from <u>memory</u>
- Quarter note = **_90_** for 16th notes or Quarter note = **_180_** for eighth notes.
- Perform scales in all possible octaves with **_<u>no mistakes.</u>_**
- Full Range Chromatic Scale (page 45)

   Foundations for Superior Performance, by Richard Williams and Jeff King
   © 1997, Kjos, Neil A., Music Company

Etude segment
- Required Etude
- Supplemental Etude.   <u>Acceptable tone</u> is required on all exercises.

Symphonic Band
Scale segment
- Play the Concert C, G, D, A, E, B, Gb, Db, Ab, Eb, Bb, F scales
- Quarter note = **_75_** for 16th notes or Quarter note = **_150_** for eighth notes.
- Perform scales in all possible octaves with no mistakes in **_<u>10 of them.</u>_**
- Full Range Chromatic Scale (page 45)

   Foundations for Superior Performance, by Richard Williams and Jeff King
   © 1997, Kjos, Neil A., Music Company

Etude segment
- Required Etude
- Supplemental Etude.   <u>Acceptable tone</u> is required on all exercises.

Concert Band
Scale segment
- Play the Concert C, G, D, A, E, Db, Ab, Eb, Bb, F scales
- Quarter note = **_50_** for 16th notes or Quarter note = **_100_** for eighth notes.
- Perform scales in all possible octaves with no mistakes in **_<u>6 of them.</u>_**
- Two Octave Concert F Chromatic Scale (page 43)

   Foundations for Superior Performance, by Richard Williams and Jeff King
   © 1997, Kjos, Neil A., Music Company

Etude segment
- Required Etude.   <u>Acceptable tone</u> is required on all exercises.

Concert Ensemble
Scale segment
- Play the Concert C, G, Db, Ab, Eb, Bb, F scales
- Quarter note = **_50_** for 16th notes or Quarter note = **_100_** for eighth notes.
- Perform scales in all possible octaves with no mistakes in **_<u>4 of them</u>_**.
- Two Octave Concert F Chromatic Scale (page 43)

   Foundations for Superior Performance, by Richard Williams and Jeff King
   © 1997, Kjos, Neil A., Music Company

Etude segment
- Required Etude.   <u>Acceptable tone</u> is required on all exercises.

Scale Octave Requirements for all Instruments

	C	G	D	A	E	B	Gb	Db	Ab	Eb	Bb	F	Chr.
Flute	3	2	2	2	2	3	2	2	2	2	2	2	C-C.
Oboe	2	1	2	1	2	2	1	2	1	2	2	2	Bb-D
Bassoon	3	2	2	2	2	3	2	2	2	2	3	2	Bb-Bb
Clarinet	2	3	2	2	3	2	3	2	2	2	2	3	E-G
Bass Clarinet	2	2	2	2	2	2	2	2	2	2/3	2	2	E-C
Alto/Bari Sax	2	1	2	1	2	2	1/2	2	1	2	2	2	Bb-D/Gb
Tenor Sax	2	1	2	1	2	2	1/2	2	1	2	2	2	Bb-D/Gb
Trumpet	2	2	2	2	1	2	2	2	2	1	2	1	F#-C
French Horn	3	2	2	2	2	3	2	2	2	2	3	2	C(bass)-C
Trombone	3	2	2	2	2	2	2	2	2	2	2	2	F-Bb
Bass Trombone	3	3	3	3	3	3	3	3	3	3	3	3	F-Bb
Euphonium	3	2	2	2	2	2	2	2	2	2	2	2	F-Bb
Tuba	3	2	2	2	2	2	2	2	2	2	2	2	C-C

Recruitment Practices

Good planning and implementing instrumentation ratios when recruiting Beginning Band students is critical to providing balanced instrumentation at the Middle School and High School level. Knowing the whimsical nature of 6th graders when it comes to selecting an instrument, it is important to put limitations on the number of students per instrument on recruitment night in 6th grade.

Single high school districts have more of a challenge dictating to their feeder elementary and middle schools how to do recruitment. They have less control over this matter other than a general understanding between directors at the high school and directors at the feeder schools. Without it, there can be years when the high school band might come up short on French horns or have an overage of flutes, for example. The value of having a unit district is the ability to establish district-wide policies on instrumentation at the beginner level so that the Middle School and High School ensemble are assured the proper number of instruments in each category to form wind ensembles with proper instrumentation all the way through the system. Within the Keller ISD, the high school and middle school programs are viewed as one system. One of the elements of a unified instrumental program is that policy can be established at both ends of the spectrum. In the case of Keller Central High School, the head director at the high school directs policy and various practices through the entire band program. This includes the supervision and evaluation of both certified and private lesson staff. Middle School directors have a good about of autonomy in their position, but all staff in the entire system must work in tandem to assure quality throughout the program.

Ensemble Barriers & Required Instrumentation

With some assurances that balanced instrumentation will occur throughout the system, the Keller Central and Hillwood directors are able to establish the wind ensemble format for all bands throughout the program. As was mentioned earlier, the wind ensemble format, championed by Frederick Fennell at Eastman, is the format preferred by Keller Central and Hillwood Bands. The Keller Central program believes that the size and instrumentation of what has now become the standard wind ensemble works best for their program. The following standard instrumentation is used at Keller High School and Hillwood Middle School.

IDEAL WIND ENSEMBLE INSTRUMENTATION	
1 Piccolo	6-8 Trumpets
7 Flute	8 Horns
3 oboes (1 Eng. Horn)	4-5 Tenor Trombones
2 bassoons	1 Bass Trombone
9 Bb Clarinet	2-3 Tuba
2 Bass Clarinet	2-3 Euphoniums
2 Alto Sax	6-8 Percussion
1 Tenor Sax	
1 Baritone Sax	

Keller Central uses the same Numerical Scale when issuing raw scores for auditions in the spring and assessments throughout the year. You will recall that the middle school and high school bands are aligned with this Numerical Scale at different locations as displayed in the chart below.

KELLER CENTRAL ~ ENSEMBLE SCALE			
4 Minimum 4.0	**5** Minimum 5.0	**6** Minimum 6.0	**7** Minimum 7.0
0 .1 .2 .3 .4 .5 .6 .7 .8 .9	.0 .1 .2 .3 .4 .5 .6 .7 .8 .9	.0 .1 .2 .3 .4 .5 .6 .7 .8 .9	.0 .1 .2 .3 .4 .5 .6 .7 .8 .9
CONCERT ENSEMBLE	**CONCERT BAND**	**SYMPHONIC BAND**	**WIND ENSEMBLE**

What, then, takes precedence? What would be the choice of Keller Central directors if too few students on a particular instrument or group of instruments, failed to meet the audition standard for, say, the Concert Band? Would the decision be made to take fewer clarinets if they did not achieve a higher score? If so, where would those clarinets go? Technically they would go to Concert Ensemble. But this is not a good choice since both ensembles would have an imbalanced number of clarinets. The preference of Keller Central directors is to "fill the ensembles."

In the early development of this system, directors placed students on certain instruments in ensembles higher than they scored - to keep the instrumentation of the wind ensemble intact at all levels. As any high school music director will attest, high schoolers and, for that matter all musicians, get better quicker if they are playing with musicians who are more advanced. What the Keller Central staff has noticed is that each year, fewer students are in ensembles with barriers higher than student-musicians scored. Keep in mind that the standards for these ensembles are drawn from the <u>High School Standard.</u> As of the printing of this book, directors have fully qualified students in the two top ensembles with a smattering of students in the bottom two ensembles playing below the minimum set for those ensembles. The solution lies in the further development of students coming from the Middle School.

Students well-below a 4.0, who switch instruments, or transfer students from another school below the Keller Central standard, are placed in a 5th band class called **Instrumental Techniques** that duplicates the training offered at the Middle School. which gets them up to the required 4.0 standard.

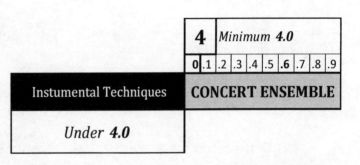

ASSESSMENT

As was stated previously, successful leaders in any endeavor 1) understand where they'd like to be, 2) do an honest and valid assessment of where they are currently, 3) create a plan and 4) **create a system to regularly measure how they are progressing.** Examining the two case studies presented herein indicates that both BBCHS and Keller Central are practicing these four tactics to improve the quality of music performance in their respective programs.

Keller Central assesses its students on a regular basis. The Symphonic Band and Wind Ensemble are advanced players whose assessments focus more on the literature they are performing from solo and ensemble work to full ensemble. The Concert Band and Concert Ensemble assessments cover a broader range of materials. Both formative and summative assessments are used in all four bands. Eighty percent of the assessments are summative and, on average twenty percent are formative. Both assessments are graded and entered into the grade record. As is the case of the BBCHS model, behavior and talent levels are not part of the assessment process. This is consistent with valid assessment policy that is being used nationwide. As was discussed earlier, we still see a large percentage of music performance programs grading on behavioral elements such as attendance, attitude and other non-academic elements.

Like BBCHS, Keller Central has a system in place to **regularly measure progress.** And like BBCHS, Keller Central utilizes the same standard in their <u>assessment system</u> that is used in their <u>audition system</u>.

BBCHS String Program – Assessment Components

1. Measures **Student Achievement** against their <u>*Program Standard*</u> which occupies a portion of the <u>*High School Standard*</u> for string players and established through the prism of the director's background and experience.

2. Assigns a **Raw Number** to each student performance that ranks all students that play the same instrument.

3. Aligns the **Numerical Scale** with a **Four-Level Scale** (by Grade Level) which adds clarity and meaning to the numerical ranking.

4. **Assigns Grades** to individual students based on the degree of deviation a student performance has from the level achieved by other students at their level (Grade Level) .

Keller Central Band Program – Assessment Components

1. Measures **Student Achievement** against their <u>*Program Standard*</u> which is the same as the <u>*High School Standard*</u> for wind and percussion players and established through the prism of the directors' background and experience

2. Assigns a **Raw Number** to each student performance that ranks all students that play the same instrument.

3. Aligns the **Numerical Scale** with a **Four-Level Scale** (by Ensemble Level) which adds clarity and meaning to the numerical ranking.

4. **Assigns Grades** to individual students based on the degree of deviation a student's performance from the norm established for their specific ensemble (Ensemble Level)

COMPONENT	BBCHS	KELLER CENTRAL
Standard	Program Standard	High School Standard
Numerical Scale	100 Point Scale and Level Scale	100 Point Scale
Levels	4 Grade Levels	4 Ensemble Levels
Grading Formula	Deviation from Grade Level Standard	Deviation from Ensemble Level Standard

In both cases, a raw score determined by using the Linear Scale (Impression-Analysis-Comparison) is converted to a letter or numerical grade for each assessment.

The Keller Central Grading Scale

Wind Ensemble	
Raw Score	Percentage
7	100
6.9	99
6.8	97
6.7	96
6.6	94
6.5	93
6.4	91
6.3	90
6.2	89
6.1	87
6	86
5.9	84
5.8	83
5.7	81
5.6	80
5.5	79
5.4	77
5.3	76
5.2	74
5.1	73
5	71
4.9	70
4.8	69
4.7	67
4.6	66
4.5	64
4.4	63
4.3	61
4.2	60
4.1	59
4	57
3.9	56
3.8	54
3.7	53
3.6	51
3.5	50
3.4	49
3.3	47
3.2	46
3.1	44
3	43
2.9	41
2.8	40
2.7	39
2.6	37
2.5	36
2.4	34
2.3	33
2.2	31
2.1	30
2	29

WIND ENSEMBLE: The entry level for Wind Ensemble is at 7.0. Therefore a score of 100 indicates that a student is achieving at the Wind Ensemble Level. Anything short of 7.0 is graded lower

Raw Score	Percentage
Symphnonic Band	
6	100
5.9	98
5.8	97
5.7	95
5.6	93
5.5	92
5.4	90
5.3	88
5.2	87
5.1	85
5	83
4.9	82
4.8	80
4.7	78
4.6	77
4.5	75
4.4	73
4.3	72
4.2	70
4.1	68
4	67
3.9	65
3.8	63
3.7	62
3.6	60
3.5	58
3.4	57
3.3	55
3.2	53
3.1	52
3	50
2.9	48
2.8	47
2.7	45
2.6	43
2.5	42
2.4	40
2.3	38
2.2	37
2.1	35
2	33

SYMPHONIC BAND: The entry level for Symphonic Band is at 6.0. Therefore a score of 100 indicates that a student is achieving at the Symphonic Band Level. Anything short of 6.0 is graded lower

Raw Score	Percentage
Concert Band	
5	100
4.9	98
4.8	96
4.7	94
4.6	92
4.5	90
4.4	88
4.3	86
4.2	84
4.1	82
4	80
3.9	78
3.8	76
3.7	74
3.6	72
3.5	70
3.4	68
3.3	66
3.2	64
3.1	62
3	60
2.9	58
2.8	56
2.7	54
2.6	52
2.5	50
2.4	48
2.3	46
2.2	44
2.1	42
2	40

CONCERT BAND: The entry level for Concert Band is at 5.0. Therefore a score of 100 indicates that a student is achieving at the Concert Band Level. Anything short of 5.0 is graded lower

Raw Score	Percentage
Concert Ensemble	
4	100
3.9	98
3.8	96
3.7	94
3.6	92
3.5	90
3.4	88
3.3	86
3.2	84
3.1	82
3	80
2.9	78
2.8	76
2.7	74
2.6	72
2.5	70
2.4	68
2.3	66
2.2	64
2.1	62
2	60

CONCERT ENSEMBLE: The entry level for Concert Ensemble is at 4.0. Therefore a score of 100 indicates that a student is achieving at the Concert Ensemble Level. Anything short of 4.0 is graded lower

GRADING SCALES
Keller Central Bands

Below are the grading scales for each band in the Keller Central Band Program. These scales convert the **RAW SCORE** into a **PERCENTAGE SCORE**. Keep in mind that students in each band achieved the **MINIMUM SCORE** to gain entry into their respective bands. In order to maintain an "A," they must maintain that standard. The standard for each band is different. Note that each band has a different position on the **LINEAR SCALE**.

GRADE MATRIX - Wind Ensemble

4		5		6		7	7.0 STANDARD
0 .1 .2 .3 .4 .5 .6 .7 .8 .9	.0 .1 .2 .3 .4 .5 .6 .7 .8 .9		.0 .1 .2 .3 .4 .5 .6 .7 .8 .9		.0 .1 .2 .3 .4 .5 .6 .7 .8 .9		.0 .1 .2 .3 .4 .5 .6 .7 .8 .9
F	60's		70's	80's		90's	100

GRADE MATRIX - Symphonic Band

3		4		5		6	6.0 STANDARD
0 .1 .2 .3 .4 .5 .6 .7 .8 .9	.0 .1 .2 .3 .4 .5 .6 .7 .8 .9		.0 .1 .2 .3 .4 .5 .6 .7 .8 .9		.0 .1 .2 .3 .4 .5 .6 .7 .8 .9		.0 .1 .2 .3 .4 .5 .6 .7 .8 .9
F	60's	70's	80's	90's			100

GRADE MATRIX - Concert Band

2		3		4		5	5.0 STANDARD
0 .1 .2 .3 .4 .5 .6 .7 .8 .9	.0 .1 .2 .3 .4 .5 .6 .7 .8 .9		.0 .1 .2 .3 .4 .5 .6 .7 .8 .9		.0 .1 .2 .3 .4 .5 .6 .7 .8 .9		.0 .1 .2 .3 .4 .5 .6 .7 .8 .9
F		60's	70's	80's	90's		100

GRADE MATRIX - Concert Ensemble

1		2		3		4	1.0 STANDARD
0 .1 .2 .3 .4 .5 .6 .7 .8 .9	.0 .1 .2 .3 .4 .5 .6 .7 .8 .9		.0 .1 .2 .3 .4 .5 .6 .7 .8 .9		.0 .1 .2 .3 .4 .5 .6 .7 .8 .9		.0 .1 .2 .3 .4 .5 .6 .7 .8 .9
F		60's	70's	80's	90's		100

Rubric Descriptions

Another view of the Keller Central Scoring Levels, along with some general rubric descriptions can give the reader an additional sense of the level of demand present in each Ensemble Level. Rubrics are not criteria but give a general idea as to the requirements of each level. This simply adds some additional clarity to the Numerical Scale used to measure student performance.

Raw Score	Goal Level (7=100 for Level 7, etc.)	Description
10 / 8.6	**Level 9** — Professional Musician	**Professional in all aspects:** • challenges the concept of the ideal
8.5 / 8	**Level 8** — College Musician	**Technical execution is perceived as flawless:** • among the best at the high school level • worthy of selection for the All-State Band
7.9 / 7	**Level 7** — HS Wind Ensemble	**Artistic expression is present:** • all notes and rhythms are performed correctly • dynamic expression is frequent and accurate throughout the performance • the chosen tempo is steady and appropriate for performance • the performer should advance to Area
6.9 / 6	**Level 6** — HS Symphonic Band	**Meets all technical demands fluently:** • minor rhythmic/note errors are handled without stopping • musicianship is shown with adequate dynamic phrasing throughout • the performance tempo is steady and in the assigned range • the performer *should* earn a chair in a Region band
5.9 / 5	**Level 5** — HS Concert Band / MS Wind Ensemble	**Performs with confidence:** • errors may include minor stops that are recovered from quickly • rhythms are correct, but may sound uneven or change tempo • dynamics and phrasing are observed occasionally • technical passages may cause lapses in tempo, phrasing, or sound quality • the performer *may possibly* earn a chair in a Region band
4.9 / 4	**Level 4** — HS Concert Ensemble / MS Wind Ensemble	**Comprehension is demonstrated:** • errors may include minor stops or restarts • technically challenging passages may cause note or rhythmic errors • the performance tempo is steady, but may be below the assigned range • dynamics and sound quality are demonstrated in less technical passages
3.9 / 3	**Level 3** — HS Instrument Techniques / MS Symphonic Band	**Preparation is evident:** • performer has good command of the fundamentals necessary • note and rhythmic errors may be frequent, with occasional stops • a characteristic sound is prevalent, but may suffer in extreme ranges • tempo may fluctuate from the assigned tempo
2.9 / 2	**Level 2** — MS Concert Band	**Demonstrates the appropriate fundamental skills:** • performer demonstrates the fundamentals necessary for the assignment • a characteristic sound is evident throughout the performance • wrong notes, rhythms, and articulations may detract from performance
1.9 / 1	**Level 1** — Beginner Level	**Demonstrates acceptable effort and attitude:** • some preparation is evident, but stops and errors may be frequent • performer lacks confidence, but a characteristic sound is prevalent • performer demonstrates some of the necessary fundamental skills
0.9 / 0		**An attempt was made, but preparation is inadequate:** • severe lack of preparation • performer lacks the fundamentals necessary to perform the assignment • performer might not finish the selected assignment

A sample list of music played by the top 3 ensembles in the Keller Central Program adds additional insight into the playing abilities of Keller High School students as of the date of this publication. The Concert Ensemble, which is the 4th band and the Level I ensemble, regularly performs Level III music.

Concert Band

"Bonds of Unity"   Karl King
"La Tregenda"   Giocomo Puccini (arr. Brian Beck)
        © 2012, Alfred Reed Publishing
"Brook Green Suite" Gustav Holst (trans. James Curnow)
        © G. Schirmer

Symphonic Band

"Variations on a theme of Robert Schumann (The happy farmer)"   Robert Jager
        © 2005, Alfred Reed
"Shepherd's Hey"   Percy Grainger
        © 1913, British Folk-Music Settings,
"King Cotton"   Sousa
        © 1895

Wind Ensemble

"Comrades of the Legion"   Sousa
        © 1895
"Aegean Festival Overture"   Andreas Makris
        © 1967, Galaxy Music Corporation
"Dream of a Witches Sabbath"   Berlioz (arranged by Merlin Patterson)
        © 1830

Assessment Practices

- Course weights for band are 80% Summative and 20% Formative

- All formative and summative assessments are graded

- Students submit recorded assessments to teacher's phones or utilize SmartMusic©

- Behavior and talent are not considerations in the assessment process

- 5-6 Summative Assessments are issued per semester based on the performance schedule

Types of Formative Assessments
- Playing Tests based on rhythms, scales, music excerpts from concert pieces, short written quizzes (lower level bands)

Types of Summative Assessments
- Ensemble Placement Auditions (each Spring)
- Individual Post-Concert Performance Reflection (writing component)
- Key Signature, Rhythm Counting Assessments (written and performed)
- Playing tests based on cumulative skills tested in formative assessments
- Perform concert literature for instructor following an absence from a concert.

Other Assessment Elements
- Reassessment on Summatives is permitted for written and playing tests but not for Concerts
- Students have the opportunity to re-play/re-take the excerpts for instructor within a designated time period
- Students who miss a performance due to illness/athletic event/family emergency will have the opportunity to perform the music selections for the instructor

Interventions for Students before Re-Assessments

- Continued practice through Sectionals and Rehearsals
- Instruction with Director
- Self-assessment of Needs
- Work with other students

Common Seating and Ensemble Assignment Factors

- <u>Standard Ensemble Size</u> is the total size of an ensemble based on accepted practices, the scope of literature, director's preference and other factors
- <u>Section Size Limitations</u> are the sizes of one section or voice to the others, that assures balance, sonority and other requirements as dictated by the literature performed by a given ensemble of a given ensemble size
- <u>Breakpoints</u> are points on the scale were parts normally split, or ensemble barriers exist
- <u>Spreads</u> are the point distances between competing musicians on either side of a breakpoint
- <u>Pressure Points</u> are breakpoint areas on the scale that contain a large number of students with insignificant spreads between their scores. This challenges your decision to cut a student that is close to the last one seated

Summary

Auditions and assessments are intended to measure the achievement of our kids. But it is not fully representative of the way our students perform as a group. A high percentage of our "product" is group performance. If we only measure our success "one student at a time" we have yet to measure our finished product. That can only be realized in its final form – on the concert stage, before a live audience where our intended purpose comes to fruition.

We take our ensembles to contest, but that assessment is performed by other professionals with their own standards. While it is good to learn how other professionals feel about our ensembles, it should not be the means by which we determine the quality of our groups and the growth of our students. Let others focus on us from their point of view. What matters is that we focus on us from *our* view of us. For we know what is really inside. We know our kids, our strengths, and our weaknesses. If you focus on that, you will always get better.

Whether you've spent one month in the classroom or forty years, you already know that musical perfection forever elusive. There is no "perfect" in our business. There is no 100%. The performance of a particular work may be the best you've ever heard. But there will be other performances to come that will be better. There is always "more better."

No director should allow outside factors to determine the quality of their program. Contests and public performances can give us road signs, direction, and destinations for our program. But the standard we hold for ourselves is the most important one to use to measure. We can only do what can be done. We should never become complacent about what we can do. While directors know, intuitively, year-to-year about the quality of their ensembles, the consolidation of data collected each school year can reveal opportunities for improvement, help shape programming, improve our teaching, and provide students, parents, and administrators with empirical evidence of student success.

Those of you who have spent many hours, days and years in the classroom are blessed with an intuition about what you do. But all of us, I included, can become complacent and possess "blind spots" in our vision that we are not aware we have. The only solution to that is to hear other groups, watch other directors teach, and continually ask questions.

In the end, systems such as those presented herein are not perfect. They measure human achievement which always possesses variables because humans execute, learn and improve in various ways. Therefore system evaluation should occur every year. Regardless of what system you use for your program, it should never distract from the teaching process. It should enhance the learning process. It must measure things that are important but also measure things that are relevant. The number we use to rank and rate our students must be based on the standards we own and set for every student we teach.

Appendix

SPRING ORCHESTRA AUDITIONS

VIOLIN
(Student Handout)

The Spring Orchestra Auditions are the annual comprehensive assessment of individual string performance skills. The audition is used to determine individual, section, class, and orchestra achievement levels in preparation for the ensuing school year. **This audition determines which orchestra you will be in for the next school year**. It also determines the final seating for the current school year.

PURPOSE OF THE AUDITIONS

1. Assess student ability in the areas of tone, intonation, note accuracy, pulsing & counting, string technique, artistic expression, sight-reading ability, music theory understanding, and audition preparation.

2. Rate Students using 1) prepared musical excerpts, 2) scales & arpeggios, 3) sight-reading materials and 4) music theory & notation written content. Grades are determined by each student's final rating in each category - against the standard for students of the same level established since 2012. Reassessments are permitted to determine final Semester Grade but not to change seating or Orchestra Placement for the following year.

3. Rank individuals, sections, classes, orchestras and other groupings against a four-tier high school orchestra standard of excellence using a 1 thru 4 rating system.

4. Determine seat-placement for the 4th quarter and Orchestra placement for the subsequent school year.

5. Establish standards of excellence for the Orchestra program and measure those standards against current national school orchestra standards. This provides data for future course content, lesson planning, curriculum expansion and improved instruction methods. **THE STANDARD** The standard has been designed based on:

1. Standard for High School String players
2. Assessment of BBCHS students since 2011
3. Requirements established by the Orchestra Course Curriculum
4. Demands of music performed in past years and planned for the subsequent year.

WHAT COMPRISES THE AUDITION

		Best way to Prepare
Prepared Music	35%	Practice musical excerpts issued for the audition
Scales & Arpeggios	30%	Practice the scales starting with Level I then move up
Sight Reading	25%	Practice sight-reading music you've never played
Music Theory & Notation	10%	Study hand out prior to taking the written exam

HOW STUDENTS ARE AUDITIONED

Students audition "one at a time" with the director. Scales are done from memory. You can use your own copy of the prepared music. All students must begin at Level I and move up if they choose to.

FOUR RATING LEVELS

		Level I	Level II	Level III	Level IV
35%	Prepared Music	1st Year Etude	2nd Year Etude	3rd Year Etude	4th Year Etude
30%	Sight Reading	1st Year Demand	2nd Year Demand	3rd Year Demand	4th Year Demand
25%	Scales & Arpeggios	3 - 1st Level Keys	3- 2nd Level Keys	3 - Third Level Keys	3 - Four level Keys
10%	Written Exam	60-69%	70-70%	80-89%	90-100

WHAT THE LEVELS MEAN

Your Level Rating demonstrates how you rate compared to standards set by BBCHS for orchestra string playing by grade. Students are rated above, below or at their grade level depending on their audition:

LEVEL I (1.0-1.9)	1st semester FRESHMAN	to	2nd semester FRESHMAN
LEVEL II (2.0-2.9)	1st semester SOPHOMORE	to	2nd semester SOPHOMORE
LEVEL III (3.0-3.9)	1st semester JUNIOR	to	2nd semester JUNIOR
LEVEL IV (4.0-4.9)	1st semester SENIOR	to	2nd semester SENIOR

Note: Pre-high school levels are ranked below 1.0. This rating is for beginning students or students not yet at a Freshman Level. Post-high school levels of 5.0 or greater are used for advanced students playing at a college level. The standards set by these students each year become the new Level IV for the following year.

WHAT YOUR SCORE LOOKS LIKE

- Numerical ratings represent 10-month periods during a school year.
- A student receiving an overall rating of 2.8 would be considered achieving at a level equal to standards associated with a Level II Student (sophomore) in his/her 8th months of study.
- Since auditions are held in the 3rd quarter of each year, to achieve an "A" grade students must rank at the .6 level of their appropriate year playing their instrument in high school.

AUDITION MATERIALS

1. Prepared Music   35%   See Prepared Music Handout

LEVEL ONE
    "Sevilla," Isaac Albeniz
        Beginning to 20
        No slower than 110

LEVEL TWO
    "Finale from 5th Symphony," Beethoven
        Two before 1 to nine after 2
        No slower than 110. NOTE this is cut time.

LEVEL THREE
    "Concerto for Two Violins and Orchestra," Bach (excerpt)
        Play at brisk pace (quarter note = 112 minimum)
        Use fingerings and bowings indicated.

LEVEL FOUR
    "Preludium und Fugue, Opus 117 No. 1," – Max Reger
        Beginning to Letter Coda
        Reference MP3 on Orchestra Web Page

2. Scales & Arpeggios   30%   Refer to Scale Fingering Guide (memory)

	LEVEL I	LEVEL II	LEVEL III	LEVEL IV
Violin	G M (3) - CM (3)	A M (3) - Gm (3)	G Arp (3) - Ab M (3)	Cm (3) - C Arp (3)
Viola	C M (3) - FM (3)	D M (3) - Cm (3)	C Arp (3) - Db M (3)	Fm (3) - F Arp (3)
Cello	C M (3) - FM (3)	D M (3) - Cm (3)	C Arp (3) - Db M (3)	Fm (3) - F Arp (3)
Bass	E M (2) - FM (3)	Bb M (2) - Gm (2)	E Arp (2) - Ab M (2)	Db M (2) - F Arp (2)

3. Sight Reading   25%   No advanced materials – practice by sight-reading

4. Music Theory   10%   See Study Guide (written test)

    Level I   60 to 69 %
    Level II   70 to 79 %
    Level III   80 to 89%
    Level IV   90 to 100%

SIGHT READING (25%)

The only way to get better at sight reading is to practice sight reading. To improve your sight reading, pull out some music you've never played before, each time you practice. Practice sight reading using the tips below as if you were actually in an audition setting, even in front of family or friends.

TIPS FOR SIGHT READING

Take a BRIEF moment to look over the entire passage. Glance over the whole piece to familiarize yourself with any dynamic markings, tempo changes, key changes, articulation markings.

1. Look at the key signature. First things first! Take note of any sharps or flats. Also, glance over the piece and take note of any accidentals added to certain parts of the music.

2. Identify measures with lots of notes. Look for clusters of notes (or lots of black). These are spots that will most likely be the trickiest. Look for patterns in these busy note passages. Is it a scale? Is it an arpeggio? Is it something familiar like "cascading thirds?"

3. Identify measures with complex rhythms. Note dotted rhythms or clusters of sixteenth and eighth notes. You will base your tempo on how quickly you think you can play the tricky passages.

4. Look at the tempo marking. If a passage is marked andante, largo, lento, or moderato, do NOT play it faster than it should be. Playing a piece quickly with the intention to show off will not gain you points. In fact, you're more likely to trip over challenging passages if you start playing too fast. If you cannot determine the tempo - ask your examiner to demonstrate the tempo. Take your time. Concerning the tempo, it is perfectly okay when sight reading to play the passage a little slower than you might in a real performance.

5. Keep a steady tempo. Don't speed up or slow down. One of the most important things you can do is play the passage at a steady, consistent speed. This is something the examiners are specifically looking for. Varying your tempo will give the judges the impression that you don't have a solid sense of rhythm or you are pausing to analyze something you do not understand.

6. Read ahead as best you can. Play one measure as you look ahead to the next measure(s). An experiment on sight reading using an eye tracker indicates that highly skilled musicians tend to look ahead further in the music, storing and processing the notes until they are played; this is referred to as the eye-hand span.

7. Don't sweat the bowings. Start with a down bow (unless otherwise marked) and take it as it comes. Generally speaking, pick-up notes will often use an up bow so look for any markings. If there are none - an up bow should be used to establish a down bow on the first full measure.

8. Don't stop or repeat measures if you mess up. This is also something the examiners look for specifically as you can't stop and repeat a measure in a real performance, especially with an accompanist or when playing in an orchestra. Forge ahead!

9. Don't apologize or say, "Oops!" In fact, don't say anything. Not even a disclaimer before you begin, like, "Oh, wow. Okay. This is probably going to sound really bad, but here goes!"

10. Stop playing when instructed. Always stop immediately when the examiner says so. Usually, they stop you because they've gotten a good impression of your playing abilities based on what you've already done. Don't misinterpret an early start as a failure, necessarily.

WRITTEN EXAM - STUDY GUIDE (10%)

VIOLIN (string) HISTORY

Stringed instruments first appeared in Europe in the medieval ages (400 to 1400's). By "stringed" we refer to instruments played with a bow. The early instruments were simple "fiddles" used to accompany singers. They did not have much in common with a violin. It was in the 15th century when, slowly, violins developed. The violin as it is known nowadays was built in the early 16th century. At the same time, the viola and the cello also emerged.

Everything that is explained about the violin and its structures can be referred to the whole family of stringed instruments. This group of instruments has been developed in order to satisfy new ideas of sound that emerged in those times in Italy. Gradually, the violin took the place of the "gamba" (a type of crude viola) that preceded them.

In Italy, violin making reached an enormous upswing between 1535 and 1610. Violin making then occurred over the whole continent of Europe. But it was Cremona, Italy (in the north of Italy) that was home to the most famous of all violin makers: The most famous was Antonio Stradivari. For more than 150 years, violins made by Stradivari have been the most desired concert instruments.

The decline of violin making began in the second half of the 18th century (1750's on). Caused by a permanent growth of the demand for instruments the violin makers were forced to produce more and to produce faster. Therefore the quality diminished from the early Italian masters.

The sound of the modern violin is not the same as it was in Stradivari's time. The instruments today do not have such a variety of sounds as in earlier times, and they do not have the ability to reach the most distant rows of a concert hall with sufficient clarity. Much know-how, manual skill and plenty of experience are necessary in order to replicate the tone of the old instruments

For the violin maker, wood is the most important material; it is only natural that the correct choice of wood is vital in order to achieve the best quality of sound. Wood that is too heavy because of its specific weight cannot be used – although it may look marvelous.

Mass-production of violins lowers quality. It will never fulfill the fundamental aspect because each piece of wood needs to be treated differently, even when the wood is chopped out of the same trunk; the single pieces are very different from each other. At the lower end of the trunk, the wood is generally harder than at the top, also, parts which grew in the sunshine obviously differ from parts that grew in the shadow. The finest maple wood comes from Bosnia, the most adapted spruce comes from central European countries.

PRINCIPLES OF STRING ACOUSTICS

1. When the bow sets a string in motion, the string vibrates clockwise on the down-bow and counter-clockwise on the up bow.

2. In motion, the string regularly oscillates back and forth "so many" times per second. The number of times in one second the string oscillates back and forth in once second determines its pitch. The note "A - 440," which is the fundamental turning note for the violin, means that the string is oscillating 440 times per second and that rate has been determined to be an "A."

3. The string vibrates from the bridge to the nut (or from the bridge to the depressed finger if you have the string depressed). In addition, while the string is vibrating at its primary oscillation (i.e., "A - 440"), it also vibrates from the middle of the suspended string to both fixed ends. This is the halfway point in the string and represents an octave above the fundamental.

4. A "harmonic" fingering occurs when the musician touches the string lightly at the midpoint. This forms a pitch perceived one octave higher than the fundamental pitch. Other subdivisions also occur at different locations on the string but are less perceived by the human ear. The relative amplitude (volume) of these "extra vibrations" (often called "overtones") is a major part of the tonal sound of all instruments.

5. The hollow nature of the string instrument provides an air chamber that serves as an acoustical (non-electrical) amplifier. The placement of the bridge, the internal sound post, the quality of the wood, strings, and bow all create (and impact) the tone quality and volume of the violin and other string instruments.

6. Finally, the technique used by the performer can hinder or enhance the natural acoustical qualities of the string instrument. Location of the bow, free movement of the right hand and arm, proper bow hold, and left-hand method all impact the tone quality of the violin.

FACTORS that affect your sound

- Amount of Bow Hair used (tilt)
- Pressure of the bow on the string (weight on the string)
- Bow Placement (fingerboard, bridge or middle of the two)
- Bow speed (linked to pressure)
- Bow location (tip, middle or frog)
- Bow angle (place bow at "right angle" to the strings)
- Proper use of vibrato (allows the string instrument to "sing")

BOWING

BOWING TERMS you must understand

- arco — bowing as opposed to pizzicato
- down-bow — the bow moves in the direction from the frog to the tip
- up-bow — the bow moves in the direction from the tip to the frog
- legato bowing — a group of notes played smoothly in one bow motion
- tenuto — alternate bows, full length at certain tempos, sometimes a slight 'push' at the beginning to give it definition if marked
- staccato — short up and down bows indicated by dots placed over/undernote
- spiccato — staccato with a bounced bow, usually for fast tempos
- detache' — a single bow stroke per note
- marcato — heavy, separate storing with pressed accent played near the heel
- con legno — string is struck with the stick portion of the bow
- pizzicato — plucking the string with the finger or thumb

GOOD PRACTICE HABITS

- Always consider your practice session AS a performance.
- Do not practice differently than you would play. Establish "performance quality" in practice.
- Do certain things every time you practice. Tune similarly, establish a warm-up, start slow then work up speed on technique. Attack your weak spots before you start working on your music.
- There are times to practice alone and times to practice with your stand partner or friend. Use both methods but early on, spend 80% of your time on your own so you can focus on your weak areas.
- Set a length of time to practice before you start and hold to it.
- If you are just not in the mood to work on certain things (i.e., scales or technique) on a given day, then have a productive rehearsal on items you find acceptable but do not avoid the more complicated skills if you need work in those areas.
- Don't practice mistakes, play up to your mistake and return over and over until you've passed your roadblock. Slow tempo on difficult passages and then work up to speed.
- Don't play a piece beginning to end – work the piece in "chunks" so that each section is "worked out, and then connect the chunks together. At the end of your practice DO play the piece front to back.

COUNTING & NOTE READING

- Part of the written exam includes two pages of written rhythms. Students will be asked to mark the official counting verbiage over each rhythm pattern.

PROPER INSTRUMENT CARE

- Maintain a properly rosined bow.
- Guard against your instrument getting too dry (especially in the winter months).
- Always wipe down your instrument to remove rosin when you are finished playing. Built-up rosin on the strings, fingerboard, and body of the instrument impact the sound of your instrument.
- Exposure to excessive heat or cold can damage your instrument. Heat can melt your rosin. If your instrument is exposed to extremes in temperature, leave it in the case for 15 minutes once inside so it can gradually adjust.
- Always store your instrument in its case. It can easily be destroyed if it is not protected.
- Do not allow the bow hair on your bow to deteriorate. Missing hair, grime and other signs of wear are an indication that it is time to change the bow hair (average $50).
- Tune slowly and gradually to avoid breaking strings. If your instrument is over 1/4 of a pitch off, use your pegs. Do not over-rely on your fine tuners. They are for final and last minute adjustments.
- Take caution when carrying your instrument, music, and bow to your seat. Make sure you have solid control of all three to avoid dropping your instrument and be aware of the space around you to avoid banging your instrument against other objects or other instruments.
- Do not toss your instrument in its case into your car or on your bed etc. This can cause damage and your bridge to collapse.

MUSIC THEORY

Major Scale is a series of notes that begins on a specific note and ascends in a consistent pattern to the starting note's octave and down again.

There are 8 steps to every major scale (1 through 8). Some notes are ONE STEP apart, and others are TWO STEPS apart. The order never changes.

1 to 2	2 to 3	3 to 4	4 to 5	5 to 6	6 to 7	7 to 8
whole-step	whole-step	half-step	whole-step	whole-step	whole-step	half-step

Minor Scale is a series of notes that begins on the 6th step of the major scale and has the same key signature as the major scale.

Key Signature appears at the beginning of a song or new phrase that lists the sharps or flats present in the key. These sharps and flats correspond to the major or minor scale that is used in the song and also refers to the "key" of the song (for example D Major).

Order of Sharps in a key signature is always the same. The order can be memorized using the following:

Fat**C**ats **G**o **D**own **A**llies **E**ating **B**irds

Order of Flats in a key signature is exactly the opposite of the order of Sharps

B♭ E♭ A♭ D♭ G♭ C♭ F♭

An Arpeggio is comprised of the 1st, 3rd, 5th and Octave Notes of a major or minor scale

A Triad (chord) is comprised of the Arpeggio notes played simultaneously

A trill is created by playing a note and rapidly playing the note (in the key - unless indicated) above the note a number of times depending on the tempo

A Time Signature indicates the number of beats in a measure (top number) and the type of note that gets (bottom number) the beat.

A Fermata indicates a hold in the music. All members of the orchestra look to the conductor for the release of the fermata

Chords have names (C chord or G chord), but they also have **numbers** based on the scale degree the chord is based on. The C Chord in the Key of C is the I Chord. In the Key of F, the C Chord is the V Chord.

The distance between notes (played consecutively or simultaneously) is called an interval. Notes that are three scaled degrees apart are called "3rds." Notes that are 5 scaled degrees apart are called "5TH's."

References

References

"William Billing of Boston: Eighteenth-Century Composer," David P. McKay and Richard Crawford, (Princeton, N.J.: Princeton University Press, 1975)

"Training Working Memory" The ADHD Report, 14(1), 6-8. doi:10.1521/adhd.2006.14.1.6, Klingberg, T. (2006).

"Faculty of 1000 evaluation for A Tunable Mechanism Determines the Duration of the Transgenerational Small RNA Inheritance in C. elegans." F1000, Boag, P. (2016). - Post-publication Peer Review of the Biomedical Literature. doi:10.3410/f.726236698.793524091

Science of memory: Concepts. Roediger, H. L., Dudai, Y., & Fitzpatrick, S. M. (2007). Science of memory: Concepts. Oxford: Oxford University Press

"Cognitive psychology," Matlin, M. W. (2014). Hoboken, N.J: John Wiley & Sons.

"An overview of American Public School Bands and Orchestras before World War II" Jere T. Humpreys, Arizona State University, Tempe, Arizona, University of Illinois, University of Illinois Press, 1989

Achieve.org. (2017, March 29). Retrieved from https://www.achieve.org/history-achieve

"Susanne Langer's Theory of Symbolism: An Analysis and Extension," Mary J. Reichling Philosophy of Music Education Review, Vol. 1, No. 1, Indiana University Press, 1993

"Foundations and Principles of Music Education," by Charles Leonhard/Robert House (McGraw-Hill, 1972)

"Philosophy in a New Key, A Study in the Symbolism of Reason, Rite, and Art" by Suzanne Langer, Harvard University Press, 1941

"The Practice of Assessment in Music Education: Frameworks, Models, and Designs," Tim S. Brody, Editor, (GIA Publications, 2010)

"A Kid from Momence…Growing up after the War," by Kevin McNulty, Sr., (KMC Publishing, 2016)

"The Activities of Teaching," Thomas E. Green, (1971, McGraw-Hill, Inc.)

"Classroom Assessment in U.S. School Band Programs: Methods, Purposes, and Influences," Phillip Matthew Kancianic, Doctor of Philosophy, (University of Illinois, 2006)

"Handbook of research on music teaching and learning," by Richard Colwell (Schirmer Books, 1981)

"Measuring Music Education: A Philosophical Investigation of the Model Cornerstone Assessments" by Lauren Kapalka Richerme, (Indiana University Jacobs School of Music,

"Choral music education: A survey of research1996-2002," by Amber Turcott (University of South Florida, 2003)

Books by Kevin McNulty, Sr.

"Around Momence" by Kevin McNulty, Sr.
Copyright © 2007 Kevin McNulty, Sr.
Published by Arcadia Publishing
Charleston SC, Chicago IL, Portsmouth NH, San Francisco, CA
ISBN   978-07358-57289

"Lt. Pat O'Brien" by Kevin McNulty, Sr.
Copyright © 2013 KMC PUBLISHING COMPANY
All rights reserved.
ISBN: 10-0615852114
ISBN-13: 978-0615852119

"The Barns of Kankakee County" by Kevin McNulty, Sr.
Copyright © 2014 KMC PUBLISHING COMPANY
All Photography is the property of Kevin McNulty, Sr.
ISBN-10: 0989796515
ISBN-13: 978-0-9897965-1-4

"Finding Pat O'Brien
Copyright © 2014 KMC PUBLISHING COMPANY
All rights reserved.
ISBN-10: 0989796523
ISBN-13: 978-0-9897965-2

"A Kid from Momence...Growing up After the War"
Copyright © 2015 KMC PUBLISHING COMPANY
All rights reserved.
ISBN-10:   098979654X
ISBN-13:   978-0-9897965-4-5

"Assessing Music Performance...
     A Valid System for Measuring Student Performance and Growth"
Copyright © KMC PUBLISHING COMPANY
All rights reserved
ISBN 13 978-0-9897965-8-3

ABOUT THE AUTHOR

Kevin McNulty, Sr. published his first book in 2007, following a twenty-five-year career in association management. He became interested in writing during his business career as his writing, and speaking responsibilities increased as President & CEO of the National Association of the Remodeling Industry and later as President and CEO of the Chicago Southland Chamber of Commerce, where he served as publisher of *"Chicago Southland Business"* magazine.

But McNulty's first career was as a high school band and orchestra director. He spent fifteen years teaching prior to his business career and added five additional years in the classroom between 2011 and 2016. He has instructed for the Marian Catholic High School band in Chicago Heights, Illinois since 1987, and has stayed active as a jazz drummer with a Chicago area big band since 1995. He has actively judged marching bands and drum & bugle corps since 1977.

He was Executive Director for the Central States Judges Association in the 80's where he first learned the craft of judging He also served as Associate Executive Director of Bands of America for five years in the 1990's. He was an instructor for the Cavaliers Drum and Bugle Corps in the early 80's and judged for Drum Corps International (DCI) in the 70's and 80's. He continues to compose and arrange for both band and orchestra.

In his latest publication, *"Assessing Music Performance...A Valid System for Measuring Student Performance and Growth,"* McNulty brings together his forty-plus years of judging and student assessment in the performing arts. His ground-breaking book, based on his forty years of applied judging research and his grading system he developed over the years, is a must-read for administrators, music supervisors, music directors, music education majors and judges in the performing arts activity.

His first published book was published in 2007, His most extensive work is an eight-hundred-page novel entitled "Lt. Pat O'Brien" © 2013, KMC Publishing Company. He has published four additional books and published for other authors. His current book is his first on music education.

Kevin McNulty holds a Bachelor's Degree in Music Education from Illinois State University, a Master's Degree in Music Education from the University of Illinois and did his MBA studies at Keller Graduate School of Management in Chicago. He resides in Matteson, Illinois with his wife of forty-five years and has three adult children including a son who is a band director in Texas. McNulty is a frequent speaker, clinician, and judge and is currently on the adjunct faculty at Prairie State College in Chicago Heights, Illinois where he teaches the history of American Music and Music Appreciation to both music majors and non-majors.

Made in the USA
San Bernardino, CA
02 August 2019